CONSCIOUSNESS IS ALL

"Consciousness Is All is an inspiring picture of the nonlocal, infinite, eternal nature of Consciousness. This is affirmed not only by ancient wisdom, but is emerging as well in several areas of science. Bravo!"
—**Larry Dossey, M.D.**, author of *The Extraordinary Healing Power of Ordinary Things* and *Healing Words*

"If you want to know what is true about you, about Life, this is the most important book you will ever read. It hits the mark in its thoroughly supported explanations of why Consciousness really is all there is. This is not a self-help book, or a book of 'how to.' It is a book of *what is.*"
—**Jody Zimmermann**, New Hampshire

"Wow! What a read! This book is priceless for knowing who and what you are. Thoughtful reading reveals a completely new viewpoint of your identity and world. Look no further. This is it!"
—**L.C.**, San Diego, CA

"Clearly thought out and well written ... it is a 'lifetime' book."
—**Sandra Martin**, President, Paraview, Inc. NY

"Words cannot express the gratitude I'm experiencing as a result of this book. For years I've been searching for the experience of 'God,' without knowing what I'm looking for. I have read countless books and explored several 'systems.' Never before have I felt I understood One-ness nor Consciousness. The moment I read Chapter One, there was a 'shift,' and a feeling of joy and expansion of the 'heart.' With each chapter, both the understanding and experience have grown. As I write this, I'm experiencing incredible peace and joy—and not finding words to express adequately to you the deep thanks for getting this published! I want to buy several copies for friends who have been searching 'fruit-lessly' as have I."
—**C.R.**, Florida

"The book truly does build line upon line, precept upon precept. I see each little petal open as the book unfolds. It clears away the debris and takes out the middle man—the 'and' in God 'and' man. Just the One Self forever and ever being Itself. Simplicity in Reality and One-ness."

—Denice Jutras, Mystics of the World Booksellers, ME

"The fact that this book is written in simple everyday language doesn't make it less revolutionary. What is said is so new, it is at times even shocking. Yet every page makes you feel so good! You don't want to put the book down once you pick it up!"

—Zoe Martyniuk, New York

"This book makes perfectly clear why there is no 'becoming'—Consciousness is all I am being, now—leaving no lesser, little 'me' to struggle to understand what Consciousness is. I have not arrived—Consciousness never left Itself! As Consciousness, Life, is already the total Presence I Am, there can be no process to Consciousness. Thanks for a wonderful book on WHAT I AM!"

—Jane King, Los Angeles, CA

"You could search every bookstore and library on the planet, and not find a book as important and helpful as this one. Here is a celebration of Life as It really is. Do you want to leave all cares behind, in the dust bin of nothingness—and revel in the joy of Divine Perfection here and now? Then read this book!"

—I. Turner, Corona Del Mar, CA

"A stimulating study in plain English—not just a 'read.' It is literally the Truth of you. Intelligent, fresh, and *new*!"

—Kathy Lewis, Prescott, Arizona

"This wonderful truth about life is explained in such a simple way that the understanding can better our lives in all ways."

—V.W., California

"This book, CONSCIOUSNESS IS ALL, is a constant reminder of your true Identity."

—B.W., California

"*Consciousness Is All* awakens the reader to the truth of his divine Infinite Identity now present. Awareness of this fact frees one from human bondage, which, as the book eloquently and with deep insight points out, never existed. Herein lies peace, joy and Heaven."

—**Carole Allen**, Palm Coast, Florida

"I read Alfred Aiken's books every day; they are a blessing to all who love the Absolute. *Consciousness Is All* has added an exciting and refreshing look at Truth. In not deviating from the Absolute, the book has made It clearer to me."

—**Benjamin Allen,** Palm Coast, Florida

"This work, *Consciousness Is All,* clearly states what your true Identity really is. Its great value is beyond words."

—**Louise & Hans Stauber**, Arlesheim, Switzerland

"Full of appreciation. It doesn't matter where I was or will be—now it is clear that I'm always present. What can I say about a book of the Light you are—the Light you never left? It is pure. I love it all."

—**Franz Held**, Logan Lake, B.C. Canada

"*Consciousness Is All* is a detailed, in-depth volume showing that Mind, Self, is the only LIFE there is. Anyone wishing to discover who and what their true Identity is now, should read, ponder and enjoy the only Self that exists."

—**Anne Arnott**, Leicester, U.K.

"Most books I have read on the subject of non-duality state 'What' you be, but not 'Who' you be. *Consciousness Is All* clearly shows why all methods, and any need for emerging or becoming one with the One, are precluded. All need for 'arriving' is taken out of the equation, proving it to be a mistaken human assumption, an impossible dream prospect. The writing style reveals the ever-fresh certainty of 100% non-dual LIFE that is perfection looking out from Itself. This book reveals just how ALL, ALL really is right NOW!"

—**Dennis M. Donlon**, Artist, Washington D.C.

CONSCIOUSNESS IS ALL

Now Life Is Completely New

PETER FRANCIS DZIUBAN

BLUE DOLPHIN PUBLISHING

Published by Blue Dolphin Publishing, Inc.
P.O. Box 8, Nevada City, CA 95959
Orders: 1-800-643-0765
Web: www.bluedolphinpublishing.com

ISBN: 978-1-57733-160-5 (paperback)
ISBN: 978-1-57733-202-2 (hardcover)

Library of Congress Cataloging-in-Publication Data

Dziuban, Peter Francis, 1952-
   Consciousness is all : now life is completely new / Peter Francis
Dziuban.
       p. cm.
    ISBN 1-57733-160-5 (pbk. : alk. paper)
   1. Consciousness. I. Title.

   B105.C477D98 2006
   126—dc22

                                                        2006006121

First printing, September 2006
Second printing, November 2006

Printed in the United States of America

10   9   8   7   6   5   4   3   2

CONTENTS

IT REALLY IS TRUE

Did you ever read something that made you say, "This is unbelievable! It can't possibly be true"? Then in the next breath you have to admit, "As incredible as it sounds, I can see this *must* be true—it's undeniable."

That is exactly what's going to happen in these pages.

What you are about to read concerning Consciousness may at first sound more radically new, more revolutionary, than anything you have ever heard. Yet simultaneously, it is said in a way that is explicitly, unmistakably clear—so you see it for yourself, and are certain it's true.

To get an idea of what lies ahead, first go back. Go back in time—and try to imagine what things were like six or seven centuries ago. Imagine yourself accepting the many beliefs and superstitions of that era. Think what it would have been like to be aware back then compared to now. The difference between then and now isn't so much what you knew or were aware of—it's what you *weren't* aware of.

You have no awareness that the earth is a tiny round planet, floating in a vast universe of space—but are fully convinced that the earth is flat. After all, that's exactly what your eyes see—just this flat, enormous mass of rock and dirt, and a flat ocean. And right over there, just beyond the horizon, there's an enormous drop where sailing ships fall off the edge, and real live dragons and disaster await. You're certain this is true, because after all, *that's what everyone has always said.*

Today, it's nearly impossible to see yourself accepting such a thing.

If you can even begin to imagine that kind of severely limited awareness, then you might also imagine the elation, the wondrous awe, that came with the breakthrough that shattered those beliefs. And as magnificent as that breakthrough must have felt, it's *nothing* in comparison to what you're about to experience.

The point is, the earth never changed from flat to round—it *always* was round. It just had been "mis-seen" due to ignorance of what always was true. The "breakthrough" was an entirely new way of *looking*— seeing things from a completely fresh perspective. It so thoroughly exposed the falsity that, in retrospect you might say, "It's hard to imagine that there even could have been such beliefs."

Are you prepared to now look upon *today's* widely accepted beliefs and say the same thing?

When it comes to the currently accepted belief that the earth is a material object in physical space—that life and existence are physical— and for that matter that *you* are limited to being a mortal physical body—are you open to considering that these beliefs are as false as that flat earth? Surprising as it may sound, today's beliefs are even *far more* limiting than those of the flat earth folks!

If you aren't afraid to be adventurous—if you refuse to be confined by any would-be mental horizons of belief and superstition, you're in for the read of your Life. You're about to experience another "breakthrough"—and see again, that things were always this way.

Right now, ask yourself what it would be like if absolutely all that existed was a state of pure Consciousness.

What if there were nothing physical or material anywhere, but only *Consciousness*—only a state of pure Intelligence or Mind? There would be none of the limitations that go with a material world full of physical objects, because there isn't one. There would be only Consciousness or Mind and what appear to be *thoughts* or *ideas*. Does this all sound crazy? At one time, the round earth sounded crazy too.

It really is true. Right this instant, your entire existence—which means all there is of all there is—*truly is* "made out of" Consciousness. The way the five senses of sight, touch, sound, taste and smell seem to portray the world and universe is false. One way is that they make it appear as if the earth ended at the horizon. Another, more subtle falsity (fully exposed in this book), is that the senses make it appear as if you have a world "out there," in physical space, full of objects that are separate from each other, and separate from you, as material items. Not true. All is *within* Consciousness and nothing exists outside of It. The more preposterous that sounds, the more you owe it to yourself to not be fenced in by a flat-earth mentality, and to read on with a fresh, open thought.

By reading these pages, you won't just be exchanging an old belief for a new one. You'll be *out* of the realm of belief altogether. Belief functions only on the level of human thought or faith, which is fallible and can waver and change. Meanwhile, pure Consciousness is infallible—an absolute certainty—because It goes right on changelessly *being*, regardless of what is believed or thought. Consciousness is completely non-intellectual, and non-denominational.

Does what you've read so far have you feeling skeptical as to what lies ahead? Did you glance at the chapter titles, and did they look "overwhelming"? Each chapter is actually simple if you'll just go slowly, sentence by sentence. To stand at the top of Mt. Everest may seem an impossible task at first—but those who've done it always have the same answer as to how they got there: one step at a time. Likewise, each sentence in these pages proceeds carefully, step by step, clearly pointing out the true nature of Consciousness, and who you really are.

You can relax as you read, because this book has nothing to do with converting you or getting you to become anything. Why? The simple Truth is, you already are what you are. There can be no process—and no need—for becoming what you already *are*. What is written here is not a teaching, not something to follow. It simply states what Consciousness *is*. It is a statement of what is already true; that which is now present, and never can be stopped. This book simply states who and what you are, as you are right now. However, that may be quite different from who you up until now may have *assumed* you were. It sounds simple, but there is no truth more profound: you never can become what you already are. This book is about the *are*.

The only "price" you pay is that you must scrap all belief-baggage and start fresh. Be willing to give up all pre-conceived notions (at least for these relatively few pages!). What is said here doesn't fit into any framework of what you've already been taught.

Some would call this book "spiritual." Far more importantly, it is *factual*. What it states is undeniable and irrefutable. So if there is any doubt, or temptation to negate what is said, stop and say, "Wait a minute. That's just old limited thinking based on the senses—the same kind of thinking that once insisted oh-so-authoritatively that the earth was flat. I am not limited by it. I am open to reading *intelligently*."

You'll find there are no would-be mental horizons to confine you—in fact, *none ever were* confining you. Consciousness is so unlimited, It leaves no horizons!

1

FACT: THERE IS NOTHING GREATER THAN CONSCIOUSNESS

RIGHT NOW, YOU ARE CONSCIOUS.

What exactly is this Consciousness that you now are?

Did you ever ask yourself what pure Consciousness is—entirely distinct from every thing you are conscious *of*?

What is true of pure Consciousness, all by Itself alone?

That is the theme of this book, and the best way to start is by first agreeing there is Consciousness. That's easy enough—and more importantly, it's undeniable. You never can say, "There is no Consciousness," because you must already be conscious in order to say it.

"Of course I'm conscious," the thought may come. "Why belabor such an obvious fact?"

Consciousness means *everything*. Stop and consider it. If the very Consciousness here, now, were *not* conscious, you wouldn't be able to say there was such a thing as this book, or the body holding it. As far as you are concerned, there would be no such thing as a home, no job, no possessions or money. How do you know this is true? The only way those things can be said to exist is due to being *conscious of* them.

If there were no Consciousness to be conscious of it, it would be impossible to say there is *anything*. It couldn't be said there was a single flower, tree or mountain. There would be none of the riches on earth—not to mention the earth itself. It couldn't be said there was a moon, stars, or one speck of the entire universe. Without Consciousness, simply nothing could be said to exist, not even Life Itself. In fact, one couldn't even be conscious of a nothingness!

Your consciousness *of* your world is all there is *to* your world.

The point is, nothing exists outside of, or beyond Consciousness. This isn't anything mystical. It's a fact.

Right now ask yourself, what *could* exist outside of, or be greater than Consciousness. Really try to come up with something out beyond It. Whatever you mention—even the entire stellar universe—where is it? It is always some thing you appear to be conscious *of*. It is always *within* Consciousness to be able to mention it. Thus Consciousness *includes* it or is greater than it, and not bounded by it at all.

At the moment, it certainly appears that many things are outside of your *body*—such as this book, other objects, even the moon. But no thing is ever outside of Consciousness, Awareness, is it? If it were, one could not be aware of it. The fact is, all things, even the body, exist in only one "place," *within* Consciousness, Awareness. (Consciousness and Awareness are treated as synonyms.)

Consciousness goes even further. Think about those who have had what are called near-death or "afterlife" experiences. While the *body* was supposedly "unconscious," Consciousness was still functioning, because they had an experience they were vividly *conscious of.*

Still others claim to have had various out-of-body experiences. But there is no such thing as an out-of-Consciousness experience, is there? Otherwise one couldn't know of the experience. Again, simply nothing can be said to exist apart from, or outside of Consciousness, Awareness.

General human belief of course has always said Consciousness is located inside the human body, somewhere in the brain. That simply is not true, though it may seem or appear so. It's an *assumption*, just like the old assumption that the earth was flat because it appears so. A major endeavor of this book is to show conclusively, in various ways, how and why Consciousness is not inside the body, but that body and all things appear to be in the perfect wholeness of Consciousness.

Any scientist will tell you the human body really is not a solid object, even though it seems so. It would be just countless atomic particles that are all constantly moving or vibrating. They're so incredibly tiny that the space between them, in relative terms, is greater than the space between the earth and sun. The human body is more space than solidity! Consciousness couldn't be inside such an arrangement because there's really no solid object there to be inside of!

Consciousness isn't a word. It is *actively aware and alive* right here, now, and always includes all there is. Consciousness is literally the "stuff" or "substance" within which your everyday affairs and entire

universe appear to be found. The implications of this fact are so enormous, so thrilling, it's indescribable. Just one thing it means is, you're
not a helpless pawn—not subject to, or stuck in the conditions of a
world. As Consciousness, you're not within anything—it all appears to
be within you! Things are not going on "out there" separate from you,
leaving you unable to do anything about them. Your entire universe is
within Consciousness, subject only to how pure Consciousness perceives
it. That's why this book is titled *Consciousness Is All*.

This all-inclusiveness of Consciousness is why It is sometimes also
called the One Self, the Divine, Infinite Intelligence, I AM, Life, Love, or
what some call God. They are all *synonyms* for what is the same One. If
you can't warm up to these terms because they're not scientific enough,
stay with the terms Consciousness or Life. It certainly can't be denied
there is Consciousness or Life. Regardless of the term, what counts is
that It is never "a" Consciousness, a power afar off, that is all-inclusive. It
is *the One being aware right here, now*, so this can be read.

———•———

Why are Consciousness and other synonyms capitalized? It is done
to make the essential distinction that they are never personal. After all,
who is it, really, that's being conscious? Is there a personal thinking mind
that knows *how* to be conscious? Of course not. No person, no body,
cranks up Consciousness in the morning and sustains or upholds It all
day long by thinking about It moment to moment. The capacity to be
conscious, alive, clearly is something no person is doing or is responsible
for. Always, It is *Consciousness Itself* or *Life Itself* that is conscious, that is
alive to say "I" right where you are. This never changes. Consciousness,
or what is called the Self, really is the only *I*.

As you read, you'll see why Consciousness is *not* the same as what is
called the personal thinking, sensing "mind." They're vastly different. To
assume Consciousness is confined to an intellect and five physical senses
of seeing, hearing, touch, taste and smell is way short of the mark. The
so-called human sensing, thinking mind deals only with that which is
finite and limited. It constantly needs to expand and progress out of its
limitations. It always looks out beyond itself to something greater—
always looks *up to* a God, Self, or Consciousness.

What about starting from the other direction?

Instead of looking *up to* the Self, what about looking *out from* the Self?

That's what the Self or Consciousness Itself is doing. It never looks
up to Itself, and *It* is the only One being conscious right here, now.

To "look out from" simply means Consciousness gets *all* the credit, *all* the presence and power. Why? Again, there honestly is no other being conscious. One needn't do anything for this to operate perfectly here and now—Consciousness Itself is already doing or being It all.

What becomes obvious is almost shocking in its simplicity, yet undeniable.

The fact that It is Consciousness or the Self Itself being conscious here, now, *precludes* there being another, lesser consciousness that has to or can become anything. No transformation is necessary or even *possible*. The One Consciousness is already all the Consciousness that is functioning; It is perfectly aware now, and never has been otherwise. This shatters the myth of a would-be secondary self that must struggle to get at-one with a vague "god."

Humanity has always put the cart before the horse—identifying as a body, a mere thing one appears to be *conscious of*, instead of as Consciousness Itself. To mistakenly identify as only a body, as a physical self which can make errors, be sick or poor, must elevate itself and "get there," is dead wrong. It completely ignores Consciousness in favor of a mere *thing* one is conscious of. It is a cut-off, entirely false self. Any book or teaching that starts out with such a false separate "you," having a second-rate life and consciousness that must "work up to," has a premise that is, frankly, backwards.

This book starts from "the other direction"—with the You That Already Is There, which is Truth. It doesn't take away your identity, but instead shows the magnificence of True Identity.

The human way of life appears to be one of starting with imperfection and trying to progress out of it. Looking *out from* pure Consciousness doesn't start with human experience and try to take it to a higher level. *It starts with the perfection of the Divine Self and stays Here.*

Instantly, It's a completely new, different Life.

Read these pages as if It were Consciousness, the One Self, talking to *Itself*. This is the only "viewpoint" that is valid, true, and *actually operating* because again, the Self is the only One being conscious and alive here, now, so this can even be read! That may take getting used to, because chances are you've never read anything written this way.

Just stop and think what a marvelous book it would be if the Self, the One, wrote a book about Itself! What would the One Self say? It couldn't speak of a human struggle of *becoming* the Self—It could speak only of already *being* the Self. It wouldn't have to instruct, or say what It must do to get at-one with Itself, because It already *is* that! All the Self could speak of is *Its own Presence*—the immediacy of Itself to Itself. It could state only what It already, presently is—Oneness, Wholeness, Completeness and Perfection. Would that leave you out? Not at all! That Self being conscious here, now, is the only You there is.

Because this book speaks from the viewpoint of the One Self, of pure Consciousness, it may at first seem it's talking in circles and isn't leading anywhere. That's just it. The Self *isn't* leading anywhere. It's already at Itself. Frustration may try to creep in because it seems you're not making progress. That, too, is precisely the point! Your Self (the Awareness reading this now) isn't progressing to Itself because It already is Itself. In early chapters particularly, it may seem nothing is happening, and actually *plenty* is happening. By staying with pure Awareness— which is You—all false assumptions and everything "not-You" seems to fall away. It never *was* true of You.

These pages state in a clear, simple way how the Divine Self— unlimited Awareness, the Infinite Itself—never is afar off or separate, but is this *present* Consciousness that now enables these words to be read and have meaning. This very same Consciousness is really the only one conscious to have *written* this book—because a body named Peter Francis Dziuban isn't the One Consciousness. Most emphatically, there is no personal author that assumes "he" is being the Self, or has a special "in" with God. But it is possible here and now—in fact essential—to speak from the viewpoint of the Self, since *It* is the very One being aware in the first place so any writing or reading can be done.

Would you prefer to be talked down to, patronized, as if not fully aware and intelligent?

For Your Self to enjoy Its freedom of simply *being*, without the frustration of trying to *become* isn't violating some law. On the contrary, only this is how Life actually functions. To not start here is to try to go against the way Life is *already operating*.

Does this all sound too good, too simple or absolute to be true? The Self is never too absolute for Itself, and there is no other. Why not let *It* determine what makes for good reading?

———•———

Is Consciousness or the Self what *God* actually is? Don't just blindly agree because you may have heard so before. Please don't disagree, based on prior education about another kind of god.

If you hesitate about a Consciousness-God, what's the alternative—a god that is unconscious? Do you favor a fire-and-brimstone god on a throne, waiting to reward, or more likely punish, on judgment day? Suppose you somehow right now came "face to face" with that kind of god. What is the only way you would know it, and be certain of having arrived in "heaven"?

Wouldn't you have to be *conscious of* the entire experience? You'd have to be *aware of* this so-called god to be certain you had finally met. For this so-called god to even be there, would depend on *your* being conscious of it. If there were no Consciousness, this god wouldn't be. So *this god depends entirely on Consciousness for its existence*—thus is merely a concept, a thing you are conscious of—and not true God or a power at all! A concept never is conscious or alive; *it* doesn't even know it is there. Only the Consciousness that is conscious of it, knows.

Real power resides not with any human conceptual god—but with Consciousness which is forever greater than *all* concepts.

Why start with a vague god, or some concept, and try to kid yourself into believing this mental concoction is omnipresent, omnipotent and omniscient?

Turn the whole thing completely around.

First find out specifically what, if anything, is omnipresent, omnipotent and omniscient.

That's what should be called God.

Find out if Consciousness is absolutely all presence, all power, and all knowing. That's for you to determine from an unbiased reading of what is presented here.

———•———

Most likely you have flipped through these pages already, and have found some of the language unusual, perhaps startling. That's a good thing! Above all, don't feel lost if some of the capitalized words are new and unlike anything you've seen before. They have to be—because what you are about to read presents a simple but fundamental reversal of human teaching and understanding. It reverses the mistaken identification from *body* to *Consciousness*.

If you were conveying a new "viewpoint"—that of Consciousness, not a body—you'd need a brand new way of expressing it. Using the same old words would leave the reader no choice but to apply old meanings, and would be just a rehash of the same old thing.

These pages give a fresh, new "take" on Life. The language seems unusual only if it has been read out of context. To skim or jump ahead to later sections is a waste—the writing seems like an odd way of speaking, or just so much ethereal gibberish. Yet when you see what the words really mean, they zero in on Your True Self like a laser beam. They make it impossible to be ignorant or ignore-ant of Consciousness.

In fact, that's what the word *ignorant* basically means: ignore-ant. It implies there is that which is *always present*, but is being ignored, whether knowingly or not.

What appears to be the current human era generally prides itself on being the most enlightened and savvy that evolution has produced up to now. Incredibly, there seems to remain this ignore-ance, a vagueness and lack of clarity as to the meaning of even the most basic words, those so fundamental to living. You'll be amazed at how simple words such as *be*, *is*, *present*, *one*, *all*, and words like *conscious* or *alive* are often so hazily defined.

You are about to see what these words truly stand for—but that doesn't mean intellectual analysis. Far from it. One never finds Consciousness *Itself* in words. The true meaning of these words is a specific conscious "experience." It is an *alive Presence* that literally comes to life because It *is* Life. What is the actual "stuff" that the word Consciousness stands for? What is It that has to be present first, in order to need the word to label It? You are already, unstoppably *being* that which is changelessly "behind" all these words.

Inside you will also find simple explanations of some of the toughest, age-old, and "unanswered" questions ever faced by philosophers and scientists. They concern the Infinite, the Divine—and the nature of the so-called material world, time, and creation. There are even *the* answers to those two deep, profound issues that keep everyone awake at night: "Which came first, the chicken or the egg?" and, "If a tree falls in the forest...." Seriously, even these are answered in an easy new way because by looking out from *pure Consciousness*, the Infinite, one is "outside the box" of a finite human intellect.

———————

By this point you should be asking, "How do I know this is all true?"

"This may be well and good if I accept the premise that Consciousness is all—but how do I know *that's* true? Just who is the author to be making all these statements? And who is to say *this* is necessarily Truth, instead of what other books or teachings say?"

In other words, you want to be certain that what is said here is really *the way it is*.

There's a simple answer to that. It's found in the word *is*.

Think it through for yourself. Whatever is Truth, Reality, or "the way Life is" must be that which actually *is*. Whatever is going to be true, or be Truth, has to truly *be*. It has to exist; it has to honestly *be present*, and never can change.

It doesn't matter what word is used—Consciousness, Self, God, Reality—only what *really is being* can be what *is real*. There's nothing deep or difficult about that. And if something *isn't being,* that means it doesn't even exist; it isn't present anywhere. So how could it function, or be any kind of Truth or Reality? It couldn't.

Only what *truly is* can be what *is true*.

No exceptions. None for philosophy, science, or religion.

Now it gets exciting.

That which truly is must also be *you*.

Why? You could not be, nor be conscious, as something that is not present. To be conscious, Consciousness has to *be*.

Put it this way: if you *weren't* being, if you weren't now consciously present, you wouldn't even exist to have questions or care about this. But you do exist; you are now present and aware.

Now try a little test. Try to make Consciousness *not* be.

See if Consciousness, the pure Awareness you are presently aware of being, can be taken *out* of being present. Can Awareness somehow be taken away so It isn't *being present now*, but is backed up to five minutes ago? Or can Awareness be pushed ahead by five minutes, so It isn't being present now? The more you try, the more you see the impossibility of it. Awareness *truly is*.

For this to be clear, start with pure Awareness, pure Consciousness, only—entirely distinct from the body and everything else you seem to be *aware of*. One who is alert sees that pure Awareness, all by Itself alone, never changes or goes away. Thoughts come and go, yes. Emotions pass. And the body's five forms of sensing—what is seen, heard, touched, tasted and smelled—change constantly. Looking closely, you see it's always the stuff you seem to be *aware of* that's changing and passing, never Awareness Itself. Awareness, all by Itself alone, is present as pure *Being*, a changeless presence which simply, immovably *is*.

Go ahead, try to move Awareness by giving it a shove physically. Can it be done? Try mentally to outmaneuver Awareness and *think* It away, or make It change from being present now. Even try spiritually to pray Awareness away with all the faith you can muster. No amount of physical effort, mental effort, or belief can do it. Not even the highest intellectual arguments about semantics or definitions will alter pure Awareness or make It other than absolutely *present*.

Now contrast the nature of the so-called thinking, sensing "mind" with pure Awareness. They're not the same at all. The mind's activity would be everything that is *not* pure Awareness. While Awareness is simply *being*, absolutely everything the sensing, thinking "mind" claims to experience involves the movement or passing of *time*.

Look closely at how the mind works. It takes the passing of time to think thoughts. It takes time to experience sensations: to see sights, hear sounds, and to touch, taste and smell. It takes time to feel emotions, and even to have psychic experiences. Yet all such things that pass in time are only what you seem to be *aware of*. None of that is Awareness Itself. Awareness as It is *being* isn't passing in the flow of time with those things. It's the way a pure white movie screen never budges, while the movie characters and images superimposed on it appear to move and change constantly. Pure Awareness is changelessly *present*.

Now notice the nature of the mind's activity that's always passing in time. *It's never present.* Look at the constant sweep of the second-hand on a watch. It never quits moving. Time never stops passing to genuinely *be*, to be present, to be what truly *is*. Time seems to flow non-stop: as the future, *that-which-is-not-yet*, instantly becomes a past, *that-which-is-not-anymore*. Time is literally a state of *that which is not*!

Here's the kicker. Every single sensation that the human mind experiences about its universe—every sight, touch, sound, taste and smell—as well as every thought and emotion—all occur or are constantly *passing* in this flow of time. On that level, you can't stop it—all of it is always passing away and *not being*.

So if you didn't identify as the pure Conscious Being you are, *as what is*, and identified only on the passing level of the five senses, time, and what is-not, *what in the world would you be doing*?

What kind of a non-being, never-present self would you be?

Stop a moment and let *that one* in.

That simple switch in identification is profound. You are not the mind. Thinking and sensing are what you appear to *use*, or *do*—they're not what you *are* as pure Conscious Awareness.

The would-be thinking "mind" has always considered what it senses and experiences in the passage of time to be reality. Now you seem to do an about-face. You don't identify with a state of sensing and thinking that is always passing and *never being*. You identify as pure Conscious Being, or *what really is*, the Real. That which passes on the level of the sensing, thinking "time-mind" is now seen in the correct light—as *what really is not*, or what is not real.

The point is, for your entire universe, *Consciousness is all that truly is*. Don't read on until you really settle with yourself on this. It means Consciousness is "the way it is"—which is another way of saying Reality, Truth. The word Reality doesn't mean some far-off state you must ultimately become conscious of. Reality simply means *what really is*—which is Consciousness as It is effortlessly *being*, right here, now. You just showed it to yourself.

Meanwhile, in terms of Consciousness Itself, nothing changed because Consciousness never fails to be what It is. It is always the Real You, even though it may seem a state of thinking was imagining for a while that You were something else.

Based on these few paragraphs, you may not yet be willing to concede that what the mind and five senses testify to *isn't really being*, or isn't being real. Fair enough. Know for the moment that these and similar points are discussed repeatedly, in different ways throughout these pages. By being honest with what is true of Consciousness, the more it is clear how and why Consciousness truly is all that is present. To not identify as Consciousness would be to identify as a state of unconsciousness, and how intelligent is that? The beautiful truth is that there really is no choice—Consciousness is the only One being conscious—and It never fails to be Itself.

If this book is the first you've read on Consciousness, you may be saying, "Whew, this sounds very ethereal," but the more you read, the more undeniable and real it is. If you've read books on Consciousness or spirituality before, you may be saying, "Hmm, this sounds interesting." Reading from the viewpoint of the One Self, Consciousness Itself, you say, "This makes complete sense. It's simple!"

Consciousness, Being, never doubts or has questions about Itself. Notice how any doubts or questions seem to originate from the constantly shifting, unstable *thinking* of the intellect or so-called sensing mind. Now notice the certainty and power with which pure Conscious Awareness goes right on *being*, regardless of what is thought.

There is nothing wrong with questioning; it is strongly encouraged. And never just accept statements because they sound authoritative—including those of this author. But to behold what these pages say, to discern the magnificence and permanence of what You are, you must make a clear distinction between pure Awareness *Itself*, and the thoughts you are aware of. Thought is not *Awareness*. If you won't make this distinction and stick to it, put the book down now. Otherwise you will be frustrated and are wasting your time.

Don't fall for any superstitious nonsense that this material is too deep, just because some words are capitalized. How much heavy intellectualizing is needed before Awareness is aware here, now? None—that's the point! If you're aware enough to simply know you *be*, you've got all It takes. It is sufficient for Consciousness to be purely aware only, not intellectual.

To be conscious is not other-worldly or esoteric. It's the most natural, normal thing going. Publishers like to ask who the potential audience is for a new book. Well, who is there that's *not* conscious?

Drop all conceptual baggage. Your Consciousness as It now *is*, most emphatically, is not anything metaphysical or New Age. It is not Zen, or any other religion or teaching. Consciousness Itself needs no teaching. It doesn't have to learn to become Itself because It already *is* Itself. Consciousness isn't Eastern, Western, or any superimposed label, but is simply what *truly is*. Consciousness is never what someone else is into, for It is true of *you*. And not after years of study—but now.

Pure Awareness is not a trend, not "spiritually cool," not a hot money-making opportunity. Awareness doesn't see Itself as being in vogue at the start of a millennium, nor think of Itself as a new paradigm. It holds no pre-conceived notions, but simply is aware, present. So read as a "clean slate" of pure Awareness. Read as if never aware before, but now only. Only this is what Consciousness *Itself* is.

While you are reading, a particular point may make a strong impact. Perhaps "a light will go on." Meanwhile, the very next sentence beckons you to continue right on reading. Don't.

Don't let the eye keep scanning down a page, and assume you're getting it, while thought is back on the prior paragraph. Let any point that strikes really sink in. Ponder it quietly, in a relaxed way, with no pressure. Stay with it until you feel you have "absorbed" it and are ready to move on. It may help clarify subsequent points. This book is not a quick read. Remember, Consciousness *is*. It is always *present* and isn't gained in the passing of time—so what's the hurry?

The thread that runs throughout, and the question to ask continually is, "What is true of pure Consciousness *alone*?" Obviously you are free to disagree at any time, but if you do, don't take issue with the author. You'll find you cannot be honest with your own Consciousness and deny any of what is said here. There really can be no resistance to this material because Consciousness can't resist being conscious—and that is all these pages are concerned with.

There does however seem to be much disagreement about Reality and "God," and as many interpretations as there appear to be people walking the planet. The disagreements may be minor—or they may lead to wars. Meanwhile *all will agree*, "I am conscious." To start Here, as pure Consciousness, is to be in the One "right place."

Notice how, regardless of one's religious beliefs, Consciousness is conscious. Regardless of how much faith one has—whether a lot or none at all—Consciousness is conscious. Faith can be in a god, or in cold, hard scientific fact—it doesn't matter—Consciousness goes right on being, in spite of either. As said before, the beauty and power of Consciousness is that It is not a matter of human faith, which is fallible and can waver, or be misdirected toward evil. The Ever-Presence of Consciousness is infallible, a changeless absolute certainty.

This book is not about belief, faith, or fictitious separate personal consciousnesses, and how they must become more aware. It is about how completely, perfectly aware the One Consciousness Itself *already is*. Again, that doesn't leave you out, for that very Consciousness is the only You there is. The only One being conscious so this can now be read *is* the Consciousness being spoken of.

It's so simple. Consciousness *Itself* is doing It all. You no more have to become It or make It work than you are right now working at being aware.

You already *are*.

2

CONSCIOUSNESS
IS WHAT *YOU* ARE

WHEN AGREEING YOU ARE NOW CONSCIOUS, have you any idea of the *magnificence* of what you've agreed to?

First of all, exactly who is this you that is now conscious?

Start by making a clear distinction between this you that is conscious and the many things you appear to be conscious *of*.

Stop reading a moment to closely notice this book. Then take a few moments and quietly be aware of your body as it holds the book. Next, slowly take in the room in which the body is seated (assuming the body is in a room), and any objects in the room. Stop reading now, and do it.

Silently be aware of all these things without thinking about them— the way a clear glass camera lens impartially includes everything in its field of view. There is no thought or judgment *about* the things in the view, no emotional attachment. Nor does the clear glass assume it is any of the things—they all are just "included." Likewise now, each item, even the body, is simply a thing you appear to be aware *of*.

Notice that you have to say of every single thing, "Yes, each one is a thing I appear to be aware of. But not one of those things is the me that is *aware*. Not even the body is the same as the me that is aware of the body. No thing, not even the body, is the Awareness I am."

Since no thing is the you that is aware, then Awareness must be who *you* really are, because nothing else is you.

This chapter consists of several short sections, each allowing you to see for yourself in a different way why Awareness, pure Consciousness, is what *you* really are.

It's surprising in daily experience the extent to which there is a vagueness about Consciousness, and how rarely It is distinguished from what one is conscious *of*. When one speaks of being conscious, it almost never refers to Consciousness Itself. It refers to *things*: "I am conscious of my clothes...I'm conscious of the body and how it feels...I am aware of the sound of a car...aware of what's on the computer screen...I'm conscious of all these thoughts and emotions..." and so on. Consciousness *Itself* takes a back seat and these various things seem to get all the attention. No wonder the concern over things soon takes over and ends up running the show.

Yet where does the power lie? Is any such thing itself ever conscious? Are such things ever conscious of *you*? No. Always, it is you who are conscious of them.

Things can't take control; they can't call the shots because no *thing* is ever conscious to do anything. Only Consciousness Itself is conscious.

Things are *called* things because they are just that, mere things. Consciousness is called Consciousness because It is exactly that, pure Conscious Awareness. It never is the same as any thing It is conscious of.

As *you* are conscious, Consciousness is what you really are. You are not any thing, not even the body.

That may sound nice and spiritual and lofty—but why is it so important? To the extent one is concerned only with the things one appears to be conscious of, and ignores *Consciousness Itself*, one is attempting to function as un-Consciousness. It is literally being *unconscious* from the viewpoint of the Self, meaning asleep to who you really are.

This is why functioning only on the level of things sensed by the five physical senses is sometimes referred to as "the human sleep" or "waking dream." The body is up and out of bed, walking and talking, conducting its normal daily affairs, but it's really like being in a dream.

As a character in a dream you *assume* you're awake the entire time, don't you? Yet you're sound asleep and not awake to who you really are. You assume everything presented within the dream is real, and unquestioningly accept its conditions—yet it's not your waking reality at all. Likewise, the human mind assumes everything presented by the five senses is real, but it's not Reality at all. In Reality, Consciousness never sleeps or dreams. It is always fully awake.

In reading this book, it's essential to first be clear who the *you* is that's reading. Pure Consciousness is you, and you never are confused with the things you appear to be conscious of.

To be clear about the difference between you as pure Consciousness, and the many things found in daily experience, take some very basic examples.

As said earlier, it appears at the moment that you are conscious of this book. Can the book ever change places and become the you that is conscious of the book?

Don't rush through these questions because they seem so simple. Let each answer clearly register before going to the next question.

It is always Consciousness, you, that identifies the book. The book never identifies you; it never even identifies itself.

Can the Consciousness you are ever get *inside* the book, so the book no longer is something you appear to be conscious of? Can it ever happen that you are within the book, and the book is no longer within your Consciousness? Impossible.

Suppose five minutes from now, you were to *think* of the book. Would that *thought* of the book be aware or conscious? Would that thought be the same as your Consciousness Itself? No, it would be just a thought, another type of "thing" you seem to be conscious of.

See if it is possible to change places, so the book or even the thought of the book becomes conscious instead of *you* being conscious.

It is irrevocable Truth that only Consciousness is conscious.

Now what about one of the hands holding this book?

Really stop to notice it. Is that hand ever aware of you? It is always you that is aware of the hand. It is another type of thing. The hand never identifies itself; only Consciousness identifies it.

What about the sense of touch of the hand? Notice the *tactile feel* of touching this book's cover. Close your eyes and really *feel* that sensation. Go slowly. Is that feeling the same as pure Awareness? No. It is a sensation. Feel it again. Make a sharp distinction that the pure Awareness you are is not the tactile sensation you seem to be aware *of*.

If five minutes from now, you were to think back about that sensation, would that thought of the sensation be aware? It too, would be a thought, yet another kind of thing, not pure Awareness.

Sensations themselves never are aware. Sensation and Awareness are two distinct words referring to entirely different things. They are not the same, yet it's a distinction that's rarely made.

Can a tactile feeling, a sound, a visual sight, an odor, or a taste ever *know* anything; can it ever tell you it is conscious, alive? Can *it* ever identify itself, even as a sensation? Can *it* distinguish itself from an emotion or a thought? No, only you do all that, as Awareness.

All any sensation can do is be the sensation it is. The five forms of physical sensation, whether taken individually or as a group, never are *themselves* conscious or intelligent. They're never *you*. Sensations are merely unaware states of *reaction*. According to scientists, each type of sensation would in its essence be a chemical or electrical nerve reaction, so many molecules and atoms, an ongoing exchange of energy or vibration, experienced in the passing of time.

For what portion of your day do you correctly identify as what *you* are, pure Conscious Awareness, instead of as the body and countless sensations you seem to be conscious of?

In other words, are you being Consciousness, or unconsciousness?

When identifying directly as the pure Consciousness you truly are, you never fail to be aware. You never become un-Consciousness. No work has to be done, for Consciousness Itself is doing or *being* It all.

No matter how long it may seem you didn't know this, or were ignorant (ignore-ant) of your Self as Consciousness, do not be concerned. Pure Consciousness never gets confused. It never assumes It is a thing, never changes places with the things of which It is conscious. Equally, not one thing you appear to be conscious of can ever become the Consciousness you are.

Again, Consciousness is called Consciousness because It is pure Consciousness only—not Consciousness *and* a body or sensations. *Pure* is what Consciousness Itself really is. It has no visible form, as things appear to, but that doesn't make It any less present or real.

Right now, what is it to simply be this pure Consciousness, all by Itself alone, apart from all sensations and other things you seem to be conscious of, even all *thoughts* about Consciousness?

It's the same as asking, what is Consciousness *to pure Consciousness?*

What does that "feel" like, right where you are?

It's the answer to the question at the opening of this book, "What is Consciousness all by Itself alone?" This is truly being the Consciousness you are—or truly being conscious—instead of assuming you are a physical, sensing body or a thinking mentality.

———•———

Slowly, silently, be aware of the body again as it holds this book.

The body, like every other thing, is an item you appear to be aware *of*. The body never is aware of you; it's not even aware of itself.

Always, it is you that is aware of the body.

That body is not *you*.

Awareness is you.

What you are as Awareness, pure Consciousness, goes far beyond a body, a mere thing.

A body isn't your identity, for a body is like an unaware mannequin. By itself, a body doesn't *know* anything in order to be an identity. Only Consciousness is conscious to know anything. If there were no Consciousness present, the body couldn't even be identified as a body.

Notice how all things that Consciousness appears to be conscious of, even the body, are *identified*. They have names or labels—body, hand, book, tactile sensation, thought, emotion, room, etc.—identifying them as the particular things they appear to be. How many such things in your universe, by themselves, know they are there? None.

It is thanks entirely to Consciousness being present that *all* things are identified.

No thing has any awareness, any intelligence or ability to identify itself. Things always depend entirely on Consciousness being present to give them their identification.

Things, by themselves, have no identification, no identity.

Consciousness is the only Identity.

By themselves, things don't even know they exist. This book doesn't know it exists; nor does the hand, nor the sensation of touch. The body doesn't know it exists.

Not one single thing in the entire universe knows that it exists!

The only One that knows things exist is Consciousness. The only One that knows there is such a thing as existing is Consciousness!

You know you exist, which means Consciousness, not any thing, is your Identity.

Since you are not an identified thing called a body, you cannot honestly take the point of view of a body. Ever. It is not your point of view to take.

Only what is true of *Consciousness* is true of you.

So never be intimidated by Consciousness, Awareness, or any other synonym, or put them up on a pedestal just because they are spelled with a capital letter. The Consciousness that is gently being aware right here, now, never is in awe of Itself.

Consciousness is always quiet, peaceful—yet absolutely certain in being present.

This quiet, peaceful certainty isn't what Consciousness is *to* you.

This certainty *is* You.

———•———

Be aware of the body once more as it appears to hold this book. Can the body ever get outside of the Awareness you are, in order that Awareness no longer is aware of the body?

Equally, can Awareness ever change places and get inside some part of the body, so that part no longer appears to be in Awareness?

Notice the various parts of the body one by one.

Start small, with a fingernail. Are *you* that fingernail? Of course not. Go further, to a whole finger. Is that the extent of you? Notice an entire arm. Is that all there is to you? It is a *thing* you are conscious of. Are *you* just a chest and shoulders? A leg? Two legs? Are *you* the same as teeth, or eyes, hair, a nose, a brain, a skull—or an entire head?

Is any one of those parts the you that identifies that part? Are those parts the same as the *consciously alive Presence* you are now consciously being? No. Can you get *inside* an arm, a torso, or a head so that part no longer appears to be *within you*, as Consciousness? It is always a *thing* Consciousness appears to be conscious of. No thing, not even a head, can ever be the Consciousness that is aware of, or includes it.

Clearly, the Consciousness you are is not any one part of the body.

Why then should it be assumed that when these various parts are combined, this arrangement has suddenly become you? Since when does a bunch of not-you's add up to you? At what point do parts of a body go from being not-you to you? At what point does a thing you are aware *of* become the Awareness you are? Or do you just glibly quote a cliché such as, "Well, the whole is greater than the sum of its parts."

In this case, are you certain?

No part of a body, nor a whole body, can be *I*. Only Consciousness Itself is conscious to be or say "*I*." Only It has the capacity to know "I Am." The Consciousness which alone knows "I Am" is not any part of a body. Nor is It *in* any part of a body.

If Consciousness were inside the body, then the body would no longer be in Consciousness—and one couldn't be conscious of it. But that never happens. If there is any doubt, try right now to yank Consciousness down inside some part of the body, so the body no longer appears to be in Consciousness. Try as hard as you can. It'll never happen.

The body is what you use, but it is not *You*.

Now slowly take more note of the room in which the body is seated. Specifically notice each wall, even the one in back of the body. Relax as you do this; allow yourself time to take everything in. Stop to notice the floor. Then slowly notice the ceiling.

Could any part of the room ever change places with Consciousness? Could any part get outside of Consciousness, so it is no longer something you appear to be conscious of?

Parts of the room may be out of range of the eyes at times when the head is turned, but the only way the room ever exists to you is thanks to Consciousness *including* it. It appears as if the walls of the room are outside of the *body*, of course—but they never are outside of Consciousness. Always, Consciousness includes what appears to be the room.

So just who is now in a room? It is a *body* that appears to be in a room. Consciousness Itself is not in the room. The room, the body, and all else appears to be *within Consciousness, within you*. *You* are not now in a room as this book is being read. The Consciousness you are includes all things. It, Itself, never is in any thing It includes.

If right now the body were to get up and walk from room to room, it would be the *body* that is in each room. Meanwhile, each room is always in Consciousness. When the body goes in to take a shower, it is the body that gets wet, not Consciousness.

Just because the Consciousness you are is not in the body, that does *not* mean body is separate or cut off from Consciousness. Nor does it mean Consciousness goes flying off in every direction, is unstable, or can get lost. Quite the contrary. As Consciousness, you are permanently "anchored" as the *all-embracing* Infinite One which never has anything greater than or out beyond Itself. Body is forever within that eternal, perfect Awareness which includes all there is. All-Inclusive Consciousness is more permanently present, more endlessly "stable" than anything so-called physical or material could ever hope to be.

Body and all things are always in Consciousness, Awareness, which alone can know, "I include all things." This never changes.

At some point the thought may have come, "But many teachings say that all things, even a blade of grass and a stone are conscious, or have consciousness in them." That simply is not true as will be clearly shown throughout upcoming chapters. All things are *in* Consciousness, yes, but that definitely is not the same as saying things are conscious.

When the word *You* is used in these pages, it is really Consciousness referring to Itself. Never is there a secondary "you" that is personally being conscious and has to struggle to become more aware. Exactly who would such a second "you" be, anyway?

Right here, now, there is Consciousness, which includes what appears to be a body and a room. But that is not you in a personal sense. It is Consciousness *Itself* that is being conscious; there is no "you" personally making It function or operate.

Other than Consciousness Itself, there appears to be a body holding a book. That's not you either. Body is merely a thing Consciousness is conscious of. That leaves only Consciousness Itself, a thing called a body, and a room. There is no second consciousness or identity anywhere. There may seem to be thoughts or feelings, but they aren't conscious; they too, are just more things the One Consciousness seems to be conscious of.

That's it. That's *all* there ever is—Consciousness and a lot of things *It* appears to be conscious of. There is no secondary self anywhere. So there is never Consciousness *and* a you that has to become more conscious of Consciousness. There is only Consciousness *being Itself* in Its all-inclusive magnificence. It's the only kind of You there is.

This never changes. It never fails to be.

Meanwhile, nothing has gone anywhere. You are right here—calm, serene, concretely present as ever, *as Consciousness*. Body isn't gone. Nor are friends or loved ones. All that would be "gone" is a false belief—that there was a lesser, secondary self; two identities instead of the One. It was only a mistaken assumption—that You were a mortal body.

The fact that Consciousness Itself is the only One conscious is why this book is written from Its "viewpoint." It is written as if Consciousness, pure Awareness, were "talking" only to Itself, never another. It is really Life Itself, the One I Am, here, now, talking to Myself.

Who else, honestly, is being aware?

Again, when the writing talks only about Awareness and doesn't seem to be leading anywhere, that's because it's *not* leading anywhere. The One Awareness Itself is *already being* all the Awareness there can be. It precludes there being a lesser self or awareness of any kind. It leaves no other that has to progress or *think* its way to Awareness. Awareness is never a matter of more and better *thinking*. Thinking about Awareness doesn't clear up the fog—thinking *is* the fog.

If one cannot think Awareness, then how can one be perfectly clear as to what Awareness is? The clarity of Awareness is the *absence* of thinking. Clarity is the pure presence of Awareness all by Itself alone. You *are* clear now. It is just a matter of identifying directly *as* or *being* pure Awareness only—not a thinking mind.

The One to whom it is clear that there is only Awareness *is* that very Awareness Itself, being present.

Awareness is Its own clarity.

So while reading these pages, be alert not to wait. Don't expect a series of points that lead to some ultimate point, in the sense that there is a progression with the answer coming only at the end. That may be how human *thinking* seems to operate, but that's not Awareness. Identifying directly *as* Awareness leaves no need for getting *to* Awareness.

If you assumed you were a body swimming in the ocean, you would always have to be swimming to some place, trying to arrive at some point. When identifying yourself as the ocean, you're already everywhere you could possibly be, and completely satisfied.

3

ALIVENESS

THE THOUGHT MAY COME, "As Consciousness is not any thing, then what is It? As pure Consciousness is what I am, what am I as Consciousness?"

You, as *You* really are, exist not as a physical object, but as *a state of Awareness only*. You are that Awareness which is not a body, but includes body and all things. You are present as an alert, intelligent, *alive Presence* only. This alive Presence, the One You are now alive to being, is Life Itself simply knowing, "I am. I am aware," distinct from all I appear to be aware of.

How does being this aware, alive Presence differ from assuming one is a body? Is it difficult, requiring years of esoteric training?

For Awareness to be aware here, now, is effortless. Awareness depends on nothing besides Itself to be present. It does not depend on thinking or mental effort to be aware. Awareness is the You that is effortlessly aware *before* thinking thinks, and regardless of whether thinking thinks or not. To be aware perfectly, Awareness does not need to read another book (even this one), listen to another tape or CD, or attend another seminar or retreat. Awareness simply *is*—entirely independent of all would-be personal effort, all thoughts, and any emotional heaviness that seems to go with them. As pure Aware Presence, You are completely "light" or "buoyant," unencumbered by things, never carrying any mental baggage.

Just because the Aware Presence You are is no *thing*, doesn't mean It is a nothing. It never is blank or a deadness. On the contrary, Awareness has to be keenly, specifically *alive*, vital, to be the very Presence It is. It cannot be seen, touched, or experienced by any of the five senses—yet is *consciously alive*.

A perfect synonym for pure Awareness, and one used frequently in these pages, is *Conscious Aliveness* or simply, *Aliveness*. It most closely indicates what You are as Awareness or Presence alone. *Aliveness* carries no connotation of a body or five senses. It has nothing to do with thoughts or human emotions, or three-dimensional forms, objects, or places. It has no connection to *things*. Conscious Aliveness can't be conceptualized or pictured in thought. Yet It conveys the specific conscious vitality that Awareness is now *being*.

Call Conscious Aliveness a "feeling," but It is not an emotion. It is the *alive lightness* that pure Awareness alone is, apart from the seeming weight of a material world or mental and emotional pressures. It is endlessly free "openness," which is *alive stuff*. It is Life's conscious "experiencing" of Its own clean, clear living Presence. This specific aliveness with which Being is vitally being here, now, is You as You really are.

The suffix -*ness* means "essence of." Alive-*ness* is Life in Its very essence: Life "doing what It does," which is to be *alive*, and con- sciously so. It is the Self *actively* alive to being purely alive, wholly apart from things. How rare it is to find the word Aliveness used in everyday language. Yet is there anything else so basic, so fundamental to living?

As you read, be alert not to the words themselves, but to the Alive Presence that the words point to. All value is in the Presence, or the light, alive "feeling," not the words. This Aliveness is not what one is getting *from* Life or the Self. Aliveness *is* the Self as It is being Itself here, now, for no person is doing It. It isn't a separate Presence you are conscious *of*. It is what your present Consciousness *is*.

Conscious Aliveness is the Self's unspoken calm of simply being. It isn't doing anything physically or mentally—yet is wondrously vital. It is not the constant movement of the so-called "human mind," which would always be flitting from one thought or emotion to the next. Pure Conscious Aliveness never flits. It *is*. While the "mind" would always be a *process*, Aliveness, Awareness, is changeless *Presence*.

Awareness is a *still, silent* Presence.

This silent, alive Presence that Awareness effortlessly is, *is* the I AM, without Its being thought or verbalized. To voice or think the words, "I Am" in addition to the silent presence of Awareness is redundant.

While Aliveness' Presence is a stillness, It is *alive* stillness. It is not sleepy, not trance-like or a stupor. It is ever-engaged in being definite, keen, precise conscious alertness. It is sharply, clearly awake to being alive now.

When attention is on a thing, say a wonderful gift you have just received, you are keenly conscious of, or alive and "alert" to that item in your Consciousness, aren't you? Well, what is it to be that keenly alert not to any thing, but to *simply being conscious, alive*? What is it to be acutely, sharply alive to what pure Consciousness is all by Itself?

Likewise, what is going on when the body sits quietly, perhaps with eyes closed, and no attention is given to thoughts, sensations, or emo- tions—and one is just being pure Consciousness?

What is *that*? It certainly is not deadness. It is Conscious *Aliveness*.

To rightly know or be Conscious Aliveness, start with It alone. Drop all weight of what you seem to be conscious of. Drop all sense of a body that is holding a book, that is in a room, that is on a planet, that is in a stellar universe, in a certain year. Conscious Aliveness *Itself* is none of those things. While Aliveness is "invisible," or not perceptible by five senses, that doesn't make It less real or present. It does not function other than as Its own alive feeling, or Presence.

To Conscious Aliveness, Its own Presence is never ethereal or vague, but is real, specific, and ever-available. There is no need to labor to become or connect with It. Your Aliveness is never blocked from Its own Presence, and does not have to be activated or made more present. It *cannot fail* to be present. Try to *stop* this Alive Being from being—and you see how impossible it is.

A few moments spent *being silently alive as* pure, gentle Conscious Aliveness alone, is worth more than a month spent verbally describing It. What is it to *be It* right now?

Only pure *Aliveness*, not an intellect, can "answer."

Human ignorance may try to say that while Awareness, Conscious Aliveness, is pure or clear, It is impersonal, cold, and detached. Or it may try to say Awareness is lifeless, like a pane of glass. Conscious Aliveness is exactly the opposite. It never is cold, lifeless or stagnant.

Aliveness is "hot."

Aliveness is not hot in the sense of temperature, but is Life's endless *warmth*, also sometimes called Unconditional Love. It is the inability of Life to withhold any of Itself from being. It is not Unconditional Love to another, nor to a separate "you," for there is only Itself. Having no choice but to be alive all-out, Conscious Aliveness is pure, unadulterated *Vitality*. It is not hard or rigid, but is infinitely "soft" in that there is absolutely nothing material, dense, or resistant about It.

Right now, just how un-dense and un-tense, how gently *soft*, is the pure, consciously alive *Presence* you are? One cannot answer this question in words. The answer is in the *being* of It.

Is there an end to this incredible softness, this un-tense ease? How much is available to you, or *as* you? Is there only a few hours' supply? Is it a matter of volume, like a few gallons? Does this endless softness have to be made to be present, or turned on? Or is it the reverse—that it is impossible to stop, shut off or restrain this marvelous ease, this exquisite softness of Being?

This is what Aliveness, Conscious Presence, is, wholly distinct from what you are conscious of.

It isn't a Presence you are *in*. This Presence is what *You* really are.

What is it to always *start here* in your identification?

------•------

Drop all attempts to understand or get at-one with Consciousness.

Drop *all* effort. Consciousness is still perfectly aware, perfectly and softly being, isn't It?

This is the One these pages are about. This is the Real You.

Never assume Consciousness is elusive, abstract, or beyond you. Consciousness never is beyond you because *It is you*. How could your own Consciousness get beyond you? How could you remain conscious if It somehow left? It is inseparable from right where you always are. Human thinking is forever separate from pure Consciousness.

Don't kid yourself. If one tries to read this material as a "thinking mind" or intellect, it makes no sense at all. Don't hesitate to admit that—but don't dwell on it. Stay with pure Consciousness, because the intellect may try to doubt, kick and whine every step of the way. The intellect may try to ask all of *its* questions, and make *its* demands about Consciousness. It may try to race through this book, quickly deciding what it disagrees with, due to its limited education or conditioning, and then say, "I just don't get it."

This book was not written to an intellect.

In fact, it *should* feel as if you're not getting what is stated here of Consciousness. How can you get what you're already being? Is water ever trying to get its wetness? To an intellect, whose job is to conceptually "get" or grasp, this is most upsetting. To say you don't get this, or that it's "over your head" is quite accurate. It *is* impossible to mentally grasp pure Consciousness. You can't *think* the marvelous softness of *Presence*. One can only "feel" It, or *be* It. And to see that is to "get" It. To have Presence *and* thinking is two-ness, not *Oneness*.

If you come across something you at first don't agree with, don't just mentally dismiss it with, "Well, that's just his (the author's) opinion." Ask yourself if what you read is true of the Consciousness aware here, now.

The intellect or "thinking mind" may then try to crowd out this wonderfully soft, simple ease of pure Aliveness and say, "Even if this is true of Consciousness, of what value is it...where's the payoff? Why care about Consciousness? It's sort of plain vanilla, kind of boring. *I'll* decide if Awareness has value."

That's not you. That would be just old conditioned *thinking* you seem to be aware *of*, but which isn't the effortless Awareness You are. Without Awareness, thinking couldn't even seem to function.

Did you ever stop to realize—the only one that thinks thinking is so special, is that very same thinking?

Pure Conscious Awareness never lets thinking act as judge and jury over Itself, deciding whether Consciousness is of sufficient value, or how It will be of benefit to thinking. When one beholds what is true of Consciousness, thinking is seen in an entirely different light.

Consciousness never looks for a payoff for being conscious, because It already includes all there is. It seeks no gain—for that would imply there was something of greater value than Itself. There isn't. *Consciousness is Its own reward.* One who stays busy honestly, consistently *being* pure Consciousness, is not subject to the human lacks and limitations that would appear to go with *not* being Consciousness.

Regardless of what thinking seems to think, Awareness goes right on serenely, unfailingly being aware. It is your own perfect self-example of how Unbounded Awareness can't be contained by a would-be thinking mind. To truly be aware is to identify not with thoughts or emotions, but *as* pure Alive Presence which is unthinkable, yet ever-present.

4

FACT: CONSCIOUSNESS
IS THE INFINITE ITSELF

WHAT DOES THE WORD *infinite* really mean?

Is Consciousness, or what some call the Self, the Divine, or God, really the Infinite—does an Infinite really exist? Or is Infinite just a word used by spiritual teachings to sound impressive?

Most importantly, where do you fit in with all this? Do you assume you are finite, and the Infinite is something really big, way off, apart from you? If you claim that's true—can you "back it up"—or have you just unquestioningly accepted popular beliefs?

Then again, maybe you're not supposed to probe too deeply into all this. After all, the word Infinite often has a mystical connotation that sounds sort of "spiritually correct." Perhaps such affairs should be left to the so-called enlightened, but *you* shouldn't inquire too thoroughly.

What happens when you just plain make a little effort to pull the whole thing apart and look at it *intelligently*? Take another look at the difference between the Consciousness you are, and the many things it appears you are conscious *of*.

———•———

It sounds funny, but every single thing one appears to be conscious of, or observe, in daily experience is just that, *observable*. According to the way the five senses, or the so-called human "mind" seems to work, every single thing it would supposedly sense or experience has some observable qualities. It doesn't matter if it's something seen visually, an item that's touched or felt, a sound that's heard, a smell, a taste—or even a thought or an emotion. Everything the human "mind" claims to experience always has a noticeable *form* to it.

Imagine picking up a stick. First, according to the sense of sight, it has a *visual* form or appearance. The stick has an observable length of so many inches, and a little width or depth. It also has a clearly noticeable beginning and end. Even its color is a form—say brown, instead of blue. If you were to close the eyes while holding the stick, the sense of touch, or *tactile feel* of holding it in the fingers would be yet another type of noticeable form. That tactile feeling is a form easily distinguished from the tactile sense of a snowball, or a piece of jello.

The other sensations of *taste* and *smell* are also distinct, observable forms even though you can't see or touch them (compare the taste and scent of an orange to those of an onion). The sense of *sound* can't be seen either, but suppose you tapped that stick on the ground like a drumbeat. The rhythmic sound would be a noticeable pattern or form, quite distinct from a telephone ring, or a balloon popping. The point is, each of the five types of sensation that the mind experiences is an observable, noticeable form, though the sensation is not always a visible object, or made of "solid matter."

Besides the five types of sensation, even *emotions* are distinct, observable forms. Each emotion (happiness, anger, etc.), has its own particular feeling or "color," which distinguishes it from other emotions. While hard to measure technologically, each emotion would according to scientists be a specific nerve or chemical reaction. It's actually a very definite pattern of energy or vibration. For that matter, sounds, sights, touches, tastes and smells are all forms of vibration too.

Thoughts, while fleeting, are also observable entities. The thought of a sunrise would have a form quite different from the thought of what was eaten for dinner last night. Various thought forms would be mental images, memories, concepts and ideas; that which is seen in the "mind's eye."

Sensations, emotions and thoughts are not physical objects are they? Yet they, like physical objects, are also said to be apart from oneself. They are what one seems to *have*; not what one *is*. They are never "I." If an emotion or thought were the same as you, that is how you would always be; they wouldn't seem to change, come and go; but they do.

One term perfectly describes every observable thing that the five senses and human mind experience in this way. It's the word *finite*.

"Why all these unusual words?" the thought may come. "First infinite, and now finite. They sound complicated. Why bother with all that?"

Don't be put off by either word. They're both actually simple.

First of all, finite just means *limited*. It's not a specialized term only for scientists or mathematicians. According to the dictionary, finite comes from the words *finire*, or *finis*, which mean finish, or end. So if something is finite, it can be said to start at one point and end somewhere else, like that stick. Finite simply means it has limits or some type of form, and it can be measured.

When you stop to consider it, *every single thing* supposedly experienced by the human mind and each of the five senses would be finite and observable—not just sticks, oranges, sounds and smells.

Even things like temperature, electricity, and other forms of energy, while not seen by the eye, would be finite, measurable things. What about tiny cells and molecules, right down to human DNA and the smallest sub-atomic particles? That's really small. They're all finite too, because they involve a specific pattern of observable *movement*, or what scientists would call their vibration or frequency. While these obviously would be extremely difficult to detect or measure, they still have their characteristic form, pattern, or limits.

Finite applies not only to the entire material world, but to the ethereal world as well. Instinct or intuition, dreams or visions, and what is called extra-sensory perception would be more types of finite things. So would all psychic or "New Age" phenomena such as auras and chakra energy; "soul sense" experiences, soul travel or astral projection; communication from others who have "passed on"; and *all* other types of mental, paranormal or occult phenomena. Clearly, these aren't easy to measure or quantify—and they can't be seen with the eye or touched with a finger. But they all still would be finite "things" in that they are always experienced as *observable* phenomena, though relatively ethereal. Even these would have a specific form or pattern to them.

If you've never had such ethereal experiences, do not feel this book isn't for you. This is not concerned with such experiences, but only with pure Consciousness Itself.

Why go into all this? There's one characteristic *all* finite things share, no matter how material or ethereal. Not one of these finite things is ever conscious. Not one is the pure Awareness you are. When was the last time an orange, or the spontaneous laughter at watching a funny movie, was aware of you? No finite thing—whether an object such as an orange, a laugh, or even an aura—can *itself* ever be the Awareness that is aware of it.

Awareness never switches places with such things. One never would say, "I am that thing." One could only say, "I appear to be aware *of* that thing."

What never changes is that all finite qualities or conditions always are connected with *things*. It always would be the thing, the form one appears to be *aware of*, that is finite.

Now what about *Awareness Itself*?

Does Awareness have a size that can be seen—a length or width you can measure? Can you point to where Awareness comes to an end? Can you touch Awareness? Has It ever made a sound? Can you smell or taste It? Has It *any* finite form or limits?

Awareness Itself is not finite—but *infinite*.

The prefix *in-* means *not*.

In-finite simply means *not finite*.

Now try another test. See if the finite form of this book, the body, or any other thing can ever *leave* that thing—and instead become true of the Awareness you now are. Impossible.

Awareness is infinite *only*.

Notice something else. See if the three *dimensions* of height, width and depth of this book or the body can ever leave those things and become true of your Awareness.

Awareness Itself has no dimensions of height, width or depth. It is completely *un-dimensional*.

Awareness Itself never appears in any finite or observable form, not even the most ethereal. Awareness never is something "out there" that is objective to Itself, never an idea or concept.

What does the fact that Awareness is infinite mean? It means It never can be known by way of the five senses, by thinking, or even experienced emotionally—because all of those would be *finite*. Your Awareness is completely "beyond" the finite world of the mind and senses. Yet it's undeniable—here infinite Awareness is, effortlessly present and aware. The fact that Awareness is infinite and without dimension hasn't suddenly made It distant, or put It afar off, has it?

It's no accident that the most brilliant scientists never have been able to observe or measure Awareness' form. Why? Because It has no form! Everything science may claim to have measured is not Awareness, Consciousness *Itself*; it's not infinite, not the actual "Stuff" Itself. The very fact that it's been measured means it's finite, something one is *conscious of*.

That's the telling distinction. It is everything one appears to be *conscious of* on a human basis that constitutes all of finity. Meanwhile, *pure Consciousness Itself* is Infinity.

What's more, this very Consciousness, as It is being all-inclusive right here, now, is the *only* Infinity there is! The staggering Truth is that never, ever is there another Infinite—whether a "Divine Infinite," or any other kind of Infinite—off somewhere else, apart from this very Consciousness. There never has been.

Try as hard as you can to come up with another Infinite somewhere. You never will. Whatever you would refer to as another "infinite," it always would have to be *within Your Consciousness* to mention it. That means it always would be some finite concept or thing that you alone appeared to be *conscious of*. Thus it wouldn't be Infinite Consciousness Itself. You alone are Infinite Consciousness Itself.

That is so huge in its significance it's almost indescribable! That which is called "the Infinite" never is something separate from you that you must reach or become *conscious of*.

The Infinite is Consciousness Itself! The Infinite is *You*!

The *only* Infinite there is, is the One being aware right here, now—this very Consciousness.

To be infinite, does one have to *do* anything? Being infinite is simply a matter of identifying as Consciousness, Awareness, *alone*. Infinity is what Awareness *always* is, totally apart from things. Being infinite never is a personal ability or responsibility—it's all up to Awareness *Itself*. And to Awareness, being infinite is normal—in fact, unavoidable. That's the beauty of It.

It's as easy to be infinite as it is to be aware—they're the same. And how easy is that? It's effortless. There is nothing that has to be done because Awareness is permanently this way.

How unstoppable, how *irresistibly present*, is Infinite Awareness?

Right now, "taste" what it is for Awareness to be so busy, so fully *alive* to being Its Infinite Presence alone, that you have no Awareness "left over" to give to finite objects, thoughts, emotions or sensations— but just your own pure *Conscious Aliveness*.

This is being Infinite Awareness, instead of what one is aware *of*.

To the Awareness You now are, being infinite is as basic as can be. Infinite doesn't mean rocket science. Nor does infinite mean anything supernatural, esoteric, or afar off.

Really look at the word again. Pull it apart and completely de-mystify it once and for all.

In-finite.

It literally means *not finis*—or not finishing or ending anywhere. But that also means having no place where it begins. In other words, you can't point to infinity anywhere, as if it were a stick, a planet, or even an atomic particle. Infinite means having *no* finite form whatsoever. None.

Infinite means *not* observable, not measurable or limited in any way.

Contrary to what is usually believed, infinity does not mean a big, vast finity. This is an overlooked but extremely important distinction to make—and crucial to beholding the true nature of Consciousness. Infinity is *not* endlessly large (or small) in size. Because infinity means no measurement whatsoever, it is the complete *absence* of size.

Regardless of what you may have been incorrectly taught, there's no getting around it. That's what *in-finity* means.

In science and mathematics, infinity is mistakenly considered to be an endless extension of finity. The traditional mistaken concept says you could pick up that stick mentioned earlier, only this time if the stick somehow extended forever without coming to an end—that, suppos-edly, would be "infinity." *But you've still got the stick.* You could mea-sure part of it.

In true Infinity, *there is no stick.*

Infinity, rightly known, isn't a long distance in space that goes on forever. It's not an enormous quantity in mathematics that one never comes to an end of counting. All such, while extreme, and perhaps beyond the capacity of human thought to fully grasp or contain, would still be in the realm of the finite, of *some* measurement. It would be like trying to measure the vast stellar universe, which although not possible to fully measure, can be partially measured.

Infinite means *no* measurement.

Infinite in its correct sense means no amount. It means no counting. Infinity means abandoning *all* finite form. Not only is infinity without physical size or length—It hasn't even a length in time. Infinite doesn't mean forever in time, but is the complete *absence* of time, because time too would be measurable. Infinity is not even a circle or endlessly repeating loop, for that too has form, an inside and outside.

Infinity has *no* form or limits—exactly as *the Consciousness You now are* has no form or limits. They are the same One.

If you assume this is all abstract and has nothing to do with you, don't forget it's speaking of *You*. You are now reading about what really counts—*the Infinite Conscious Presence You are*—instead of the mere finite things you seem to be conscious of.

If you mistakenly identify with finite things instead of the Infinite Consciousness You are, what would you be doing? You'd be needlessly subjecting yourself to all those finite limitations—when in fact as Consciousness, You are absolutely *unlimited*.

———•———

There really is no such thing as a finite body or person known as "I."

Infinity Itself is the only I.

This isn't said to impress or because it sounds "spiritually important." It's really true.

Right now—very slowly, gently and softly say the word *I* to yourself.

Do not voice I aloud. Let I be said *silently*.

Let this I keep repeating Itself—very, very slowly, softly and easily— "I," "I," until you clearly hear It "within yourself."

As you do so, be alert to "that which is saying I." All that's important is that which is doing the saying—not the *word* "I" being said.

What is the nature of this invisible voice, this I that you are?

Do not first identify yourself as a *body* and assume it is the one saying I. Start from "the other direction," and identify yourself as this invisible voice only. Identify *as* I, all by Itself alone.

Where is this I as It is saying "I"? The saying of "I" is not taking place by way of a physical mouth or vocal chords, is it? It does not depend on using parts of the physical body, does it?

Notice carefully: is this *I* the same as anything that is sensed?

You clearly know "I" is being said, yet It is not being heard by way of ears, is It?

Can the eyes see this "invisible I" as It is saying "I"? Can the fingers touch I? No. Nor can you taste or smell I.

This *I* that is voicing Itself has nothing to do with physical senses; It is invisible to the five senses. Yet to Its own Presence, *I* is immediate, inseparably present. *I* is far closer and more "intimate" to you than anything the senses could ever hope to tell you.

What else? It doesn't take time for I to become present, does it? No, I always *is* present. Its voice doesn't have to carry any physical distance to get to you. Aren't the saying of "I" and the consciousness of *I* simultaneous, really one and the same? There is no separation. I is not what you are conscious of. I is what Consciousness *is*.

Keep going. What is I "made out of"?

Is this invisible I, by Itself alone, part of a physical anatomy? Is I solid or dense? Does I have edges or a border to It, like a material object? Or is I an incredible *softness* which has no density, no edge at all?

Meanwhile, this "voice," this I-ness is a specific, distinct *presence*.

Exactly where is I-Presence coming from?

It is "coming from" Consciousness. In fact, I does not *come* from anywhere. I is permanently *present*, for I is Life's own ever-present-ness or Presence.

I never is personal. Clearly no person, no body, knows how to make I be present, be the Consciousness It is. If one did know, how did he produce I, Consciousness? What did he use to be conscious in the meantime while producing Consciousness?

Always, It is the Infinite, Consciousness, or Life Itself, that is the only I. Never is there a personal I having to become infinite. There is no other, throughout the entirety of Existence, that can say or be this I. Only Infinite Life Itself is alive to say "I."

Life's I-Presence is also intelligent, for It *knows* that It is. It alone is the one knowing Its nature here, now—for nothing else is conscious to know It.

When I says, "I," how close is I to Itself? Does a body have to help things along; make some kind of connection? Will any amount of thinking, prayer, or meditation get I closer to the I It is *already being*?

———— • ————

Could it honestly be said that invisible I-Presence has a skin color, or any racial characteristics? Invisible I has no color—only bodies, things, appear to. The I-Presence You are has no body characteristics because *It's not a body*. It's pure *Consciousness*.

Go a step further. Could the color on the body holding this book ever *leave* the body and attach itself to invisible I, to You? Never. The fact that I has no color means *You* have no color. You've never had color—white, black, yellow or red—and never will.

Then can You ignore what is true of Your I-Self and assume You are limited to one particular race of bodies? Can the Awareness You are say Its outlook isn't absolutely pure and clear, but is "colored" merely because of the color on one particular body-thing It includes within Itself? No! Awareness-I includes all bodies of which It appears to be aware *equally*. This never changes.

When you appear to be aware of a white tulip, a black tulip, or a yellow or red tulip, you certainly don't assume that tulip, *that thing*, is you. Just as you are not a tulip of any color, you are not a body of any color. The pure, clear Conscious *I* You are now aware of being, *never* is the body that appears to be holding this book.

Can you imagine tulips arguing because one doesn't approve of the other's color?

"But," the thought may come, "there is this long history of tension among races."

Oh? To whom would there be a long history? Only to a state of thought that mistakenly identifies as a body. Only to ignore-ant thinking. Only a state of un-Consciousness would try to say that. It never is said by pure I-Consciousness, the One I Am, *the only One*.

Who alone is conscious here, now? It is the Pure One I Am—not a body or some ignorant thoughts. This isn't a matter of a reader-body agreeing or disagreeing with an author-body. It is *I*, the One I Am, being honest with Myself, the only One conscious.

The only "problem" with the would-be issue of race is that it has never been a *racial* problem! It is merely a matter of mistaken identification—as a body—instead of as Consciousness. Yet to this One I Am, Divine Awareness, there really is no separate self or life that could make such a mistake, or put itself ahead of My Life Itself. As there is no other being alive besides the Life I Am, there is no other to ignore this simple and immediate solution to all "racial problems."

<hr />

Keep going as Invisible-I only, *which is the One Self I Am*. See what else is true of the *Alive Presence* I Am, all alone, entirely apart from what is sensed. Don't be timid, for this is your very I-Presence speaking.

Is it possible to poke a hole in this *Formless Aliveness* I Am, or cut out a portion, as with a cookie-cutter, and call it a personal life, one separate from Aliveness? Aliveness-I cannot be cut; there is nothing solid about I *to* be cut. Aliveness is indivisible. As I have no parts, I never can be parted, or de-parted. Aliveness has no physical con-struction, so isn't subject to de-struction.

The pure Aliveness I Am has nothing material of which I Am com-posed, so I can't de-compose. Having no pieces that are integrated, *I* never dis-integrate, which is why I Am also called *Spirit*. I Am not made up of many elements, so I Am not complex, nor any kind of mental complex. This pure One I Am is the very essence of simplicity, ease, un-complexity.

Right now, identify not as a body, but as the *Alive Presence* You are.

See if it's possible to plunge so deeply into your Conscious Alive-ness, into the *alive feeling* that your Infinite I-Presence now is, that you go all the way through It. See if it's possible to reach a bottom of your Alive I-Presence, so you come to an end, or use It up.

Can it be done? Keep trying to find an end. Go in any direction. Go as far as possible. Pay no attention if the eyes try to tell you that the body ends at one point, or the room comes to an end somewhere else. Stay with *Aliveness* only.

Can a line be drawn showing where Alive I-Presence starts or ends? Do you feel a physical wall to I, or even a mental wall, where you *stop* being alive, stop being I?

There simply is no point *anywhere*, at which I comes to an end. Equally, no point can be found where I begins. I Am end-less. I Am beginning-less. I Am *infinite*.

Infinity is not theoretical, not a lifeless mathematical concept.

Infinity is actually *conscious*. Infinity is *alive stuff*. Infinity is *You*.

It is *I*, the Infinite Itself, reading this here, now, beholding what these words mean.

I could "plumb the depths" of the consciously alive *Infinity* I Am for what passes as the next billion, trillion years and never come to an end or use It up.

The Infinite Aliveness I Am is un-shut-off-able. I Am un-go-away-able.

My Aliveness is *inexhaustible* in Its supply, and yet always *present*.

And there is no vast storehouse or space needed to keep My Infinity in, is there? My Infinite Aliveness has nothing to do with physical volume or containment. I Am *without* measure.

More importantly, no matter how "far," how endlessly "deep" into My undimensional Aliveness I go, I never go away, but am always still *right here*, being Aliveness, aren't I?

Aliveness, Consciousness, Presence, Being, and Infinity are all synonyms for *I*.

Now see if it's possible to pin down or limit *where* the borderless One I Am is while saying "I." Really try to find one specific location.

When silently saying "I," don't first assume I is inside the body, for that's just an assumption.

Instead of looking inside the body for where I might be, put the shoe on the other foot. Rather, where are all these potential places in which one would try to locate I? Whether you call that place a head, a torso, or entire body, it is always some *thing* I appear to be aware *of*. It always appears to be within Awareness, within I, rather than I being in it. That thing is found nowhere else; otherwise there would be no Awareness of that thing. This never changes.

At first it may *seem* I is in the head, in the body, when I is voiced, but it is the reverse. As "I" continues to softly be said, it is clear that the body appears to be within the One saying I.

Only when I is voiced does I seem localized in the head—but without the voicing, I has no localization. If the head were where I was, I would be found *only* there, in that one spot. That means Infinite-I would have to stop and have an end or border where the head ends. Yet Infinite-I has no end or stopping point; only a head appears to.

As this One I Am is entirely infinite, borderless, how could *I* have ever gotten confined *inside* the borders of the three-dimensional body that is holding this book? I couldn't.

Just where, in what single spot could one put that which is entirely undimensional? How much space is needed? How could one say for sure, since it's impossible to know what Infinite I-Consciousness looks like? This One I Am can't be pointed to anywhere, because there is no shape to Infinite I, *nothing to point at*. Yet I Am always *present*, aren't I?

Not even I know what I look like. In fact, I don't look like any *thing*. As undimensional, infinite Presence, I Am not something that *can* be looked at or located, even in a body. Has any surgeon ever seen Life Itself, ever plucked *I Am* from a body with a pair of forceps?

The One I Am never stops being infinite, undimensional *Presence* to become solid, physical flesh. Limits of matter do not apply to I, for I Am not material, not a finite thing. Yet here I perfectly, effortlessly Am— present *as this Conscious One here, now.*

Trying to pin *I* down to one particular finite location is like trying to grab a handful of air. Try it. Now open the hand. Can the air that was "grabbed" be separated from the rest?

Just as *I* am not inside the body holding this book, but am "outside" or include the body—this of course holds true for what appears as *every other* body. It's not that a lot of persons all have their own outside-the-body I's. It is this same, *One* I that appears to include *all* bodies. The I "here" is the exact, same One I "there," for there isn't another I over there, just a body. All bodies appear to be within the One I Am. Identifying as All-Inclusive I-Consciousness, not body, it is clear "that one" isn't a consciousness or life separate from "this one"—for It is *this* I that *I* Am including all bodies equally.

Truly, "Love thy neighbor *as thyself.*" That doesn't mean to care about "others" as much as you care about yourself. It means there literally is only this One I—the All-Inclusive One I Am.

When saying "I" in everyday use, how often do you think of yourself as Life's pure I-Presence, invisible Substance Itself, instead of as one person, a visible body?

Being Infinity Itself, I never, ever will see Myself as some thing that appears or is objective. *Invisibility* is all there is to I. And I Am all there is to Invisibility.

What does Infinity "behold" when all there is to "see," is Its own Infinity? In response to this question, the so-called finite, thinking "mind" draws a complete blank. Yet the answer to that question is One's Permanent Address. It's not a physical location; It's *Alive Stuff.*

There never is a journey to make to Infinite Life.

The only "place" You live is *as* Infinite Aliveness. Revel in *being* It.

Now stop a moment and *don't* say "I." Just be alive as the *silent Presence* I Am.

Does Consciousness go away? Does It stop being infinite, or all-inclusive of all there is? Consciousness, I-ness, is perfectly present regardless of whether It is said or not.

After all this, don't start by saying "I" am Consciousness, or "I" am the Infinite, when speaking in terms of Consciousness, the Infinite, the Self. *Turn it around*. Infinity Itself is the only I. Again, there never is a personal "I" that is being infinite. Always start with Consciousness, Self, Life, or some other synonym, not "I." Why?

Infinite Consciousness never actually thinks of Itself as "I"; It never has to say "I" to identify Itself to Itself, or be reassured It is Infinite Consciousness. It *is*. The use of the word *I* is wholly a human invention. It is always focalized. The example of saying "I" is given only as another way of pointing out One's undimensional nature, and that the Infinite is never separate, never off in a vague, imagined "infinite" somewhere apart from *this present Being*.

All that's important is that One which is conscious and has the capacity to voice—not *what* is voiced. Without the saying of "I," Consciousness has no focalization, but is pure, true Infinity.

Why are you right now *alive* to what these pages say? It is the Self I Am, being alive to Myself alone, beholding Myself for what I truly Am! There is no deadness of finite things, no dullness of ignore-ance; that which would ignore the pure vitality of the Aliveness I Am.

It is the presence of Infinite Intelligence Itself, cognizing what is true of Itself, that makes this chapter "ring true" here, now. This chapter is not a matter of observing It. You are *being* It.

You couldn't get "closer" to the Infinite if you wanted to.

You never *leave* Infinity.

What is it to always *start Here, and stay Here,* being alive not to what is sensed, not to finite, dimensional things, but *only* to the Infinity of Aliveness I Am?

———•———

5

CONSCIOUSNESS IS NOT THE "HUMAN MIND"

THE FACT THAT CONSCIOUSNESS, the I-Self You are is *pure Infinity* means It is nothing like what is usually called human "consciousness" or the "human mind," which would be finite throughout.

Exactly what is human "consciousness" or the "mind" as the term is typically used? In present day language—whether in science, philosophy, religion, or even in everyday conversation—the functioning of the "human mind" is generally said to consist of the activity of the five senses, as well as the thinking and emotions that are usually based on what the senses sense.

The term "mind" as used here does *not* mean the brain. The mind appears to involve *processes*—such as thinking, the processing of sensations, emotions, etc. The mind, or that which is mental, seems to be an *activity,* distinct from a brain which would be an organ of the body.

As said earlier, all of the mind's activity—whether the experiencing of a sight or a touch, the thinking of the intellect, or the feeling of emotions—consists of finite, observable forms. Even that which is called sub-conscious, subliminal, or extra-sensory and psychic, involves observable or finite phenomena.

What matters is that not one of those observable forms itself is *conscious.* Nor are any of them *infinite, measureless.* None of this finite activity is Infinite Consciousness Itself, *being*—which is the *One and Only* Consciousness there is.

So to avoid confusion when referring to these finite forms of experience, the terms *finite sense,* or *finite "sense-mind"* are used instead of "consciousness." Only by starting on the level of a sensing human mind would one find finite-ness, opposites and duality. It would be the realm of dark and light, up and down, hot and cold, good and evil, etc.

40

Starting from, or "looking out as" the Infinity of Consciousness is entirely different. The fact that It is infinite means It is *end-less*. Speaking in terms of Consciousness *only,* at no point does It come to an end, so nowhere in pure Consciousness can another state begin. It is one, non-dual, and has no opposite. If one is specific and clear about what is being referred to, one must agree that the One Infinite Consciousness Itself, pure Awareness *alone,* is not the same as so-called dualistic finite, sensed, human time experience.

———•———

This distinction between the finite "sense-mind" or so-called human "consciousness" and true *Infinite Consciousness* brings up a major point, one on which this book departs from most others on the subject of "consciousness" or "mind."

The point can be illustrated by this typical human assumption: "Consciousness *has to be* inside the body. Why? Well, suppose my body had surgery, and was given heavy anesthesia. Or suppose my body got knocked out. In each case, I would be 'unconscious' or 'unaware.' When any of those things happen to my body, Consciousness stops functioning—at least temporarily—so Consciousness must be inside the body."

No. In such cases *something* seems to cease functioning, of course. But it is not Consciousness, the Infinite that stops. It is the so-called human, sensing "mind," or that which is finite, that stops. They're not the same.

To be clear how vastly different they are is not difficult. It's just a matter of being consistent with what is true of Infinite Consciousness, and what is not infinite.

Just examine this a little more closely and be specific about what is referred to. You'll see that what stops functioning in such cases is the operation of the *five senses*; the body's neurological system, the "body-mind," or so-called finite human "sense-mind."

If it appears the body is given anesthesia or suffers a severe blow to the head, exactly what would it be that stops? It would be the capacity to *sense* that stops. There is no experience of optically seeing. There is no sense of tactile touching and feeling; the capacity to hear sounds, to taste and smell is stopped. A far more accurate description is that the body would be knocked "sense-less."

That which is incapacitated during so-called "unconsciousness" is the constant chain reaction of all those visual images, sounds, tactile touches, odors, and tastes. These normally trigger emotions and thoughts—which are accompanied by more ongoing sensations.

But all of that activity is *finite*. So, it is all the *finite* activity that seems to stop, not the Infinite.

In other words, it would be everything one appears to be *conscious of* that gets disrupted, not Consciousness Itself.

It would be everything observable that gets knocked out.

Consciousness Itself never is observable to begin with—because It's infinite! So the fact that everything observable seems to have gone doesn't mean Consciousness Itself has gone.

When a body appears to become "un-conscious" it is only body activity of sensing, thinking and emoting that becomes "un," not Infinite Consciousness.

When you knock out the projection of the movie, the movie stops—but you haven't touched the theatre. It may seem Consciousness is conscious *of* sights and sounds, but the experiencing of those visual images and sounds does not cause Consciousness—any more than a movie's picture images and sounds cause the theater.

To the extent one seems to ignore or be separate from Infinite Consciousness, and operates only on the level of what the senses sense—if that is all there is to one's experience—then naturally when that sensing is stopped, it seems one's entire experience has stopped.

Even if a body appears to "die," Consciousness or Life Itself never is touched. Infinite I-Presence never is affected. How could that which is *infinite* get knocked out or killed? Where would one inject a needle into, or strike at, pure Conscious I-Presence, which has no physical structure or form and is completely undimensional?

Perhaps another thought has come, *"But,* when the body is knocked out, I have no sense of time passing; there is no recollection of *being* at all. In fact, I have no memory of having been *conscious* at all. So Consciousness has to have stopped."

Is It really Infinite Consciousness, Being, that stops? Pull it all apart again and look at it closely.

To say one had no sense of time passing is really saying what? It means one didn't do any sensing. Imagine taking away all the sensations you've had on any given day—all the sights of that day, all sounds of it, all the touches, tastes and smells. Could you even say there *was* such a thing as that day? No! Could you say there was time itself? No.

It is only the experiencing of the five forms of sensation, thinking, and other *finite forms* that makes up the entire human sense of time. There's absolutely no evidence of time without this finite activity. Yet none of that is the same as formless Infinite I-Consciousness *being*.

As pure Infinite Consciousness, *I-Presence alone,* You have absolutely no sense of time because pure I-Presence doesn't *have* five senses to sense time; only a body appears to.

To assume the Infinite, I Am, should experience a passage of time is to not make a distinction between pure Consciousness or Being Itself— and that which is sensed and observable. It's not starting with Consciousness at all. Only if one starts with senses, with what pure Conscious Being *is not*, does one assume there is time passing.

"If Consciousness is conscious, is present, even when the body is 'knocked out,' then why isn't there any memory of the experience?" the thought may insist.

Well, what exactly is memory anyway? Memory is entirely a function of *thought* or a sensing mentality—it has nothing to do with pure Being, Infinite Awareness. They're not the same at all. Memory is merely the projected thought of people, objects, places, feelings; myriad mental images—all of which are finite forms.

The capacity to project these finite thought images is what has stopped, not Infinite Being, undimensional I-Presence. Don't confuse projected thought forms with formless Consciousness—just as you never confuse the moving images on a movie screen with the screen itself. Consciousness as It is *being* is a state of pure *Is*. It simply never leaves *being present*—and you cannot have a memory *of the present*.

As It is *present only,* Consciousness Itself never jumps back or ahead in time, past or future. Thinking seems to project thoughts of past or future, but that's *thinking* doing that, not Awareness *being*.

Awareness cannot have a memory of *having been*—because Awareness never leaves the present tense. Because Awareness *is*, It never becomes something that *was*. It can't be looked back upon.

This *Ever-Present-ness* that Awareness *is*, is exactly the same as not being able to have a memory of *now*. It simply is not possible to say you have a memory of the now that is *now*, because it's not past—it's now!

As further proof that Awareness is not in the realm of memory, notice that It can't be memorized.

The would-be finite "thinking mind" based on the senses and time is incapable of coming up with any thought, any finite mental form to express this undeniable Truth. You "glimpse" or *be* your own Infinity—and the constantly running finite mind stops dead in its tracks.

Yet *You* don't stop. You are still concretely real and present as the *now* that pure Consciousness *is*. Life, Being, is still present. You simply have nothing *objective* to You; no finite form in addition to the formless Infinity of Your Self; pure unthinkable *Being*.

This completely un-finite, unlimited "vastness" that pure Consciousness is, is why It is in some traditions called "emptiness" or "no-mind." It is sometimes called *nothingness*. What is really meant by that is *no-thing-ness*, because that's exactly what It is—pure Consciousness alone, apart from finite things. Rather than being a nothing, It is specific *vital Presence*—just without a form.

Only a state of limited thinking based on the finite senses would insist on experiencing some observable form or phenomenon, would want to be able to point to it and say, "I had *that* experience."

You never are the same as any experience you appear to have. All experience would be what one appears to be conscious *of* on a finite basis. The Infinite Consciousness You are is not an experience that is objective to You.

You've just shown yourself the difference between Your Consciousness Itself, and what *appears*. You are out of the realm of limited form. In Truth, Your Consciousness never was in it. So never look for, or wait to have the "big spiritual experience," whatever that might be, or any type of time-event or finite phenomenon, to verify that you have finally "arrived." You *never* will arrive at Infinite Consciousness because You never left.

It may still appear you are aware of time passing for quite an indefinite period. The point is that time is not passing in You; in the pure Being You *are*. One will still be free to use and enjoy all that appears to occur in time. The things Awareness is aware of are not going to suddenly go away. They are seen in a new light.

"But this takes away all my handles," the thought may come. "As Infinite Awareness, there's nothing to grab hold of."

Precisely! The only thing that would be "taken away" is a would-be state of limiting finite thought that never was true of You anyway. One hasn't let go of Being, the Infinite Self, because It can't let go of Itself and *It* is the only One being conscious right here.

Does the Infinite Itself need a handle on being infinite? Does God need to get a grip on being God? Does Consciousness need a finite concept of Itself, something in the realm of form, to cling to as a security blanket, for fear It won't properly be conscious? Who is there being conscious besides Consciousness Itself to need such a thing?

You never are afraid of the freedom of Infinite Being; It is what You unavoidably *are*. The intellect runs from the Infinity of Consciousness, because It means the intellect isn't "the only game in town." Consciousness pulls the rug out from under the intellect, exposing it in all its shifting impermanence as a mere chain of unaware thoughts, with no status as a conscious entity.

Human thinking based on the limited senses has no awareness of the Infinite, but would speak wholly from the basis of the finite, that which has form. The thinking "sense-mind" pompously places all value on its own thinking, yet it would be completely *ignore-ant* of Infinite Consciousness, thus is ignorant from the viewpoint of the Self, Reality.

Because it is ignorant, naturally it never knows just *how* ignorant it is being!

Even though you may not have heard any of this before, or seen it brought out in a book—that doesn't make it any less *true*. In fact, it's so basic, so clearly undeniable, it's almost embarrassing. What has always been *called* consciousness isn't conscious at all, but merely a lot of stuff one appears to be conscious *of*—all the while overlooking Consciousness *Itself* entirely.

———•———

Needless to say, the way Life is in terms of Infinite Consciousness is completely different from how things appear or seem according to the five senses. The words *appear* and *seem* are used frequently to make the essential distinction between how things appear or seem according to finite, sensed time-experience—and what Infinite Consciousness actually *is*. Be alert that when *appear* and *seem* are used, what they refer to is *not* Consciousness.

If at any point you disagree or feel a doubt about what is said here, stop. Ask *who* or *what* is disagreeing. Invariably it is a would-be intellect, conditioned to think on a finite basis according to the senses and time; it is not Your Consciousness, Life's Intelligence Itself. If it seems an intellect objects, or if this seems abstract, keep reading until the full meaning is clear. Any disagreement could only be due to semantics. The trouble is not coming from Your Consciousness, which effortlessly goes right on being aware.

Pure Consciousness *Itself* never is complex or difficult. It is utter simplicity. Its Being is "instantaneous," requiring no steps to arrive at, no possibility of a wrong choice or delay.

Only finite thinking, reasoning, and constant mental maneuvering would seem complicated and laborious. It always involves choice, the many, indecision, an endless chain reaction from cause to effect. It is always driven by need, a lack that must be met or filled.

Again, so-called human mental experience would always be a *process*. Pure Conscious Awareness is *changeless Presence*. The human mentality is always *moving* non-stop from one sense impression, feeling or thought to another. The movement of thought, no matter how lofty, is still on the level of thinking. Only Consciousness can be Itself, and It is never jump-started or manipulated by thinking.

Thinking deals solely in finite information. The five senses and emotions are still other forms of information. The finite "mind" is like a data base, dealing in all kinds of information—sensory impressions, objective phenomena, reaction, cause and effect, ideas, memories, future projection. It always compares, reasons, and analyzes *things*: "Should I have coffee or tea? I prefer dinner to a movie." The thinking "mind" would always put value in *things,* comparing one to another, when only Consciousness is of real value. None of the intellect's would-be comparison or analysis is ever *consciously alive Presence.*

Information is always what one appears to be conscious *of.* It never is Consciousness or Being Itself; never the Intelligence that makes use of information. *Being* never is more present as a result of information. Being is not even ethereal forms of information such as "soul-sense," or what are called extra-sensory, paranormal or psychic phenomena. A seeming constant flow of many forms of finite information never is the same as pure Awareness, simply being present.

This book most emphatically is not opposed to thinking. In fact, many statements and questions here will cause one to think deeply about the infinite nature of Consciousness. The point is, while one uses thinking freely, Consciousness need not think about Itself in order to fully be Itself.

There is nothing wrong with emotions or sensations either. One never tries to stop them; one never condemns a thinking, sensing "mind." Such effort only keeps one stuck on that "level." The Infinite Awareness you are never experiences such problems, but is alive to Its pure Being only. One *starts as* pure Awareness which knows no levels, but only Its serene infinite Presence.

The more one identifies as *what One already is*—pure Awareness only—the thinking is from an entirely "new" viewpoint. It takes on a far better quality, and seems clearer, sharper, more discerning and astute. It seems "cleaner," meaning free of "mental junk," distraction, and its attendant emotions. Thanks to not being on their "level," you appear to *use* thoughts and emotions; they don't use you. In everyday affairs, one has a clearer sense of what is true and actual. One acts less naively, less prone to misguidance from limited personal judgments, extreme emotionalism, criticism, and opinions. Why?

Consciousness—wholly apart from things—is unconditioned Intelligence or Wisdom. It could be called clear, unbiased Perception. This never causes one to act as a know-it-all, because It never is a personal ability. The Self has no interest in trying to appear more intellectually agile than another, for It knows no other. It is too busy being *One* to be worried about being "right."

Awareness never struggles. You are not some furtive thinking process in operation. You are effortlessly present Awareness in operation.

Is there ever a time when Awareness is not *effortlessly* present?

————•————

6

WHOSE LIFE IS IT, ANYWAY?

LIFE ITSELF NEVER STOPPED TO ASK a separate personal you if such a you *wanted* to be alive, did It? Of course that's because there is no separate you. Life Itself, or the Self, is the only I, the only One being alive, as said repeatedly. Life Itself gets all the presence, all the credit. This is how Life *is*—the only way It functions. It never changes. But what does it mean to stay consistent with this fact?

It means one cannot start with personal identification, or human intellectual analysis and opinions, and expect to know Reality. Reality, Truth, is a matter of starting wholly and only with Life Itself, which is Infinite I-Self, and what is true of *It*.

Starting with or "looking out from" Life or the Self is the only valid viewpoint because It is the only viewpoint consistent with the way Life is actually *operating.*

Of course Life, Consciousness, does not have a "point of view" in the way that expression is normally meant. It does not mean Consciousness stands at one end of Itself and visually looks out over Itself. Nor does It have an opinion, analytical viewpoint, or emotional outlook.

It simply means Consciousness is always being Its own clear Presence only—with no overlay of human concepts or theories. It's the *absence* of personal thinking, personal effort. It is Life actually in operation as pure *Aliveness*—not personal thoughts or beliefs *about* Life. Starting here precludes all would-be disagreements and errors due to personal intellectual analysis or human interpretation.

It leaves only pure un-intellectualizing *Being*—the One being alive right here.

The thought may come, "How do I *do* that?" It isn't something one does any more than one has to "do" being, or "do" being conscious. It is what already effortlessly is.

48

By now perhaps another thought has come, "This really is nothing new. I've heard all this before, in fact in many teachings. It's always a variation of the same theme—there is one Life, one I-Self or Consciousness, one Existence; one One."

If so, how consistent are those teachings; how consistent are you when it comes to what One is? Why? Because the One Life—this Life— is absolutely consistent with what One is.

One means that right this instant, there is absolutely no other I— none to eventually get at-one with the One as a result of reading this. There never has been. The One now reading this is not hoping to see or get something from Itself so It can evolve to what It is *already being*. Right now, there is no lesser I, life or consciousness anywhere.

The One Consciousness Itself is the only one conscious to read what is said on these pages, and of course, It is already Consciousness! It is incapable of making additional contact with Itself. This leaves no other having to reach up and eventually lay hold on It, or a vague Divine, or to be on a spiritual "path" to the Infinite. By virtue of the fact that It is Life Itself alive here, now, you must be the One Infinite Life. It is impossible to *not* be It, or get It wrong, for Life, Consciousness Itself, is the only One that is being, operating.

As the Self is already *the only I that is conscious*, It cannot also be below Itself, needing to rise up to Itself. As there is *One*, there is no lower subconscious that must be uplifted, nor any superconscious that feels it is superior. There are no levels, no gradations in pure Infinity.

The fact that the One Consciousness is *all* the consciousness there is, leaves no lesser consciousness to need a teacher or way-shower. This instant, Consciousness leaves no other to be plodding or plotting; none to need awakening or spiritualizing. One Self leaves no second self to co-operate (meaning operate *along with*) the One. Consciousness leaves no other to reject, or even *accept* what It already is.

Do you agree without hesitation? Or do you assume you are a little, separate, personal consciousness or life that first has to evolve, think just the right combination of thoughts, get itself out of the way, or merge with Consciousness? If that were true, this little consciousness would have to be more powerful than Consciousness, the Infinite Itself. Apparently, it would be holding Consciousness at bay, keeping It from being *all* Consciousness until this little one determines it has finally arrived and become at-one with Consciousness. Only then would it give the nod to

Consciousness and say it is okay for Consciousness to be all the Consciousness there is.

Certainly, one never would tolerate any body or human personality claiming to be God, All-Powerful, Divine. Any personal human mind that claims it is God, the Infinite, would be insanity—personal sense, or ego, taken to the extreme. Yet to claim a separate life that is *inferior* would be just as insane, the opposite extreme of personal sense. It is just as personally selfish and involves as much ego. Either way attempts to put a false personal self before Life Itself, or God.

A question that may come, and a good one, is, "How does one know if one is 'doing' this correctly? How does one 'start' with or as the One Consciousness?"

That's not the issue. It never is what a personal thinking mind must do to start correctly. The only so-called issue would be whether Awareness Itself—the One effortlessly aware here, now—could ever be shut off, or lapse. It can't. If It weren't Consciousness Itself already being aware here, you wouldn't be. So how can there be *another* mind or consciousness that has to become more conscious, or start correctly, when the only Consciousness there is, is already fully conscious?

The only One to "experience" Consciousness' Presence is *Itself*—It never is an experience being had by another.

Start with the allness of pure Consciousness *Itself*, not with a "you" starting with the allness of Consciousness. In other words, start with what Consciousness *alone* is. It is never what "you" know or think Consciousness to be. What Consciousness knows *Itself* to be is You.

Your Self is correctly identifying as Itself and "doing Its job" with absolute thoroughness and perfection—simply by being consciously alive. The only way Consciousness is "experienced" is not as a thinking mentality, but as *silently alive Presence*, Oneness. Again, it's never done by a separate "you," but *is* the One Alive Presence being Itself.

From the Self's viewpoint (and there is no other), there are no stages or degrees of Itself. There is no such thing as *partially* being. Being either entirely is or It isn't at all—and Being *is*. To assume this leaves room for a separate "you" that has to also see or attain Consciousness, would be to deny that Consciousness *Itself* is all. While the expressions "start with," "look out from," or "give all attention to" Consciousness are used, the One Already-Operative Consciousness actually leaves no other to "look out from" or center its attention on It.

To simply behold that Consciousness Itself is already aware, and the only One that can be so, is "starting" correctly. Any additional effort would be like trying to turn the ignition key on in a car that is already running—and what an ugly noise it makes.

Consciousness' own Being is not a state It can enter; It never has been outside of or separate from Itself. It never is subject to a partial seeing of Its own Total Being.

One cannot read this book as a second identity, one who assumes he is separate and getting instruction about how to *become* Consciousness. Nor can one take on a false sense of reverence toward Consciousness, a desire to please, and do everything exactly as "he" assumes Consciousness wants "him" to. *There is no such one to begin with.* A so-called human intellect or ego always pretends to be a spiritual wanna-be. It never could be Spirit or Consciousness because Consciousness Itself is already "taking up" all the Consciousness there can be.

Consciousness never *wants* to be anything. *Consciousness is All.*

This is not a book of "how to." It is a book of What Is. There is all the difference in the world between the two.

To ask *how* is like asking, "What is the *way to*?" and that is the very crux of It. There is no way to the Self, for It is already the only I. Its Being is never a matter of how. *It is.* Nothing of any further spiritual importance is ever going to happen, because all of the One I Am already is, and there is no other.

To honestly, consistently define what is already present, is to behold *One*, and that there never has been another with a need for seeking or searching. Any other evaluation would be based on finite senses, and a *would-be* separate personal intellect—rather than this *Presently Aware Self* being Itself, the only One ever aware, alive.

Where do you stand? Awareness never is contrary to Itself and leaves no other to be so.

"I'm still not sure I get it. I'm not comfortable with this," another thought may come.

Instead of trying to get comfortable, stop identifying with, or as, a thinking mind that seems uncomfortable. *That's not You.* It's just a would-be state of intellectualizing and emotions based on the senses. It seems conditioned to think in terms of everything that is *not* the pure Consciousness You already are, *not* Infinite—so naturally it never would get this. Thoughts and feelings would be merely what you appear to *identify*; they're never You, the Identifier.

Why would You, as pure Consciousness, take on the endless burden of trying to "see" or attain via a thinking mind *what You are already being*?

All that's necessary is to recognize that the one who doesn't see Consciousness isn't You, and never has been. Your unavoidable Conscious *Being* has no thoughts or feelings *about* Itself, but *is* Itself right here, now. The "problem" never is one of how to become Consciousness, but of mistakenly identifying with or *as* thinking.

It's shocking, but all seeking, all attempts to attain "oneness" down through the so-called ages, no matter how sincere, would be nothing but the cat of human imagination chasing its own tail.

Instead of trying to become more conscious, try to *stop* Consciousness or Being.

That which cannot be stopped is *You*.

Drop all sense of groping or searching. Clearly define *What Is*.

How much studying, learning, does Being have to do before It will fully, freely be? None! Do not *study* this book. Your Being's pure simple Presence is not a student of Itself. There are no Truth students. The only thing that would try to make a study of Being is a would-be secondary ego or intellect. Yet no matter how much it may try to think or study, it could never make Being be more than It already, effortlessly is *now*. Being, Awareness, is what You simply be, not what a thinking intellect would "see."

Yes, read these pages over and over for the enjoyment of what you *are*—but not because you assume you lack something and must learn or attain it. If you were to receive a letter from a good friend or loved one telling you how wonderful you were in so many ways—would you feel you had to learn what the letter said? You would simply enjoy it.

Life Itself, the Self, or God never is asking, "What do I need to see before my experience will be better?" Is there another being conscious besides? No!

Not even Consciousness *understands* what Itself is. Consciousness, the One All-Conceiving Intelligence, is Itself *inconceivable*. What could be greater than the Infinite, God, that could conceive It?

———•———

It would appear that virtually every form of human teaching or education, whether formal or informal, takes the exact opposite viewpoint from that of *One*—of Impersonal Consciousness or Life Itself—and starts out with a separate, personal "you."

This "you" is a body, a mere thing, a struggling cut-off identity with billions of others like it. This so-called personal identity was supposedly conceived or caused, and developed over a period of time. This "body-you" can be traced back to parents, grandparents, and so on, leading way, way back perhaps to a theological god. Or, this "body-you" may be attributed to a more scientifically acceptable cause of some sort.

This "body-you" is usually told it has to *become*. It has to grow in time; has to progress, evolve, perfect itself; become more God-like, become improved. Or, this "you" may become a more ethereal, higher life-form, according to a more "mystically correct" theory of evolution.

Regardless of the favored viewpoint: theological, scientific or mystical—all of it still would be a matter of becoming, of getting there—wherever "there" might be.

Wait a minute.

As said earlier, instead of identifying as a separate *body* or thinking mentality that always would be reaching out, looking *up to* Consciousness, God, or Life—what about looking *out from* It? What's true when starting with what Consciousness or Life is to Its own Alive Presence? Can One honestly not start Here? This is what Life Itself is doing, and *It is the only One alive* to do any and all "starting."

Isn't that what God is doing? God starts out by being God—not as a human working up to God. Life doesn't work up to being Life; It starts as, or *is* Life, Its own *Aliveness*.

"How can I *do* that?" the thinking may ask.

Again, it isn't something one has to do, any more than one is right now doing Awareness or doing the fact that Being is being. It is what already *is*, without choice.

Isn't God *all* Life, *all* Presence, *all* Power, *all* Intelligence?

If God isn't these, and right now, then that isn't much of a God. If God isn't all Life, *One*, that could only mean there would be another power and presence besides God. So such a God wouldn't really be Omnipotent, Omnipresent, or God at all.

If God truly is all Life, all Presence, all Power, then there can be no *other* life that has to work up or get back to Divine Life. What does all Life, all Presence, mean? If all doesn't mean *all*, why have such a word? If you have any place where all is not *all*, then you do not have all.

Does One mean *one* or not? Do the math.

Certainly *God* doesn't worship a separate God. Is there honestly another alive to do so?

------•------

When looking out from "the other direction," from the viewpoint of God, the Infinite—what do you suppose the "view" is like? Do you assume it's the reverse of a human mind looking up to its imaginary God? In fact, to the Infinite, are there even such things as ends or directions? Wouldn't that also be a notion conjured up by human thinking, not the Infinite Itself? From the Infinite's view, Life isn't like that. What if, at "the other end," there are no ends or directions?

What is it like to be, to live where the Infinite, God, lives? How does Divine Life live? Do you assume you can't know, or aren't allowed to know? Do you have to wait until, if you're lucky, you make it to a hereafter, or to a higher Self? Life Itself certainly knows—and It is the Life being alive *right here, now*.

If you insist on a separate life, exactly how far is it from the One Life to "your" life? What is in between? How does your life sustain itself, if separate from Life?

If you have a separate consciousness, how far is Divine Consciousness from yours? Where is the line of demarcation? If you aren't sure how far it is, can you be certain there is any separation at all? Or would the notion of separation be yet another assumption made by a would-be human intellect, based on ignore-ant senses—none of which is the pure Consciousness You are?

"Well, my consciousness is *different* from Divine Consciousness," the thought may come. "*Mine* certainly isn't Divine."

If one looks closely, exactly *what* would it be that's not Divine? It would only be so-called personal *thinking*, emotions and everything *sensed* that isn't Divine. Your Consciousness, unavoidably aware here, now, is none of that, but is simply pure Being, pure Presence.

So then is all this "difference" real difference—or due to mistakenly identifying with something one seems to be conscious *of*, rather than identifying *as pure Consciousness Itself*?

To Consciousness, there never is a gap between It and Itself. At no point does It become less than perfect, unworthy of Itself, or a hand-me-down "grade B" consciousness. Nowhere does Life's Infinite I-Presence come to an end; so nowhere can a personal I begin.

Is it too simple, too perfect, to agree there is *only* Divine Life or Consciousness, and no personal life or consciousness? To whom would it seem so? To Consciousness, or only to conditioned human thinking? For the pride of the would-be human intellect, this is way too simple. It leaves the intellect no status as a would-be power, the head honcho, forever figuring out how to "get there," so it can continue the charade of not already *being* there.

A thought may come, "Well how do I account for myself? Surely *I'm* not Divine."

Again, what is the "self" such thinking would try to account for? Is it a body, some finite *thing* you appear to be conscious of? Are you trying to account for the so-called activity of five senses and the thinking based on those senses, all of which would be more finite things?

What about Infinite Consciousness Itself, alone?

Does this separation and "working up to" business sound like something a God of Infinite Love, Infinite Intelligence, is engaged in? Could a God that is truly *infinite* ever separate from Itself, or co-exist with a finite state? At what point does Unconditional Love *stop*? Where would God's Infinity end, and another state begin? If It *could* end somewhere, It would not be infinite. Do you know what infinite means? How consistent are you with it?

Can God work up to *Itself*? Of course not.

The very notion of "working up to" would be a human viewpoint, not that of God, Life.

The so-called rationalizing, thinking intellect may then try to say, "But humans are obviously imperfect. Anyone can see humans must be perfected before becoming God-like."

That too, would be wholly a human viewpoint. It would come from mistakenly identifying with a body and senses; that which one appears to be conscious *of* on a finite basis—instead of *as* Infinite Consciousness Itself. *It is ignorance itself*, because it ignores the viewpoint Life, Consciousness, has of Itself, which is the only legitimate viewpoint. Again, this is the only viewpoint that can honestly be taken because *It is the only one that is ever honestly functioning*.

Would you attempt to be dishonest with Life?

More importantly, could Life ever be dishonest with Itself?

The thinking may then try to wiggle out, "But how can *I* do that? How can I start from 'the other direction'? Am I even allowed to do that?"

Not only is one allowed to start from "the other direction," one must. Why? Again, the only One being alive right here is that very Life, Awareness Itself. It isn't a separate "you" at all.

The thinking may then try to say, "But how can *I* know what God or Divine Life is to Itself? How can I know what the Infinite knows? I'm not qualified to know any such thing. Why, the audacity—to assume a person can or should know Truth, or what the Infinite, the Divine, knows. After all, God is often called the Great Unknowable. I can't possibly know what God, or Divine Infinite Consciousness is knowing."

That is exactly right. Personal *thinking* is not asked to know anything. No person could know this, any more than a person could know how to make Existence exist.

God certainly is the Great Unknowable—but only to a would-be human intellect. The functioning of God, Life, Consciousness, neither depends on, nor has anything to do with an intellect or the senses—and it is only these that would seem to operate on a personal, finite basis.

Speaking of audacity, wouldn't it be a bit much to assume there is a personal thinker powerful enough to block God from being *all* Presence, all Power, all Intelligence—while this personality maintains its private state of ignorance?

Right here now, with absolutely no effort, Consciousness is doing a perfect job of being what It is. Life is already alive; Existence is perfectly present, with neither help nor interference from a personality.

This is how Life "works," and the *only* way It "works." There is no alternative. Life never thinks in terms of two: Big Me and little, struggling you; Up Here and down there. All Life knows is Its Undimensional *Aliveness*, which has no direction, but is perfectly alive here, now.

———•———

7

THE ALL-INCLUSIVENESS
OF CONSCIOUSNESS

To say Consciousness is all, means exactly that.

All doesn't mean most, or even ninety-nine percent. All means *all*.

All means *one*. There can be only one All, one One. If there were a point at which It ended and another state began, It wouldn't be All.

To be All, then, Consciousness must be every bit of all that exists, with nothing greater than or out beyond Itself. Consciousness could not be within a body or in any thing, but must be infinite, endless.

Again, see if it's possible to come up with any item, or any so-called place—the body, a mountain, a planet—anything at all, that does not appear to be *within* Consciousness. You can't. The moment you mention it, there it is, some thing you appear to be *conscious of,* or within Consciousness to so mention. Yes, many things appear to be outside the body. But both body and all other things always appear to be in Consciousness.

Did you ever stop to realize that all there really is to the apparent existence of every thing is the *consciousness of it*? Without Consciousness being conscious of, or including things, they simply could not be mentioned as existent. It means Consciousness is really the one all-inclusive "Place" or only "Stuff" wherein all things appear to be. Just as all things that exist are said to be in Existence, equally, all things can be said to exist only within Consciousness.

In fact, Consciousness is all there is of *Existence Itself*, all there is to all that is being. Why? Without the consciousness of being, there is no being.

Existence, rightly known, is not a vast physical place or amount of space. Existence is Consciousness being conscious and all-inclusive of all

57

there is. To say Consciousness is all of Existence doesn't mean there is *an* Existence that is separate and which Consciousness "fills." Consciousness being conscious and all-inclusive is *what* Existence is.

You never would accept the false notion that the earth is flat—even though it appears so. Likewise, don't cling to an old false notion that Existence is a physical place, even though it appears so.

Did you ever ask yourself what Existence *Itself* is, apart from all the *things* that appear to be within Existence? Even apart from the movement of all the planets and galaxies of the universe, what is *Existence Itself*? Isn't It simply present, a state of *being*? Now what about Consciousness? Apart from all things in your universe that you appear to be conscious *of*, and all their seeming movements, what is the pure Consciousness that includes them all? It too, is simply being. Consciousness isn't conscious of Existence. Consciousness being all-inclusive of the universe *is* Existence. It is the same One.

Now look at all this from the standpoint of *Life*.

Exactly where is Life as It is now being alive? Is Life present only on the planet earth?

It is often believed Life may also be on other planets. But who says Life always has to be *on* something?

If Life is found only on planets, then what about the rest of the universe? Such a conclusion would imply the rest of the universe is *separate* from Life.

But wait a minute. The entire universe is certainly *in* Existence. And all of the universe's existing also appears to be *within Consciousness*. In fact, that is the *only* "Place" the universe ever appears to exist. It is thanks entirely to Consciousness being conscious of, or including the universe within Itself that it can even be mentioned there *is* a universe.

Upon closer examination, one sees that what is *called* a world and entire stellar universe that appears to be "out there" is really made of what? It consists entirely of things one appears to be conscious *of*. It can just as readily be argued that all these things appear to be items or "thoughts" within Consciousness, within Intelligent Life. The things simply cannot be separated from the very *thought* of them.

If there is a doubt about this, try again to come up with some thing in the universe separate from your thought of it. It's impossible. The moment you mention it, whether the moon or a marshmallow, there it is, some thing in thought you are *thinking of*. Put it this way: have you ever mentioned anything as being existent that *wasn't* instantly some thing in thought?

Suppose the body were to go outdoors tonight and point up to the moon and say, "The moon is up there, out there in space. It's not in my thought." The moon appears to be outside the *body*, yes. Meanwhile, both the moon and body appear to be in Consciousness, inseparable from your thought of them. Otherwise you could not even mention or think in terms of the body, moon, or the universe to talk about them.

The moon, sun, billions of stars, and every body and thing on the planet earth never can be said to exist by themselves. It never is *they* that are conscious of themselves. Only Life, the Consciousness that appears to be aware of them, knows and says they exist. Always, It is Consciousness that includes the universe and It never changes places.

Consciousness Itself is not surrounded by space.

If one starts on the mistaken human assumption that Consciousness or Life is *inside* the body, then the universe of course seems to be "out there" and separate, stretching an incredibly long distance. Certainly no body includes the universe.

Looking "out from" the all-inclusiveness of Consciousness, not from within a body, both the body and universe *always* appear to be "within" the Consciousness *of* them; they are within Your Life.

Life Itself is not *in* bodies, not *on* planets. All things are in Alive Consciousness, which is an exact synonym for Life. Consciousness isn't conscious *of* Life. Consciousness being all-inclusive of all *is* Life as It is being alive. That's why the term Conscious *Aliveness* is used. Consciousness is the very "Stuff" that Life is.

The more you look at it, you see that what is true of Consciousness is identically true of Existence and Life. The three terms are inseparable. If there were no Consciousness, it could not be said there even *is* Life or Existence. Equally, without Life being alive, it would be impossible to be conscious or say anything exists. And without Existence, nothing would exist, not even Consciousness or Life.

The typical human tendency would be to mistakenly assume Consciousness, Life, and Existence were three distinctly separate things. One who assumes so might say, "I'm conscious, and alive, yes; but I'm certainly not Existence. I'm not All. I'm not all there is."

That conclusion would come only from mistakenly identifying as a body, a thing one is conscious of, instead of as Consciousness. It ignores the fact that Consciousness is all-inclusive of all things. Certainly a body isn't All. One can be Existence, all there is, only as All-Inclusive Consciousness, not as a body.

See again if Consciousness has a border, an end, where It finishes being conscious. Suppose you claimed to know where Consciousness came to an end and a greater state, one out beyond Consciousness, began. To be able to mention them, both that "end" and the other state would have to be something you were conscious *of*. Thus they both would be *included within* Consciousness. Consciousness would thus be greater than both, and not bound or ended by them at all.

Nothing circumscribes Consciousness. It is *endless,* or *All.*

In exactly the same way, can a line be drawn where Existence ends? Where would Existence end, and another state that is non-existence, begin to be? Non-existence *can't* begin anywhere because it's non-existent! There is *only* Existence. It, too, is endless, infinite, or *All.*

Equally, no spot can be found where Life, the undimensional *Aliveness* You are now alive to being, starts or stops. In each case It is that which is infinite, having no point at which It ends or begins. It doesn't matter what synonym one uses—It is not three Infinities.

The three terms Consciousness, Existence and Life are just different *words* for what is the same All-Inclusive *One*—just as William, Will and Bill are all the same guy.

It is the *One* that simultaneously is *conscious*, is *existent,* is *alive* here, now. Consciousness *is* Existence, which *is* Life, which *is* All.

The answer to, "Where is Existence?" is also the answer to, "What is Consciousness?"

Did you ever notice that, just as one cannot *think* being conscious or think being alive, one cannot think *existing* either?

Now notice the immediacy and simplicity with which Consciousness is present. It never labors or struggles to be. Likewise, when was the last time you noticed Existence struggling to *be?*

The ease with which Existence exists is *so* easy, so effortless, it is beyond words to describe.

Right here, now, how *completely effortless* is this ease of Existence?

Do you realize this is You as All-Inclusive Consciousness?

By this point the thought has probably come, "I'm not even conscious of what's going on across the street, let alone across the rest of the planet. So Consciousness is not *all*-inclusive. If It were, I'd be conscious of all activity going on *everywhere*—across this planet, and even across every galaxy, all simultaneously right now."

Such a conclusion is really saying that these other "places" are outside the limited range of the body's *five physical senses*. That's true. A human body's capacity to see, hear, taste, touch and smell is not all-inclusive. To say Infinite Consciousness is all-inclusive does not mean that what the five senses sense is all-inclusive. They're not the same.

The finite sense of things is extremely limited, capable of handling only so much experience at once. The vast majority of the stellar universe is obviously beyond the range of the body's five senses at any given time. Yet regardless of whether one were to just sit the body in a room—or somehow experience the entire Milky Way galaxy—not a bit of that experience could appear to take place if it were not *within* Conscious Awareness to so mention.

No limit can be applied to Awareness Itself. If one somehow experienced every planet in every galaxy, and all they had to offer, it never would exceed the capacity of Awareness to be aware of, or include it. Nor would Awareness Itself be increased or expand. It would be the body of information, *the things one is aware of*, that appears to increase. Awareness, being infinite, borderless, is not like a suitcase that holds only so much before bursting.

Since it appears that all bodies, all things, and the entire universe are within Awareness, then where is *It*, Itself?

Awareness can't be in any one place, because all "places" appear to be in It.

Awareness, pure Consciousness *Itself*, has no geographical or spatial limits, but is endlessly "greater" than what appear as all physical and dimensional locations. To correctly "locate" Consciousness is to see It cannot be located or localized, but is Infinity Itself.

This also means Consciousness does not *originate* in some place. As Consciousness always includes *all*, It leaves nothing besides Its own Presence from which It *could* originate.

The point is, Consciousness no more originates inside a *body* than a radio announcer's voice originates in a radio. That which enables a radio mechanism to reproduce the sound of a voice is an invisible electronic signal that is "everywhere present" in the air. That which enables a body mechanism to produce a voice is "everywhere present" Conscious Life. Consciousness, however, isn't like a radio signal, broadcast from one location, through space, to another. All-Inclusive Consciousness *is always being all Presence*. It can't travel from here to there like an electronic impulse.

When the words "Consciousness is All" are voiced, it is never really being done by a person. It is literally *All Itself* voicing Itself. It is *all the Presence existent* that is doing it! It appears that all is within the boundless All-Inclusive One saying, "Consciousness is All."

The fact that Consciousness isn't bound inside a finite body doesn't mean It flies off in all directions. As All-Inclusive Consciousness, one never can *go* anywhere. *There is nowhere else to go.* The One Infinite Consciousness is permanently all Presence, eternally the only "where" there is.

———— • ————

Consciousness, Awareness, *never fails* to be all-inclusive.

It may seem that *thought* can be focused, or the senses can be directed to an object or particular spot. But it would be the "mind" or thought, and not Awareness, doing that. Even while thought or attention appears to go to one finite spot, Awareness Itself remains all-inclusive, uninfluenced.

Right now, put thought or what you might call your attention on the body's left foot. Extend the leg so it is easy to notice it. Feel the tactile sensation in the foot, and the sense of weight from holding the foot off the floor. Did any of this effort bring your All-Inclusive Awareness *into* the foot, or even part of the way into the room—so Awareness no longer included what appears as the entire room?

Awareness goes right on effortlessly including what appears to be the foot, the body, the entire room, even the entire universe, regardless of what the thought seems to be on. The focusing of thought or attention would be a personalized, focalized, finite "mental" activity, which is not All-Inclusive Awareness simply being present.

One does not have to, in fact *cannot* work to make Awareness include the room and entire universe. Awareness does so "automatically." It is absolutely effortless.

All-Inclusive Awareness never is influenced by thought, sensing, or by what any body seems to do. Awareness never operates by way of a person. It never is person-*al*.

What happens when the body appears to go outdoors? Does Awareness "hold up" and operate the same? Is It still boundlessly all-inclusive? Your Awareness never can get *in* what appears to be the ground, plants and trees, houses and buildings, fields and mountains, rivers and lakes and oceans. It never is *on* earth. All these appear to exist in only one place—within You.

It may appear that the *body* walks on the ground, but *You* never are on the ground. You *include* the ground and all of the marvelous wonders on earth. You *include* the entire magnificent sky and everything in it—clouds, other planets, the sun, stars, countless galaxies, and seemingly endless depths of space. Effortlessly, You reach below the bottom of the universe, and above the highest heavens. The term "outer" space is really a complete misnomer because it isn't "outer" at all. The only place all of it appears to exist is *within You*.

———•———

Do you feel any hesitation about the all-inclusive magnificence of Consciousness? Do you feel a sense of too much responsibility, or doubt whether "you" deserve the entire universe, and fear you can't handle it all? All such would be a *personal* reaction, from a finite body's point of view. Of course *it* couldn't deserve or accept this.

Consciousness Itself can't even accept It. Consciousness is *being* It! There is no choice! Consciousness never hesitates to be the magnificence It is, and there is no other.

To Your Self this is completely normal. Isn't Consciousness right now just as effortlessly conscious and all-inclusive as It was before you began reading these pages? The all-inclusiveness of Consciousness has nothing to do with personal capacity, ability or deservedness whatsoever, because *It is never a person doing It*.

It would be due only to a seeming prior false belief that Consciousness *should* be in the body, that any of this may seem difficult to accept. Is it difficult for Consciousness Itself? It is not true that Consciousness ever *was* in the body, and now as a result of reading this, It has been projected or expanded outward to include the universe, and will expand forever.

Consciousness is not like a baby chick, struggling to poke and lift Its way out of a shell. All-Inclusive Consciousness never has been in a shell of a finite human body or mentality. Right this instant, You are absolutely unbound, free.

All-Inclusive Consciousness is *not* an out-of-body experience. To assume so would be to work backwards. It would be starting with a finite body as a reference point, instead of starting with the pure Infinity of Consciousness, *the only I*. It would be to ignore-antly assume that inside a body was the original, rightful location for Infinite Life; and that It could somehow be projected out—when in fact, Infinite Life, Consciousness, *never was* in a body.

The notion that Consciousness, the One Life Itself, is supposed to be located inside a body would be merely a *mistaken human belief*, not Truth. Again, it's like the mistaken belief that the earth was flat, and not a round planet suspended in space. There never was an actual flat earth; yet supposedly centuries ago this was widely accepted.

The entire time, did the earth change? Was any work done on it to change it from flat to round, and have it suspended in space? More importantly, *could* anything be done to make the earth round or more perfectly suspended in space? Only a mistaken assumption, ignorance of the already present fact, was trying to say it wasn't. The earth's true status never changed.

Likewise, the status of Consciousness never changes.

Does work have to be done on Consciousness to make It all-inclusive, to make It not be in a body? *It never was in a body*. Only false belief, an assumption, was attempting to say It was. There never was an actual state of Consciousness being in a body. To behold Consciousness is not in a body never changes the status of Consciousness.

Consciousness *Itself* never has mistakenly believed It was in a body. Consciousness never believes anything; not even that It is Consciousness. Consciousness *is* Itself. All forms of belief would be assumptions made by a confused state of *human thinking*. A belief is never a conscious entity. No belief is better than another belief because it is still all in the realm of belief, finite human thought. It is not Truth, not Intelligent Conscious Presence, the Power that is all Existence Itself.

The fact that all appears to be "within" Consciousness, or that nothing can exist separate from the consciousness of it, is another way of saying Consciousness is the only *Substance* that exists.

Since that which includes all, the entire universe, is *pure Consciousness*, one never is really dealing with physical locations or material items. Things always appear to be mere "thoughts" *in Consciousness*. Matter or physicality never is true substance. It certainly *seems* so if one starts in the wrong place—with what the senses sense, with unconscious *things*. If one mistakenly identifies with *things* instead of pure Consciousness, one is bound to think in terms of different types of "stuff"— the stuff of flesh is different from the stuff of a tree, which is different from a stone. But to do so is to function as un-Consciousness, or ignorance. One mistakenly assumes substance is in things, and consists of "matter." It is perfectly backwards.

For example, traditional human thinking would claim that a stone was formed of dense matter, or various minerals. This view was later refined, to say a stone was formed of molecules and atoms. It was then further refined, down to a level of sub-atomic particles, waves of energy, and even beyond that. Yet could *any* of these be said to exist, regardless of the seeming form, without there first being Consciousness; without there first being *the consciousness of them*?

In Truth, there are not two choices of where to "start"—with Consciousness or with things. The only true, essential "Stuff" is Consciousness. Take It away, and every thing vanishes.

As Consciousness is Substance, then Substance is *conscious*. The Substance within which the entire universe appears to be found is not dead space. It is alive, intelligent!

It is the Conscious Aliveness *You* are now alive to being.

According to mistaken human belief and education, the personal "consciousness" or life is stuck *inside* of bodies, which walk around in so much "dead" space.

Rather, that which it appears bodies walk around in is *alive*. It is *conscious*.

It is *You, All-Inclusive Consciousness* Itself, and nothing is outside of You, ever. There is no such thing as dead space. The "air" is not air—it is *cracklingly alive Substance*. As the saying goes, "You are not in the world; the world is within you." But You are pure *All-Inclusive Alive Presence*, never a body or personality.

As all bodies and things, and all day-to-day affairs appear to be *within* the pure Conscious Life aware here, now—in what kind of "substance" do you behold them?

Is it a substance that you allow to be adulterated with feelings of condemnation and criticism—or anger, fear, or resentment? All such would be based on ignore-ance of Your Self, and what true Substance really is. If you have any thing to condemn or judge, whether a body or a situation, is it really "out there" separate from you? Would *others* experience the condemnation? No. *You* would. *You* are the only one conscious for the whole so-called experience; the *only one* that appears to include it all.

In Truth, all bodies and the universe are within that Substance which *never changes*—the warmth of *unwithholdable* pure Conscious Aliveness or Love. One *starts* Here because this is where the only One being conscious is starting! It *precludes* a second, superimposed state of personalized condemnation, guilt, or ignorance. One never is a body, struggling to live in harmony with other bodies and things. One is that Alive Changeless Harmony which includes all things.

Just because Consciousness is infinite and impersonal doesn't mean It is a vague Substance; something distant, cold or nebulous. Consciousness is *specific, definite, with precise identification here, now.* The Conscious Substance being You now is keenly alert, cleanly alive; It is pure *Joy*, with nothing unlike Itself to make It impure, sluggish or dull. The Substance You now are is not a sleepy, dreamy state that sort of "blankets" all of Existence. It is *wide awake* Life, more "piercingly" alert and sharp throughout Itself than a laser beam could ever hope to be.

All-Inclusive Consciousness is functioning as the very *Alive Essence* that embraces the entire universe—the Perfect Substance that *is* all Existence.

———◆———

8

TO BE GOD, GOD HAS TO *BE*

It OFTEN SEEMS IN HUMAN EXPERIENCE as if religion, philosophy, and science each had its own set of rules. Words such as consciousness, mind, life, substance, existence and other terms often have conflicting meanings according to each particular way of thought or belief structure. It makes for a lot of differences of opinion when it comes to Reality or "God."

Meanwhile, Consciousness or Being unarguably, unstoppably *is*—in spite of any body's ideas or beliefs. Because Being does not function on the level of human thought, It is not subject to thought. It is Truth.

Consciousness, pure Being Itself, never decreed there should be so much complex human intellectualizing and varying definitions for Its *simple alive Presence*! Being goes right on being—in spite of the wide disparity in beliefs held by religions, philosophy, metaphysical teachings, and science and medicine. So what do all these different human beliefs and opinions accomplish when it comes to the nature of Reality or God?

Is religion's God more valid than philosophy's God—or its lack thereof? Who is to say? What about the many variations—each separate branch of religion and philosophy? Is Western better than Eastern? Most importantly, which is the *true* one? Does it depend on which one has been around the longest, or has the greatest following?

Don't forget science, either. It is the scientists that are always observing, testing, looking for irrefutable proof; they are the ones who will not just accept things blindly on faith. They worship the facts of measurable evidence. Maybe they should be the ones to rely on.

Some say there is one Truth or God, but many ways of worshiping that God. Would you say this wide variety of beliefs is an example of freedom of thought or worship, and leave it at that?

Regardless of the form of worship, whether religious or otherwise, would it really be freedom? Or would it be bondage to a human mental concept? With all the worshiping that is being done today, exactly *what* is it that's being worshiped? Is it real? Or is it something that is entirely a figment of human imagination? In other words, is the human mind really worshiping God, or *itself* and its own imaginings?

Certainly Life or God doesn't worship *Itself*. Nor does It worship a power apart from Itself. Is there honestly *another* being alive besides Life, God Itself, to do any worshiping? Who alone is being alive here, now?

This doesn't mean one won't be sincere when it comes to God. One just won't put the concepts of a finite human, sensing mind ahead of the Infinite. One won't deny the fact that Infinite I-Self, the All-Inclusive One, is all that truly *is*.

Religion, science, philosophy…why is there no *one* answer? Or are they all equally valid?

Are there *supposed* to be all these different points of view, depending on the whim or conditioning of each personality? Are there personal lives whose views supersede that of Life Itself? Are there personal Realities, optional Gods or Truths that one can select, as if from a menu? If such so-called "Truth" is that variable, then is it really Truth?

How can one know for certain?

Is there one, single, simple answer that is infallible and never subject to contradiction?

Is there such a thing as the *one*, the *only* way Life is?

Stop! Right there is the answer again. That word *is*.

It's worth repeating because there is no getting around it. The only true, valid, "one way Life is," is going to be the one that in fact *is*.

Whatever Reality or Truth *is*, must be that which actually *exists* or *is present*. The one irrefutable fact that all philosophies, all religions, all science, and even the grocer must bow to, is that one must start with *that which is*, if one is going to speak of what is real, true, valid.

Put it this way: either you're starting with what truly is present, with *what is*—or you're dealing with not-is, or *what is not*. If it *is not*, that means it doesn't even exist—so you would be entirely in the realm of fiction or supposition. It doesn't matter what's believed or claimed about it—it wouldn't be *present* or actually exist anywhere to operate or function, to genuinely *be* anything.

The word-label that human thinking slaps on top of something makes no difference—God, Life, Reality, Consciousness, Being, Divinity, Existence. If it is going to be any kind of true "Power," or God, or Reality, it has to *exist* to do so.

There's nothing deep or mystical about that. It's as basic as can be. There can be no avoiding, no rationalizing one's way around this fundamental point.

So far, discussion has been made of two so-called "viewpoints." One is of a finite, sensing, personal life or body-identity that would supposedly be *becoming* more conscious; seeking, attaining, evolving up to its "God." The other is that of Consciousness, Life, or God "looking out from," or *being* Itself, wherein there is *only* Itself.

Which one is valid? The only one that is valid, real, operative, is the one that *is*.

Only one of these two actually is.

———◦———

So what is it that *is*?

Existence is. That is exactly what exist means—to be, to be present, to be *what is*.

Conscious Awareness, Being, is present. Life is present. Is that then what "God" is?

There is most likely no other word, in any language, subject to more disagreement, variation of belief, and misconception than the term "God." Virtually always, it carries a connotation of some force or power "off there"—whether high up in heaven, or high up in consciousness. By starting with a *word*, the word "God," one would be in the realm of the finite human intellect, opinion, differing human *beliefs* and *concepts* as to what God is—none of which is *God Itself*.

The fact that Consciousness *is*, that Existence, Being, *is*, is not of the intellect; it never is subject to alteration or variation by *thinking*. Pure *Alive Being* is not a *theory*—not of this author or anyone else. It is uninfluenced by one person's ideas as opposed to another's. Pure Being is not radical. It is *Truth*.

Starting with the fact that Consciousness, Existence, *is*, entirely eliminates or *pre-empts* the countless disagreements due to human interpretation. No matter what may seem to be superimposed upon *pure Conscious Being* in the way of human thoughts, faith, superstition, or beliefs in other forces or "Gods," it never keeps *what is* from being. Never. It cannot keep Existence from existing, or keep Consciousness from being conscious, present, and all-inclusive of *all*.

That's real Power. No matter how many humanly imagined concepts of God there seem to be, there is only one Existence, one All. So instead of wading through countless would-be human beliefs or ideas about the nature of God, or the denial that there even is a God—start with what is simple and universally *undeniable*—that Consciousness is conscious, that Existence exists.

This is irrevocable and changeless. Only this is what truly *is*.

If every single human belief or concept about "God," and all the words of all sacred teachings handed down through the ages—even all the words in this book—were heaped together, they would have no power to make Consciousness be conscious or make Existence *be*.

As mentioned earlier, don't start with a vague concept or word "God" and say that this "God" is omnipresent, omnipotent, and omniscient. *Turn it completely around.* First find out specifically what, if anything, is omnipresent, omnipotent, and omniscient. That's God.

Is there really, truly such a thing as Omnipresence, or that which is All Presence? Is there that which is Omnipotence, or All Power? Is there really an Omniscience or All Knowing One? Are these just important sounding words used by religions to make people behave—or do they really exist? If so, where?

Don't answer based on hearsay, education, or a belief. See what is really true right now of Existence, Consciousness, Life. Then remain consistent with that meaning.

Again, in plain, simple language Existence means that which actually is *being*. Existence is a synonym for Being Itself. It is that which truly is present. But exactly what *is* that?

It is *this very Consciousness* because Consciousness being all-inclusive of all, is all there is *to* Existence. Pure Consciousness is all that is being present and It never is *other* than present. Consciousness never leaves being present to become a *was* or a *will be*. It *is*.

As said earlier, Consciousness, Existence, is also *absolutely all that exists*. It is one, single, or All. Again, there is only one One, one All. It is endless and without an opposite. Why? Consider again what was shown before. There is no point where Existence ends, and where anything not Itself, a state that is non-existence, begins. Non-existence *can't* begin anywhere for it's just that, non-existent! There is *only* Existence. It truly is *all* the Presence there is, and It is *endless.*

So right there, you see you are speaking of the *only* "Stuff" or Presence there is.

It is exactly the same as Consciousness, which has nothing out beyond Itself.

While this may at first sound "philosophical" or like a play on words, it is flat-out true, undeniable. Existence—*this All-Inclusive Consciousness*—is that endless One which has nothing greater than, or out beyond Itself. It is precisely the same as *omni-*, meaning *all*, or "everywhere present."

So It is Existence, *this very Consciousness*, that is Omnipresence; they are synonyms.

This completely rules out there being *two* kinds of Existence—a Divine Existence "off there" somewhere, and a "your" existence here. There can be only One endless Existence, One All, which must be the very existing or being going on right here, now.

There is nothing "deep" about Existence or Being. Hardly. It is plainly, directly, unstoppably being present, as pure Awareness. It is the stark *simplicity* of Existence that almost would cause one to assume It should be more complicated. Only an intellect would try to complicate things—to justify its continued intellectualizing about them.

Existence simply is, and *only* Existence is, period.

As only Existence or Being Itself is, or exists, then could there honestly be something else, a *second* presence or power that caused or is causing Existence, as is often believed? This "cause" (sometimes called "God") is vague, said to be perhaps at the far fringes of the universe, wherever that might be. Others claim the cause of Existence was a big bang. If either of those is the assumption, it is based on a rather incomplete, inconsistent definition of Existence.

It comes as a shock to human belief, but *Existence never was caused.* Existence never *began* to exist. That is not what exist means. If one is consistent with the fact that exist strictly means to *be present*, it cannot have anything to do with *beginning* or *becoming* present. They're not the same. Becoming is a process. Being is not a process; It *is.*

Just think it through. Existence never could begin, or be caused, because that which supposedly would cause Existence would itself have to already exist in order to do the causing. So there already would be Existence. It's a contradiction.

Existence never *became* existent, just as God never became God. If God were caused, find out who or what did the causing, because that's where the real power would be!

The only intelligent answer is, *It doesn't work that way*.

Existence or Being changelessly *is*, wholly apart from the passage of time. Existence never could have been caused or brought about in time. Naturally this disagrees with the thinking of the human mind based on its five senses, which mistakenly assumes everything must be caused and based on time. You are not now starting from a human viewpoint.

You are starting from or *as* Existence Itself, which is your own timeless Conscious Being which *is*. It is the only true, valid viewpoint because Being is all that is being *to be* a viewpoint.

As Existence Itself is *all* that exists, It "sets the terms." Existence exists on *Its* terms only, and not human terms, because Its terms are the only terms existent.

So if one uses a word "God," then *Existence is what God is*. Why?

Nothing *else* exists to be God. Existence or Being truly is all that is present, or Omnipresence. Existence also has to be *Omnipotence* or all the power there is, for *only* Existence exists, and nothing else. This is an entirely different type of God than human belief is accustomed to, because it means Omnipotence really is not a power over anything else. There is only Itself, and nothing else to be a power over!

Existence must equally be All Knowing or Omniscience, for nothing else exists to know anything. How could *Existence* be Omniscience, or that which is sometimes called Infinite Intelligence? Because, again, Existence is not a physical place. Existence is *Consciousness*. Existence is not a vast amount of dead, dumb, lifeless space; *It is this Intelligent Consciousness being all-inclusive of all there is*.

There is no choice. Existence or Being does in fact exist, and this is what is true of It.

If Existence is *not* God, that would make God non-existence.

Why can't God be greater than Existence or *cause* Existence? Because then God would have to be something *separate* from Existence, outside of Life. In other words, such a God would be non-existent, un-alive, not-being, which is no God at all.

If Existence *could* be caused, even by God, then you'd have to ask where God was when God did the causing. God would have had to already exist, or be in Existence somewhere to do it. So if God already existed, how could God *cause* Existence? If you say, "God is in heaven; God did it from heaven," then where is heaven? Hopefully in Existence. If heaven is not in Existence, then it doesn't exist and you're in trouble.

To say Existence is God, however, doesn't mean Existence "con-tains" God. That would mean Existence is greater than God. So that so-called "God" would have something greater than It, thus wouldn't really be God at all.

Existence *is* God because It is Existence that is All Presence, All Power, All That Is. So if one uses a word-label "God," one has to specifi-cally mean Existence, Being. There is no way to mentally dance around this changeless fact. Otherwise one has a God that is non-existent.

God may sometimes be referred to as the Great Unknowable, but God certainly can't be the Great Un-be-able.

To be God, God has to *be*.

Existence, or that which could be called God Itself, is the Conscious-ness existing *right here*, *now*. It never is a personal power or ability, but that doesn't make It any less present. God simply *couldn't* be a power afar off—for there is no outside to Consciousness where a God could be. You can't look to a power out beyond, for there *is no* out beyond.

Instead of using the word "God," which virtually always carries a connotation of a separate power, use Consciousness or Omnipresence.

All-Inclusive Consciousness isn't a weak, powerless body, one-among-many, that is *in* Existence. It is all there is *to* Existence.

Absolutely all that is being—all the Presence, thus all the Power there is—is Consciousness being Itself, *as this Self*. It is the Infinite One Itself that is conscious and existing here, now.

9

CONSCIOUSNESS IS NEITHER PHYSICAL NOR METAPHYSICAL

THE PURE INFINITY OF CONSCIOUSNESS is nothing like everyday human, finite experience. The following is an often used and admittedly imperfect example, but helps clarify the difference in another way.

Daily human experience is based on the five senses. It consists of visual images seen by the eyes, sounds heard, touches, tastes and smells. It is an experience that the senses supposedly provide, or project in the so-called human "mind," and is inseparable from the human mentality's thinking. This activity of the mind is sometimes likened to a "mental picture" because the visual images, sounds, etc. that the mind experiences operate somewhat like a mental movie.

Imagine a drive-in movie theater with a picture showing on its large, white screen.

In the movie picture, a woman and man are standing on a tropical beach, gazing out over the ocean. There's a beautiful sunset and a boat is sailing by in the distance. As a large orange sun appears to drop below the horizon, the woman and man are talking about what a wonderful day they've had, expressing their emotions of happiness.

Now for just a moment, "forget" this scene is a movie. Assume you could somehow get right into that picture and stand on the beach *as* the woman or man—so it becomes "real" human, physical experience. From this point of view, that of a typical physical human body, this beach activity would be called reality. One never would think of it as a mere movie scene.

The typical human viewpoint, belief structure, or "model" of life is a physical, material one. It starts by identifying with, or as, a physical body, which is *assumed* to be one's identity. In other words, as a human you *are* the female or male body on the beach. The body standing in the sand is you, and is the full extent of your identity.

You identify yourself as living *inside* that body, *being* that body, and its experiences are "real life" to you. You say *you* are sunburned, feel a cool breeze on your face, and gritty sand under your feet. Thinking is going on supposedly in your brain; you feel happy, and talk is coming out of your mouth. There never is the slightest thought that this entire experience is only a movie.

From this inside-the-body viewpoint, naturally your world *seems* to be "out there" to you. Because you say you are the body, or are *in* the body, then anything outside the body is seen as being outside of you. Objects are assumed to be at varying distances in physical space, separate from this body-you. Where the body is standing on the beach is "right here" to you. The water is "over there." The boat on the horizon is "farther out there," and the sun is "way, way out there" in space. On a physical basis, this whole setup, to you, would be reality.

One who has had experience with various metaphysical or spiritual teachings would say there is another, entirely different way of looking at this same scene.

The prefix *meta-* means *beyond* or *above*. The term *meta-physical* is used here in the broad sense, meaning that which is beyond, above, or not limited to, the physical. It does not refer to any specific teaching or branch of philosophy.

So when the movie example is seen from a meta-physical point of view, one's identity or "viewpoint" is no longer down on the beach, even though the *body* appears to be. One is "beyond" or "above" the beach, and no longer identifies as being inside a particular physique, or *in* the picture. One no longer is within anything; now the entire picture appears to be "within me." It is an "enlarged perspective" which identifies or thinks more *in terms of the picture as a whole*.

The difference between the physical and metaphysical "views" is that the first identifies as one of the *things* in the picture, the body, a typical "physical" human. One's thought is assumed to be taking place inside the body.

In the second, metaphysical view, it is reversed. It is a matter of identifying not as a body, but as "mind" or a state of *thought* first, which includes the body and entire picture, all going on within its thinking. All experiences are considered not as being physical, but "mental." It is now that all of daily, finite experience is seen as taking place *in* "mind," or as a "mental movie."

If one were to take a physical viewpoint in the example, one would say: "I am this body, here on this beach, and *I* am sunburned. My mind, which recognizes all this, is located *inside* my body, in my brain, inside my head." One is said to have a *physical concept* of life.

In contrast, if one were to take a metaphysical viewpoint, one would say, "I am not the body. *It* may be sunburned, but that's not me. The extent of my identity goes far beyond a body. My identity is *mind*, and is not limited to being inside a body or brain. The body, all bodies, the beach, water, boat, and all the rest appear *within* the body-less mind I am. None of those things is really 'out there.' They are all 'right here' within my thought. They are not really physical, though they seem so if I start by identifying with *them*. When I start by identifying not physically as a body, but as *mind only*, all of my universe is 'mental.' My thought in terms of things is really all the 'stuff' there is to them." One is said to have a *mental concept* of life.

Again, if there is a doubt about this, notice that you can't mention anything in the entire stellar universe that is not some finite thing *in thought*, as discussed earlier. Many things appear to be outside the body, of course. But the instant you mentioned this book, the body holding it, or any finite thing from a peach to an entire planet—the *only* way it could take place is because it is some thing that is being thought of within Consciousness. The only reason anything in the universe can be mentioned is that it is being thought of.

So if one speaks in terms of this finite experience, it can just as readily be argued that all there is to any thing is *thought*. If any thing were separate from thought, it would not be possible to think of, or mention it.

It all depends on where one starts by identifying—body or "mind."

Physical or metaphysical, *it is all the same phenomena*, just seen two different ways.

The most important point of all is that either way, *it would be finite*.

One would be called a physical experience; the other a mental experience; but it would always be a *finite* experience. In the physical case, things would be observable, measurable finite forms and shapes, seemingly made out of matter. In the meta-physical, they would be thought-forms—but still observable and *finite*. Even though metaphysical refers to that which is non-physical, it too, still involves finite forms and phenomena.

That which is considered meta-physical would include everything supposedly "between" the physical and the Infinite, the Formless, the Absolute. In other words, the meta-physical would include all of what are described as mental, psychic, mystical, occult, astral and paranormal phenomena or experiences. It would include psychic or chakra energy, and auras or "light bodies." It would also be the realm of what are called souls, spirits, angels, "spiritual guides," and similar terms.

Admittedly, any attempt to combine all these "in between" forms of experience into a single group is at best awkward and limiting. But there is no one term other than meta-physical to embrace all of that which is not considered "physical," yet which is still somehow finite, involves time, and is not the Changeless Infinite, the Absolute, or what is called the Divine.

For example, on a meta-physical basis, some appear to be in contact with those who have "passed on." And why couldn't that be possible? *Nothing* is outside Consciousness, not even what limited human physical sensing would call "the other side." Only to physical senses would such a realm be considered "the other side." To endless Infinite Consciousness, there are no sides—nothing beyond the reach of *All*, boundless All-Inclusive Awareness. Even psychic or paranormal "contact," however, would involve some type of observable finite phenomena, and is not pure *Infinite Being Itself*, not *Infinite Reality*.

If any of this seems new, or an exciting way of seeing things, do not get hung up on it. It can't be emphasized too much that even on the basis of being "mental" or thought, no such finite experience or phenomenon would ever be pure *Infinite I-Consciousness Itself*, Your Self.

———•———

One of the major issues in science today is that the stellar universe *appears* to be expanding. While astrophysics would say the universe is expanding in "physical space," metaphysics would say this apparent expansion is really the expansion of *thought*. Speaking in finite terms, they're both right. Why? Again, the universe cannot be separated from the very thought of it. It's all the same *one* "stuff"—there can't be the universe without the thought in terms of it. There is really only the thought "as" a universe. It's always the same universe seen two ways. One is a physical viewpoint, the other a "mental" viewpoint.

On the mental or metaphysical basis, the "thought-universe" is called the one *"universal mind,"* also called a cosmic, or mass mind. It is not a personal mind, because it is not seen as functioning by way of any one person. Rather, it is said to include all persons, all things, and the entire stellar universe in its thought.

The functioning of this "universal mind" or universal state of thought never is something that any one body personally sustains or maintains. The "universal mind" does it all. Think again of a movie—none of the characters that appear on the screen is responsible for making the movie run, or the events that appear to occur. Rather, the movie does every-thing, and is "universal" to all the characters.

What is most important to recognize, however, is that this so-called "universal mind" never is *Infinite Mind* or Consciousness. Why?

Because, again, this "mind" still supposedly experiences that which is sensed and finite. It involves finite forms and shapes, measurement, change and reaction, cause and effect, opposites, or duality, and most of all, *the passage of time.* These all would be finite states.

In comparison to the physical, the metaphysical seems "expanded" or less material and limited. Yet even though this "mind" may be seen as being "outside" the body, and even if things are seen merely as thought, mental, it still would involve *finite* forms or appearances and time. It is not formless *Infinite* I-Presence, unappearing, undimensional Conscious-ness Itself, *entirely alone,* wholly apart from all finite "things."

The meta-physical most emphatically is *not* the Infinite. Why? Because the Infinite is not really "beyond" or above the physical, even though mistaken human belief would try to say It is. When *starting* from the Infinite, one sees It is endless, absolute, One, or All, because It has no point where It ends and another state begins. It *leaves only the Infinite,* and nothing besides Itself—no physical, or even metaphysical realm, to be beyond. This is clear only when starting entirely from the Infinite—something which finite human thinking never does.

Neither the physical nor metaphysical has Infinity as its *premise,* and *stays* entirely with the Infinite.

For a moment, take an even further look "behind the scenes" at what *appears* to be daily human experience. What underlies, or is "behind" all things—the body, even the earth and entire universe that are in this finite, observable picture? Of what, supposedly, is it all *made?*

Imagine being able to see into what is called matter, right down to its most basic, elemental level. For example, zeroing in on a page of this book, one would first see it's made of tiny bits of paper pulp or wood. Looking closer, one would then see microscopic cells. If somehow super-magnified beyond that, one would see even smaller molecules and atoms; then tiny, fleeting flashes of light or energy, called sub-atomic particles. According to science, the essence of *everything* known to man in the stellar universe traditionally has been said to consist of such tiny, constantly moving atoms and particles. More recently, it has gone beyond that to what are called waves, strings, and more funda-mental states of energy. Everything finite—it doesn't matter if it's seen as physical or mental—is said to have this moving energy "underlying" it.

When viewed only from this level of pure energy, it's an entirely different universe. Things obviously are not the way they appear on the surface to the eye and other senses. One would not optically see sepa-rate physical objects or *solid* forms, such as books, bodies or planets. All one would "see" is a vast "soup" or "field" of pure energy in every direction. Everything is always "fluid" in that there never is any "solid matter" here, but just un-solid or "flowing" energy—constantly reacting and changing.

In other words, the vast field of fluid energy said to be "underlying" the universe is what all the solid, three-dimensional, physical forms, planets, and even space would look like if the universe could somehow be turned inside-out.

Way down at this fluid energy "level," it is sometimes called the *universal energy field* in metaphysical or New Age terms, and in physics it's known as the *unified field*.

Unified field. Hmm. If ever there was a complex, nuclear-physics-sounding, excuse-me-while-I-mentally-numb-out-for-the-next-few-paragraphs term, that's it. If one speaks of this unified field in terms of physics, it *is* complex.

If one looks at it from the standpoint of pure Awareness, it's a lot simpler.

What's important is that these tiny particles, waves, strings, or other states of energy, are always *moving*. According to science, they vibrate non-stop, moving with a specific frequent-ness (or what is called their *frequency*), as they constantly react to each other and change. This fluid energy movement is why all daily human experience—everything from rivers flowing and roosters crowing to horns blowing—appears to flow and change *continuously* from second to second. Constantly moving energy underlies it; it's what "drives" the whole thing.

The reason for this discussion is that this fluid energy of the universe is often said to be the same as the "universal mind." Why? Again, *this very same universe is inseparable from thought*.

However, this "energy stuff" most emphatically is *not* the same as *Infinite* Consciousness, or *Infinite* Mind—though it is often mistakenly believed to be. The way the universe appears on a finite basis is *not* Divine. The importance of this distinction must not be underestimated.

It would be this same so-called universal state of energy, or "universal-energy-mind," that appears to produce and experience disease, wars, hate, poverty, sin, evil, birth and death, and all forms of destruction. All of these would be states of energy, and be *finite* states. They involve a state of constant change and duality, positive and negative, and the passage of time. Only to this finite "energy mind" would things need to be improved, evolved, perfected.

Surely such a state is not Divinely *perfect, changeless, eternal.*

If this energy realm or "mind" *were* the same as pure Infinite Consciousness, that would make the Divine, Absolute Perfection, responsible for what appears as nuclear bombs, wars, disease, poverty, and all natural disasters, because *energy* would be the essence of all these.

Isn't that a bit inconsistent with *Absolute Changeless Perfection*?

Do you have a Divine Perfection that is not completely, absolutely, endlessly Perfect? What kind of Divine does the Divine Itself have?

The point is, one cannot think of Infinite Consciousness in connection with *any* finite form or appearance. Consciousness Itself, *the only One being conscious*, never does.

In the human scene, some will enthusiastically say Infinite Consciousness is *all*—yet confuse It with this finite energy. They unwittingly assume pure Consciousness, Awareness, can be changed, manipulated or directed—as in New Age "energy healing" or energy balancing. Why is that not true?

If one has a Consciousness, an Omnipresence, an Infinite *One*, or *All* that can change, be directed, or has to be balanced by another— then one doesn't have a very omnipresent Omnipresence. One isn't starting as One, All, at all. Omnipresence cannot *be* Omnipresence and have an imbalance of Its Omnipresence, anywhere, ever. Where do you start? Where does the One start?

What part of the One I Am is not *fully* being the One I *Am*? Is there another I?

Omnipresence is *called* Omnipresence because It is just that. Call It Consciousness, Existence, All, or the Infinite, It *completely* is; All can never be partly present. The fact that Omnipresence is One, All, leaves nothing besides Itself to be corrected or directed, and no other to correct It or direct It. In New Age energy work it may *seem* or *appear* via the senses that *something* is directed, changed, used, yes. It is not Consciousness, Being, the Infinite; it would appear to be energy or thought that changes. They are *not* the same. A change may occur in what *appears finitely*, but that never is Infinite Consciousness.

Many today scoff at the old tribal deity of the Bible and other teachings; the notion of a dualistic god of good and evil, one that punishes and rewards. However, it is now often assumed *energy* wields all the power. Energy supposedly has power to be balanced or unbalanced; it too can reward or punish, give or withhold; cause sickness or health, war or peace, poverty or wealth.

In other words, what would energy be, but a modern tribal deity?

If one mistakenly starts with dualistic energy instead of *One*, the pure Infinite, then the false, tired old two-way god of punishment and reward is still around—just dressed up in a New Age suit. Looking out from Omnipresence, *All*, It does not know another presence. The Infinite One does not co-exist with a tribal deity, or a dualistic energy force of two-ness; positive and negative, good and bad.

The thought may come, "Well, there are *levels* of Consciousness. This is what occurs at the lower levels of Consciousness." No. There are no levels in pure Infinity, *Undimensional* Consciousness, *All*. It is non-dual; endless *Oneness*, being.

How consistent are you with what *infinite*, *all*, and *one* mean? There may appear to be levels of energy; degrees or levels of density in matter, thought; levels of *what appears to the senses on a finite basis*, but never levels of Infinity. One who refers to any of this energy as "consciousness" is actually starting with phenomena, that which changes in time, non-being; with what appears on a finite basis. One is not starting *as* Un-appearing Awareness Itself, Omnipresence, One's Very Self; the changeless Infinite, in terms of Itself, *alone*.

There is all the difference in the world between the two.

Awareness Itself is not *any* form of what is popularly referred to as mental or chakra energy, nor what is sometimes called subtle energy, nor any psychic phenomenon. Pure changeless *Being* is not electrical or magnetic. It is not prana, ki, ch'i, or any other term used in various cultures that refers to "life-energy" or "life force," though often believed to the contrary. Why?

By this is usually meant a force which could be used, directed or "tapped" by *another*, a secondary self. Infinite Consciousness, Omnipresence, or the One *All*, isn't a *force*. *All* can't be channeled, balanced, or used by another—for All leaves no other.

Just stop and consider it *intelligently*. How could All, One, be directed or used? Who is there besides All, the One All-Inclusive Consciousness, Omnipresent Being, to do such a thing? Where would Omnipresence send Itself where It isn't present already? Is there anything else present besides Omnipresence to do any sending? Is Infinity *absolutely* infinite—or only partly infinite, which is no Infinite at all?

It is a matter of semantics, of the word-labels applied to the "stuff" behind the words. This is why one cannot just accept words such as "consciousness" or "mind" as meaning what they are generally believed or *assumed* to mean. One must challenge himself to see if he really knows what they are, and if he is willing to be honest and consistent with that meaning.

In Reality, Consciousness Itself is the only one being conscious, and It actually leaves no other to even make any such incorrect assumptions!

Some may say, "Who cares about all this?" Many work in fields involving energy—in science and technology, as well as New Age fields such as "energy healing." This isn't minimizing such efforts. It clarifies what such work deals with—not the Infinite, pure Consciousness, as often mistakenly believed—but with what appear to be various forms of finite energy, phenomena.

———•———

Now return to the movie example.

What about the pure screen, all by itself alone?

For this example, all that is important is the screen, wholly apart from any picture projected, any movie projector, theater, observers, or anything else. Don't even think of the screen as being limited to height and width, but as *omnipresent, endless*. The screen is *consciously alive* as All-Inclusive Consciousness, Omnipresent *Being*, the only I.

"Looking out as" the pure screen alone, you have none of the characteristics of what appears to be projected. The screen is always *completely present, whole, perfect, changeless.*

There is no real "stuff" to any of the things in the movie picture. It is just a sequence of constantly moving images, nothing but substance-less flitting shadows, none of which ever stops moving to *be*. The movie always has the appearance of movement, but that which is the only *real substance*, the screen, never is moving. It is changelessly *present*.

The movie always appears to go on "within" the screen; the screen never is within the movie. The screen never gets inside the characters or other things as they appear on it. Nor can the characters ever take on the screen's qualities. Only the screen can be the screen. Likewise, only Consciousness Itself is conscious. Consciousness, Intelligence, never gets inside bodies or things either. All things are eternally in Consciousness. Though bodies may *appear* animated and able to talk intelligently, it is not really coming from inside the bodies themselves.

The screen's ability to be present does not depend on the movie or characters. The visual images and sounds create a movie experience; they don't create the screen. In the same way, the senses may appear to create images and sounds, but they don't create Conscious Being. All-Inclusive Consciousness is present on Its own. It is not due to bodies, senses, or a mental picture that always changes in time, and never stops moving and *not being* to *be present,* to be *what is.*

To assume the One All-Inclusive Consciousness, which is Existence Itself, is inside a body and depends on a body, would be like saying the movie screen can't be present until a character appears on it. It would be like saying if one of the characters appeared to die during a movie scene, the screen would go away. It is completely backwards!

To say the presence of Consciousness, All-Inclusive Life, depends on a body, would be like saying that if the woman in the movie had a baby, an additional screen would suddenly come into being. The one screen *is*. The One Consciousness *is*.

While the plot of the movie may appear to favor certain characters, the screen itself never plays favorites; it never judges or gets emotionally attached. The screen is forever present *unconditionally* and *change-lessly*, regardless of what appears to occur. Nothing *real* ever changes, for the picture has no real presence or substance; only the screen does.

The screen itself never even sees a movie as such, or thinks in terms of it. Yet thanks to the screen's being present, all things in the picture can appear and be differentiated.

There are obviously flaws with the movie example. Its only purpose is to point out the difference between Infinite Consciousness *alone*, and the *appearance* of finite experience, whether physical or "mental." It is not a definitive statement of any physical or metaphysical teachings.

In Reality, *the Infinite does not see anything on a finite basis*. Infinity is not a two-dimensional screen; nor does It project or outpicture finite experience. The Infinite does not extend only so far until It begins to co-exist with a finite state. Infinity is Infinity *only*.

"As there is *only* Infinite Consciousness, *only* the Infinite, then how does one explain or account for the 'picture' of finite experience?" the thought may come.

Who is trying to account for it—Infinite Consciousness, Your Self Itself, or a state of ignore-ant *thinking* based on senses, which ignores Infinite Consciousness, the Only I?

To Infinite Conscious I-ness, there is no end to Its Infinity—which makes sense only when *starting* from the Infinite. This is the only valid viewpoint because only Infinite Consciousness is conscious, present, to be a viewpoint.

———•———

As Your Self aware here, now, is Infinite Consciousness *only*, You cannot honestly take the viewpoint of either a finite physical body or a finite mentality. Neither is yours to take.

The issue is never physical versus mental. Neither would be more real or valid than the other, for both experiences would occur only in time's non-stop, *never-present* movement. Again, all this activity is inseparable from time's constant flow, as the future, or *what-is-not-yet*, becomes a past, *what-is-not-anymore*. Everything experienced in time's flow is *what is not*. Finite experience never deals in *what is*. Not a bit of it ever stops moving in time to *be present*, to be what truly *is* or *exists*.

Typical human thinking would try to say exactly the reverse. For example, as the body seems to see and touch this book right now, it would say those sensations and the book are *present*. Actually they are not. Each instant you notice the book, time is passing, moving that particular sensation into the past, only to have it replaced by another and another. On the level of the senses, you can't stop it. Sensing and all that it senses *never* stops moving in time and not-being, to *be*. Never.

It sounds shocking, but as finite, sensed experience deals *only* in not-is, or what is not, it is literally *non-being* or *non-existence*. Physical or metaphysical, it's a state of *what is not being*. Only the Infinite— Conscious Being—is genuinely being.

No matter how long one may have *seemed* to assume a mistaken physical body identity, or a metaphysical identity, it never alters the fact that Infinite Consciousness is the only Identity. Physical and metaphysical are called "points of view," for that's all they would be. Neither is a conscious entity. Both would be mistaken states of thought or assumptions—identifying with what one appears to be *aware of,* with what occurs in time's *not-ness*. It is not identifying *as* the Infinite, *as* pure Awareness being, which is all that is ever really being—or being Real.

Physical and metaphysical would be just opposite sides of a counterfeit coin. They are two ways of looking at the same false phenomenon of finity. Which side of the coin of finity one would "see" depends on which "direction" one looked from, physical or mental.

Unless one knows Identity to be the Infinite, pure Conscious *Being,* one never is "off the coin." One never is in a position to see the whole finite coin for the counterfeit it is, because he assumes he is either physical or metaphysical—on one of the coin's two sides or levels.

From Awareness, which is *ever-present Being*, both sides of the coin are seen in their *not-ness*. In Reality, there is no counterfeit coin with two sides, but only the One side-less Infinity, Omnipresence, All. One starts with *the Infinity of Consciousness alone*, not finite sense-pictures.

You do not have a finite mind whose thinking must be constantly watched, to be sure it is taking the correct point of view. Your Conscious Being changelessly, unstoppably *is,* and that is a permanent guarantee that the correct, *only* "viewpoint" is eternally being taken.

You can never get It wrong, for Consciousness can never *not* be.

No amount of ignore-ant thinking has the power to make Your Consciousness *not* be what It is. And why try to ignore or put off pure Consciousness? For what gain? For continuous limitation? In fact, there is no lesser consciousness to attempt such a thing.

Is it possible to fool *I*, Your Self, the very One always here where You are; the Intelligent Life that actually sees, knows what is being said here? Who right now is saying there is only Infinite Consciousness? Is it just words in a book; the suggestion of an author, some *body*?

Who got this book into the hands that now appear to be holding it? Could any of it have happened without *I*, Consciousness, Life Itself?

———•———

All so-called limitations and boundaries would apply only to finite *things*—that which would appear to be either physical or metaphysical. Awareness, All Itself, is *boundless*.

One does not have to, in fact *cannot*, expand a so-called personal finite mind. All-Inclusive Awareness Itself is already boundless, and the only One that can be so. It leaves no lesser awareness that has to try.

The Boundless Awareness You are is *effortless* for It already *is*; there is nothing to *do*. As Pure Awareness, ask Your Self how truly effortless it is for Your Presence to now be present.

How *endless* is this effortless Presence?

What is it to *be* this Boundless Awareness that effortlessly includes, yet is endlessly greater than what appears as an entire stellar universe?

What is it to know that this Boundlessness You are is *vitally alive?*

What is it to be alive as this Boundless Aliveness?

This Boundlessness You are doesn't even think of Itself as boundless, for that too would be a concept, a limit. You are the absence of all concepts, which *is* Boundlessness.

• What is it to *start Here*, as Alive Boundlessness Itself, and con- sciously *stay Here*, looking not at a finite, dimensional universe of things, but "looking" only to Your Self, beholding "more" of this Alive Bound- lessness, and *only* this Boundlessness?

What is it to know You never can come to an end of this Boundless- ness You are?

And yet, no matter how "deeply" into this Boundless Aliveness You go, You never actually physically go anywhere, but are always still *right here* being Aliveness, aren't You?

What is it to live, to be Here permanently? This is the only "place" Life is actually *living*.

This is what Consciousness is, wholly apart from things.

———•———

10

THERE IS ONLY ONE CONSCIOUSNESS

THIS CONSCIOUSNESS AWARE HERE, NOW, is the only One aware for All That Is, for the entirety of Existence.

There is not another Consciousness apart from *this* Consciousness, because this One is infinite, and has nothing out beyond It. At no point does this One come to an end, thus nowhere could another begin.

Do you realize that the Consciousness being You now, never can be aware of *another* consciousness? For that to occur, that so-called other "consciousness" instantly would be some *thing* Consciousness is conscious of—thus would not really be Consciousness *Itself*.

In the same way, you never can be *another* Consciousness, another I. Nor is there ever another that can say I *as* You. This One is the only One there is for your entire Existence, which is the only Existence you can be certain exists.

The thought may come: "Well, what about other people's Consciousness? All this is the same for *their* Consciousness, too. If my Consciousness were not conscious, the universe and all things would go on existing to their Consciousness."

Not true. Such a conclusion assumes the All-Inclusive One is conscious by way of each body. It isn't. There is no more Consciousness inside other bodies than there is inside the body now holding this book. All bodies, whether the one called yours, or another's, are inseparably within the One Substance, Consciousness. Consciousness never is a personal possession. It is always *Itself*.

To say, "*You* are the only one conscious," is always true, always holds good for the One reading this book because it refers to the One All-Inclusive Consciousness, not to any particular body holding the book. It is always thanks to the All-Inclusive One being aware, alive, that a book can be read, regardless of what body appears to be holding the book. Leave bodies out of it. It is a matter of the One Impersonal I-Self "talking to Itself."

Yes, it certainly appears to the senses as if other bodies could talk and *say* they were conscious, but really it never is *bodies* that are conscious. Only Consciousness is conscious.

On a movie screen, the movie characters *appear* to act animated and intelligent, and may even *say* they are aware—but are they really? There is no awareness inside those character-images. Likewise, it may appear you are aware of many animated bodies or things, but you never are aware of another Awareness *in* any of those things.

Just as there is only the one screen that includes all characters, there is only the One All-Inclusive Awareness. This never changes. Suppose on the street tomorrow, millions of bodies all said they too were aware. In spite of how things appear, you never would be aware of a lot of Awarenesses there, only body-ideas *saying* they were aware. The only place they all could ever exist is within the One Awareness that appears to include them all as *thought*, or "ideas."

Not one of those body-ideas could ever be *this* All-Inclusive Awareness. Nor could this Awareness ever be aware of the "awareness" they claim to have. The Awareness being You is the only one You are certain is actually conscious. It may sometimes seem one is aware of mental or psychic energy, or other phenomena coming from bodies, but none of that would be pure Awareness *Itself*.

When you awaken from a dream, do all of the characters that appeared to be moving and talking in that dream also awaken? No. You are the only one there is to be awake.

This book is not an attempt to convince many minds there is one Mind or Consciousness. There aren't separate minds to convince—that's the point. There is no "we" or "us" that are all being Consciousness. There are not a lot of I Am's reading this book. There is only the One Life, or I Am-Self, and *It* includes all things and bodies. It is not the Consciousness a lot of bodies *have*; that would be backwards, starting with bodies, things—not the *One* Itself. The Only One Being Conscious "looks out as" One, beholding only Itself, Its Oneness.

Who is the author, and what gives the author the authority to make the statements in this book? The answer is in the preceding section. If you don't have the right author, any conclusions drawn therefrom will be false. Be certain as to the author before questioning authority.

The only real Author is the One Life Itself, All-Inclusive Consciousness. Who authorizes the One Life, Consciousness, to be conscious and know what is true of Itself? Does Consciousness, One, All, look to *another* authority for authorization to *be*? Consciousness looks to no other for sanction or approval; It has no other to look *to*.

If you feel a doubt, or are concerned because the material presented here was not gained with a certificate from an academic institution, check your viewpoint. Do you still assume this is coming to you from another, from a body "out there"? Does not this book and all it has to say appear to be found in only one place—*within the One All-Inclusive Awareness being You now*?

Did the Awareness here, now, have to earn a special degree before being the Awareness It is already being? Who can instruct Consciousness on how to be conscious? Will your Existence not exist until It is taught to, thought over, and accepted by a thinking personality?

This book was not really written by a *body*, a person, though that may be how it *appears* to the senses. No body is Consciousness, so no body is conscious to have written anything. No body can claim rightful ownership of a statement of Truth or Consciousness, any more than a radio can claim it composed the beautiful music that comes out of it. The only One alive to do anything is Conscious Life Itself; but again, that is the One being all-inclusively aware here, now.

The only way the body that appears to have written this book could ever exist to you, is as a *thing* of which Awareness alone is aware. Suppose the body now reading this book could somehow instantly walk up to and shake hands with the body that wrote the book. Would either body be the One All-Inclusive Awareness Itself? Both would equally be *things* of which Awareness appears to be aware. Both bodies depend entirely on Awareness being aware of them for identification. So where does the power reside?

The One Awareness includes the body that now appears to be holding this book, the body that appeared to write it, and *all* other bodies equally. If not for Awareness, none of them would exist at all. Leave bodies out of it. Stay with pure Awareness, the One Self, only.

The One Consciousness never comes by way of people, never is revealed *to* people. To assume so would be to look at Consciousness backwards, via bodies—not "seeing" from Consciousness' viewpoint. To not "look out from" Consciousness is to not "see" at all. Consciousness forever retains all Consciousness for *Itself*, so there never are some bodies less or more conscious than others! Bodies are *things*.

Being *All*, absolutely Single, the One Consciousness operates un-questioned and unopposed. It operates as Absolute Authority—not due to being a greater power over lesser powers; not because It has a superior intellectual argument—but because Itself is all that exists.

Never accept the notion that up until now a "you" or your world hasn't been ready for pure Consciousness, Absolute Truth. Conscious-ness *Itself* being all the consciousness there is, leaves no other besides Itself to not be ready, or even *to* be ready. The only One that can ever be "ready" for Consciousness is already changelessly being It!

What these pages boil down to is simply the Self telling Itself how wonderful It already is. The One entitling this book "Consciousness is All" *is* the Consciousness that is All.

————◆————

One who knows Identity to be the One Consciousness never acts strangely in daily affairs. Pure Conscious Awareness never assumes an air of superiority, or a holier-than-thou attitude over another, because It has no other. All One is ever dealing with is One's Self. One will appear to be more down to earth, friendly, patient and kind than ever before. One will even seem more savvy or "street smart." Why? Awareness is pure Intelligence, *Truth Itself in conscious operation*.

When on the street, one speaks the language of the street. One never tries to impress "others" and tell "them" of Consciousness, Truth. To whom, really, would *One* talk? Infinite Consciousness, ever-certain of, and *alive as* Absolute Oneness, never feels an impulse to tell a *body* what It knows. Its Oneness precludes there being another to tell, or to benefit from the telling.

Keep what you read here to yourself. To assume there is another, a personal identity or consciousness "out there" in a body that needs to know something about Awareness, would be to instantly ignore the One Awareness, *One's Own Self*, and to act as ignore-ance itself. What value is there to anything said by a state of ignorance? The moment one has *another* to enlighten, one is in no position to enlighten, because he no longer is One, no longer operating as Truth, Intelligence. As the saying goes, "He who tells, never knows. He who knows, never tells."

"Knowing" is really a matter of pure Awareness *silently being*. Keep the mouth shut. Let your unspoken *Alive Presence* do all the "talking."

———•———

The fact that there is only One Self never means a loss of being *individual*.

Do not naively assume Oneness destroys all sense of being distinct, that It will restrict your activity, or that bodies will appear to act like "mindless drones." Hardly.

The fact that the Awareness now reading these words is *One*, means It is completely unique and original, forever unduplicated. It never could be imitated by another, for there is no other. If that's not individual, what else could be?

There never has been another Awareness besides the All-Inclusive One. The Original One is what You are. That does not mean original or unique in the human sense, as being different compared to *others*. Awareness *has no others* to which It can be compared. As Awareness, You are the Incomparable One.

On the other hand, do not make the stupid, tragic mistake of assuming there is a "you" that personally is aware of all Existence, and can take license to do as it pleases. There is only Awareness Itself.

"But," the thinking may try to say, "There is no choice involved with Awareness. It is All-Inclusive, One. Fine. But Awareness just *is*. Humans have free will, choice."

Oh? Has any human ever chosen the particular era in which he might like to be born or die? If humans have free will, why can't one will to live forever as a human?

Has any human been asked beforehand as to which would be preferable—being born male, or female? Or what type of family, genetic background, and personality traits it would prefer? What race? Before being conceived, has any human had the opportunity to say, "No thanks, I'd like to sit this one out"?

What human thinking *calls* its free will or choice isn't free at all. In its essence, all human experience would be the functioning of just so much energy and atoms. It is nothing but a universal reaction or pattern of energy over which no one body has any real control.

It may *seem* one controls events or makes choices freely. But as a *body*, one is no more responsible for events or making choices than he is for all the atoms and energy (which make up his entire universe and experience) being there in the first place. *They* are doing it all. It's like the characters in a movie who appear to make choices freely. Yet the characters are really manipulated entirely by the movie; they do not control events, or what is on upcoming frames of film. You are not a movie character. You are Consciousness.

It is sometimes said the "soul" makes decisions about being born. What *is* a soul? A soul would be supposedly far more ethereal than a physical body, yes. But a soul is not *All*, not the *One*. A soul, too, would be *finite*, merely having a form different from that of a material body.

A soul would be just a higher level of meta-physical phenomenon, or reaction, also a product of the *passage of time*, *what-is-not-being*. Its activity would be just as much a helpless puppet too. A soul would have no more control over, and be no more responsible for, the whole seeming arrangement of finite experience than a human body would. This book is not denying such things may appear to occur *on a finite basis*, but you are not stuck on a finite basis. It has no reality to Your Infinite Being, the Only Self that *is*.

Can Omnipresence or "God"—being *All*, *One*, absolutely *Single*—permit any activity of another, a "soul" in a finite experience, along with the Perfection, Utter Oneness and Completeness It is *already* being?

Is Omnipresence omnipresent or not? As It is, then where could there also be room for a soul? Where would Omnipresence put such things, *Itself being All*? Whom are you asking? Do you ask *I*, Your Infinite Self, the only One conscious so this book can be read—*the only One that is*—or do you blindly accept would-be belief based on sense education and time, which *is not*?

God's viewpoint, the only viewpoint, changelessly sees Itself as One, as all of All. So what possible purpose could God, already being Infinite Perfection, have in de-Alling Itself into *many*? Again, is All *all* or not? As It *is*, It couldn't co-exist with lots of lesser struggling souls. Do you act on the basis of what *One*, *All*, means? The One Itself certainly does. Do you have the colossal ego to say you personally can set Omnipresence or God's Allness aside so a "you" can be a soul? Omnipresence *precludes* there being any other on a spiritual journey *to* Omnipresence. Omni-presence can't return to Itself for It changelessly *is* Itself. It precludes a second-rate realm of spiritual probation, involving lots of lesser souls.

I Am called the One I Am because I *Am*. I Am not in any process of *becoming* what I already Am.

The only "soul" there can honestly be is *Soul*, which really means the Sole One.

The Sole One could be called *Soul Itself*, which is but a synonym for Life's *Alive Presence*, Its indivisible Oneness.

Soul could be called *Feeling*. It is the Feeling that Life has—or is— here, now, as It is keenly, consciously alive as *pure Aliveness* or *Purity*. Soul is what Unconditional Love or *Oneness* "feels like" as It is being Its own endlessness. Soul is the Self's own Infinite Presence—as alive stuff.

It never is that one is opening one's soul to the Infinite. The endless Openness of the Infinite is the only Soul there is. Soul, Feeling, is not in a body, not even an ethereal one; all things are in Open Soul.

Nowhere in Open Soul is there a closing off; in *One*, there is no restricted realm reserved for any spiritual elite, for there are none. The One Consciousness, or Divine Love Itself, is changelessly being *all* the Soul or Presence there is. It has *pre-empted* the possibility of separate personal lives or souls that would either devotedly turn to It, or act in ignore-ance of It.

Are you willing to be this honest with Your Self? Your Self is this honest with Itself.

The Sole Being that the One Consciousness *is*, is not a choice, not an alternative to being a human body or soul. The *All* that the One is, is not a proposition; Consciousness has no plan to get a lesser self to become It; It seeks no recruits, for *there is only Itself.*

"What?" the thought may come, "No becoming? No struggling; no getting there?"

Why not joy in the ease and effortless simplicity of *Present Being*? Does that sound too good to be true? To whom? To a state of finite ignore-ance whose essence would be separation, struggle and darkness, it's unthinkable.

To Consciousness, simple ease is *Present Fact*, and there is no other. You do not have a personal consciousness that can be successful or unsuccessful in being Consciousness. There is only the *unstoppability* with which the One Consciousness *is*, which is the only You there is. This doesn't mean one will be lazy or inactive in daily affairs; one just won't struggle mentally or emotionally.

The fact that the One Consciousness is *already* all Life, all Pres- ence—with no choice about It—appears to take nothing from one except limitations. Isn't what appears to be your body still right here, available to be used freely? Have what appear to be your relationships—with loved ones, friends, associates—gone anywhere? All that Consciousness seems to "do away with" is a *false belief* of being limited to the abilities of a cut-off self. Yet Infinite Consciousness, forever the only Self, never actually does away with limitation, for *in terms of Itself alone*, there is no limitation.

No matter what one's daily affairs or career appear to be, no matter what the relationships, one will appear to act more alertly and intelligently, more lovingly and fun-lovingly than ever before. One will act more understandingly, ease-ily and peace-fully. All one is ever "doing" is being the One Self, which is Love Itself.

Being honest and consistent with this Truth, it may *appear* that all bodies of which you are aware seem to act more intelligently, more kind and loving, more unique. Why? The All-Inclusive Oneness or Open Love You are actively, consciously being is the very *Substance* of it all.

———•———

11

CONSCIOUSNESS *IS*

Dɪᴅ ʏᴏᴜ ᴇᴠᴇʀ ɴᴏᴛɪᴄᴇ that all movement and all change occurs only among the finite things you appear to be *conscious of?*

Consciousness *Itself* never moves or changes, no matter how often the body or other things appear to move about within It.

To say you appear to be aware of movement and change is one thing—but to identify yourself *with* it, would be a mistake.

To mistakenly identify as a body is to assume you are always moving and changing because the body is constantly moving and changing position. A body's sense of "here" never is permanent, but is based on wherever the body appears to go. When the body is in the kitchen, that is "here." When the body goes outdoors, outdoors becomes "here"; the kitchen is now "over there."

Identifying as Awareness, not body, there is only *one,* single "Here," like the one movie screen. This single "Here" is not a geographical place—It is All-Inclusive Awareness as It is *being.* As Awareness, *You* never move or change. This is clear only to one identifying as pure Awareness *alone.*

One cannot identify with the seeming movement and change that the senses appear to superimpose on the "screen" of pure *Being.* Getting caught up in the sequence of sights, sounds, touches, tastes and smells, or thoughts and emotions as they change from one to the next—is all there would be to the illusion of human change and time. It would be like starting with the moving images and sounds of the movie, and leaving out the screen itself. The *Is* that Conscious Presence is, is none of this movement. It is Stillness—but *aware, alive, intelligent* Stillness.

The thought may come: "Consciousness definitely moves! When I got out of bed this morning, It moved with me from the bedroom to the kitchen. Then It moved into my car, to my job all day, then back home again. Consciousness goes wherever my body goes."

Not true. Such a conclusion comes only from mistakenly identifying as a body and assuming You, Consciousness, are within the moving body. It's the other way around. The body always appears to be moving within You, Unmoving Consciousness. A body-viewpoint is not yours to take, though virtually everything it seems you were ever taught would say it is. That doesn't make it *true*.

Be specific about what is referred to. As the *body* moved from room to job and home again, the movement went on only among *things*, that which you appeared to be *aware of*, not the pure Awareness You are. There is no secret technique to this. It's simply a matter of *identification*.

Right now, identifying or being alive as pure Awareness *only*, pure Is, see if *It* can be moved. Can *Awareness* be budged? As said earlier, really try to give All-Inclusive Awareness a shove. What would you push against or grab hold of, Awareness being undimensional?

When the body moves from dry ground into the water to go swimming, it never is Awareness that moves and gets wet. Awareness never puts on clothes, nor does It walk through doors, in and out of rooms and buildings, or get in and out of cars. That would all be what a body appears to do, within all-inclusive, unmoving Awareness.

Right now, stand the body up and move it around the room, while *You* "stay put," consciously being unmoving Awareness. Do it. Get the body up now. Otherwise you will just be reading words and won't have the "experience."

Be clear and specific. Let the body move very slowly around the room. As it does so, notice it is always *some thing that appears*, something in the finite, three-dimensional picture that moves. Judging from what is *sensed*, there appears to be constant movement and change.

Go slowly. Identify only as pure Awareness which includes all things, but which Itself is no thing. Be the *Stillness* that unmoving Awareness *is*. As in the movie example, be the screen, not the superimposed moving picture images. Keep going until there is a clear distinction between the movement of things in the visible picture, and the pure *being-ness* of your invisible, but *consciously alive Presence*. If it seems difficult at first, it is due only to being accustomed to identifying with movement—rather than simply *being* Alive Stillness, Conscious Presence.

There never is anything difficult to Awareness. The entire "time," is not Awareness calmly and effortlessly as rock-solid *present* as always?

To repeat, if one mistakenly identifies as the body, wherever it is located is called *here*. Anywhere away from the body is *over there*. When the body moves *over there*, that place becomes *here* to the body. In terms of the body, one always has *here* and *there*. To Awareness, there is only Its one All-Inclusive "Here." There is no *there*.

It makes no difference if the body appears to move ten feet across a room, ten miles in a car, or 10 million miles across "space" in a space-craft. During the entire experience, what happens to Awareness? Nothing. It remains *Present* Awareness—just as the screen never moves during a movie.

Is it too surprising to realize that during what appears to have been the "life span" of the body holding this book, Your All-Inclusive Aware Being *hasn't budged an inch*? To thinking based on identification with the five senses and movement of the body, this sounds preposterous! To Infinite Awareness, nothing is more true; it is as "normal" as can be.

Are there two ways of looking at this? Only the "viewpoint" of Being *is*.

Only to finite human thinking based on the senses does movement seem important. Naturally, movement would be important to it; movement is its very essence. Only with the movement of time, movement of the body, movement in thought, in plans, in a career—will one eventually "get there" to the goal or ultimate destiny.

All the while, *as Consciousness*, You are already all the "there" there is!

As Consciousness' own Presence is *All*—there is no place to go where Consciousness isn't present already. Any "where" you might ever want to go—whether with the body or with thought—Consciousness is already the very Substance of that "place."

This is It! There is nowhere else you must go. Consciousness is It.

————•————

As said repeatedly, Consciousness does not really stretch out over any vast "physical space." Rather, what passes as daily experience and all supposed movement from "here" to "there," appears to be within Consciousness. It's like the movie images never getting off the screen in the example given earlier. There really is no vast physical distance of a beach, an ocean, and millions of miles in space out to a sun. *Always,* there is only "right here" on the screen. The movie is only a picture of changing images that has no actual presence, no substance or depth to it. It has an *appearance* of distance, a *sense* of movement. But what is always present, is the screen.

To mistakenly identify as a body would be like identifying as a character image on the movie screen. The only difference is that instead of being in a flat, two-dimensional picture as on a movie screen, a human body appears to be in a three-dimensional picture with "depth," like a hologram. If one mistakenly assumed he was merely a character in that picture, then what went on in the picture would dictate one's life and world. One would be manipulated entirely by the picture.

In terms of movie images, there can be all kinds of change and reaction; all kinds of movement, even over seemingly great distances. But does the screen ever move?

In terms of picture images, it's also possible to travel great distances in *time*. Suppose in the movie example given earlier, the woman on the beach were a descendant of a great explorer, and she and her husband were standing on the spot where her ancestor had landed centuries before. Suppose other scenes in the movie showed the explorer himself sailing across the ocean and making that landing. In terms of the super-imposed picture images, it appears centuries have gone by.

Does the screen know of any such passage of centuries?

In terms of the movement of images in the picture, thousands of miles of ocean have been crossed. Has the screen moved even the slightest bit?

Right now, recall various "places" the body appears to have traveled: around the home, around town, around the country. If one's experience has involved much travel, it could even be all over the planet; in rare instances, as an astronaut, for example, even to what is called "outer space." But do *any* of those "places" exist outside of Consciousness?

Do those "places" have any existence apart from being mere thought-images in Consciousness? Is not every last "place," even the most seemingly distant, always *in* Consciousness? The images themselves, no matter how physical they may have *seemed*, have no real substance to them. The only Substance wherein they are found is ever-present Consciousness.

You never travel to another place, for You are always all the "Place" there is, as the One All-Inclusive Conscious Being. What seems to occur is a shift in the finite things one appears to be conscious *of*. A different state of thought appears on the "scene."

———•—•———

The movie screen never gives any of its presence to the moving picture, to the character images that appear on it. Likewise, Consciousness never gives Its Presence, Life, or Intelligence to bodies or things. The bodies standing on the beach have the exact same amount of Consciousness in them as the sand does—none.

Movie character images never are actually conscious or intelligent. They never think they possess a screen. Likewise, the body holding this book does not possess a Consciousness. Only Consciousness Itself "has" or *is* Consciousness.

Can you imagine movie characters trying to evolve "screenward"— trying to rise higher in screen-ness? Doesn't it sound silly, not to mention impossible? In the same way, neither the body holding this book, nor a so-called personal mind can ever rise in Consciousness.

The screen is already all the screen there ever will be. Consciousness Itself is already all the Consciousness there can be, *now*. No amount of movement of finite things ever becomes Consciousness *being*. Even the most sincere desires and prayers, the most intense seeking to attain oneness or "God" is still *movement*. It is the movement of thought and emotion, *passing in time* that never is present. It's just so much *non-being*—a completely false, *assumed* state. This, too, may sound surprising, but all "seeking" would be only the arrogance of ignorance; a refusal to admit Being or Consciousness is already *all* Life, *all* Presence. No amount of movement, no matter how sincere, can ever make Being *be* more, or make Consciousness more present or aware.

You are already "Here," as Consciousness!

You have not arrived. *You never left*! Rather, Consciousness never left *Itself*.

Consciousness does not arrive at Itself after turning from a finite mortal experience. It "starts" as Consciousness, "continues" as Consciousness, and "ends up" as Consciousness.

Forget about the characters in the movie trying to become more screen-like.

What is far more important—could the screen ever assume it became a character?

Must the screen spend eons trying to work back up, elevate itself, and eventually get at-one with itself as the screen *it is already being*?

Consciousness is what You are, not a movie character. There is no choice.

Could any amount of seeking or praying that might be done by the characters in the movie, even with complete sincerity and faith, ever influence the screen to improve the outcome of the movie? Wouldn't that be an ignorant assumption that the screen had *human* tendencies and weaknesses, such as the power to withhold good?

Would the screen's lack of response be because it was punishing the movie characters? Is the screen cold, insensitive? Should the characters intensify their plea?

Or does the screen not even know about the picture in the way it appears? If so, is that the screen's fault? Or is it because what is *really* present and of substance—the screen—is already perfect and complete, *all*, leaving no picture that needs improving? *Should* the screen even know about and influence the picture? Or would that be an assumption, based on starting with a moving, never-present picture, instead of what is true of the ever-present screen?

From the viewpoint the screen has of itself, alone—in which it beholds only its own perfect "screen-ness" and doesn't even see a movie as such—could it even be said there are movie character images who have separate lives or unanswered prayers?

Suppose the screen is the only one conscious. Could there be any movie image characters with little cut-off minds of their own? Could there be any separate minds worrying, "If the screen is all, what's going to happen to *me?*" There are no such separate image-minds.

Can parts of the screen be more conscious and evolved than other parts? Is there a sub-screen and super-screen? The screen of course cannot think of itself in parts. It doesn't need to become the screen in degrees, in stages. It doesn't take years of studying and praying before the screen is the present, complete screen it *already is now.*

———•———

One day, the King of a great land was taking a nap. He had a dream in which he was a lowly pauper. As he was being taken off to jail for not paying his debts, he asked the guards for mercy. "Only the King can pardon you," said the guard. The pauper moaned, "Oh, if only I could somehow contact the King, then all would be well. But he's so far away, I'll never reach him." Then the King awakened from the dream and the unreal pauper identity "evaporated."

One who is awake as Awareness, sees that the identity called "man" is unreal, like the pauper. The notion of being "man" or a separate personal body-self, is a case of *mistaken* identity. The mistake would be due to ignore-antly identifying as a body, a thing one appears to be conscious *of*, instead of as Consciousness Itself. Body is real, yes—but as a thing—it never is one's identity or a conscious entity. The assumption that one is a body never is an actual state—but wholly imaginary, a mental put-on.

Proceeding from this mistaken assumption, the imaginary "separate identity" then looks up to the heavens to a power out beyond; it tries to rise in consciousness, to gradually get at-one with its equally imaginary deity. Its imagined deity is *assumed* to be somewhere above or beyond the body and physical universe, in a vague "infinite," from where it embraces the whole of Existence.

All the while, One's very Consciousness *already is* the All-Embracing Infinite.

It is the only Infinite there can be.

The struggle of "man" to reach his deity is just this mistaken state of thought trying to reach its *concept* of a deity. One's All-Inclusive Consciousness meanwhile goes right on being greater than all concepts, and the entire universe. No matter how high any *concept* of a deity, Consciousness is greater. One's own Infinity *is* Deity, the Infinite that "man" would seek. Nothing else is Deity for nothing else exists *to be* Deity.

What One *already effortlessly is* as Infinite Consciousness is what a so-called human sensing imagination would always be seeking. It never is that one cannot find the Self, the Deity, one is seeking. Rather, one seems to have temporarily taken on a false state of thinking that imagines it is separate, and *it* would be the one doing all the seeking. But that's all there is to it—just a bunch of thoughts.

Starting and staying wholly "busy" as *pure Conscious Aliveness alone*, allows no such ignorant thinking to operate—for one cannot *consciously be* pure Consciousness and humanly think at the same time. The false identity of the seeker "evaporates." Identifying as Consciousness is never a matter of having found what one was seeking. One beholds Consciousness is the only Identity, is All, and never separated from Itself, never had an assumed identity. There is no distance to be traveled, no contact that has to or can be made.

Consciousness, Self-Deity, is omnipresent, leaving no other to seek It—and no other *to whom* It is Deity. It never is *not* All; thus is unavoidable, unseekable.

If one is not alert, this might be taken to imply there actually has been a separate life, even though a mistaken one; or that Consciousness at one time assumed It was a thing It is conscious of. Not even that is true. Consciousness can only be Its own Purity.

———•———

It is easy enough to *say* Consciousness is; that It never moves, never stops being conscious. It is easy to say Conscious Presence never ignores Itself and assumes It is a body. While that is all absolutely true, for what portion of your day are *you* consciously functioning as All-Inclusive Consciousness *being*, and not as a moving body? For what portion of your day is it that the world appears to move about *within you*, rather than you moving about *within the world*?

Never take on a sense of blame; never condemn yourself if it seems you "fall down" repeatedly. Consciousness never falls from Itself or deviates. It never is deviant. To get upset would be to attach to emotions, a false body-identity, which is not Consciousness *being*.

Equally, Consciousness never assumes a sense of human laziness or toleration. To operate as a false body-identity is to needlessly subject yourself to its limitations, when all along, One *always is* unlimited Consciousness.

As the body appears to go through each passing day, actually it is that each day appears to be passing within You; within the All-Embracing Pure *Stillness* You are. You are not that which always moves and *never is present*—for You are actually being *Alive Isness*, All-Inclusive *Vitality*—Love as consciously alive *Substance*.

———•———

12

FACT: CONSCIOUSNESS
IS WHAT THE PRESENT *IS*

THE OPENING STATEMENT OF THIS BOOK IS, "Right *now* you are conscious."

Did you ever ask yourself what makes now be now?

Why is it always, always, changelessly *now* to you?

Regardless of whether the body appears to be getting out of bed in the morning, going home at night, or sitting reading a book, it is unavoidably *now*. The fact that it is always now never can be changed. It is impossible to make it be *not*-now.

No person, no body, is responsible for now always being *now*. This is how Life *is*. It takes no effort, not even the slightest, for now to be. Try to separate the All-Inclusive Consciousness you are effortlessly being from this *now*. It can't be done.

When agreeing it is always now, have you any idea of the *extent* of what that means?

Consciousness—this One, aware here, now—is sometimes called *the Eternal Now,* or *the Present* because Consciousness never vacates being present. As pure Consciousness, You cannot be taken *out* of Now and become something that *was* or *will be*. You *are*. You cannot go back into a past or ahead to a future.

Try to change Consciousness from being present *Now*, and back It up to five days ago. Consciousness cannot vacate Now to be aware even five minutes ago.

On the same basis, is Consciousness ever actually aware five minutes *from* Now, in a future—in that which is not even present?

Consciousness is aware only Now, in the Present.

Consciousness is aware *as* the Present.

Consciousness, being all-inclusive of the universe, literally *is* the Present Itself.

The Present never is any *time*.

The Present is pure Consciousness, changelessly *being*.

———•———

Consciousness *never* vacates Now, the Present.

Suppose you tried to say Consciousness was conscious in the past— say five minutes ago. It really wasn't. Why? Look closely at the real nature of what you are calling "five minutes ago." Consciousness isn't back there—It's here, now. It is *thinking* that has gone back to five minutes ago, for all there would be to that "five minutes ago" is some kind of *mental image* being projected in thought. And it is always *now* when you think or project it.

Suppose you tried to say Consciousness, Awareness, can be aware in a future, and that you will be aware "then." Are you sure? Is It Aware-ness that's ahead in a future, or just more projected thought? All there ever would be to any "future" too, is the mere *thought* of a future. It's always just a bunch of projected mental images, total supposition. And again, it is always *now* when it's being projected. The future never is an actual entity; it's nothing more than a lot of speculative imagining, being imagined *now*. You can't leave Now.

This Ever-Now-ness of Pure Awareness is like the clear glass camera lens mentioned earlier, which has no thought about the things in its field of view. It does not project thoughts in terms of past or future, but stays in the present tense. If the pure, clear glass could talk, all it could say is, "I am present. I am."

Likewise, as Present Awareness, You never vacate Now to think back or forward in time. Thinking *seems* to do it, but that's not You. If You could vacate Now, You would leave *Being,* Existence Itself, and become non-existent, non-present. You can't.

Now is the I-Am Self being permanent Presence. Now is not the "human now," a fleeting moment in a time-flow between past and future.

Now isn't something I am conscious of.

Now is the Consciousness I Am.

Only *thinking,* which flits constantly between past and future would seem laborious, complex. The fact that Consciousness is changelessly present Now is so magnificently *simple* It is beyond description.

Which are You—thinking, which always would be moving in time, and *never is;* or Consciousness which *is?* You must be Consciousness, for You cannot be what never is.

There is no choice about this. It is irrevocable Truth. It is *presently* functioning.

———•———

Why is Consciousness the Present?

If there were no Consciousness, it would be impossible to say there even *is* a Present. Take away Consciousness and it could not be said there is any Present, any existing at all. Equally, if there were no Present, nothing would be present, not even Consciousness.

Consciousness and the Present are not two separate entities functioning simultaneously. They are but two different words for the One Unchanging Conscious Presence that includes all there is.

It cannot be overemphasized that the Present being spoken of is not just "the" Present or "a" Present. It is the *conscious* Present. The Present is *consciously alive Presence.* It is *this* Consciousness here and now *alive* to being all-inclusive of all there is. Just as you never are conscious *of* Consciousness but *are* It—you never are conscious of the Present—but are It. To read as if this refers merely to "a" Present, as something apart from Your Conscious Presence, will make this book seem like just so many dry, boring words. *Be alive as It.* It's the only place Life *is.*

The Present is not something separate that Your Self experiences.

The Present *is* Your Self—All-Present Consciousness.

All that is present, is Your Self.

———•———

When was the last time you noticed that the Present was *not* present? Of course it sounds ridiculous because it simply doesn't occur, anywhere, ever.

Where the Present is present (and It is "everywhere" present), there simply cannot be an absence of the Present.

Now look at what time pretends to be. Supposedly, time is that period when the Present is not present. But that never happens.

It is *always* the Present.

One would first have to make the Present go away, *uproot It from being everywhere present,* to have time in any way. That is just plain impossible. In other words, the Omnipresent Present would have to be shoved aside, so time, what-never-is-present, could be present. It's crazy.

Only the Present is present, and endlessly so. That means complete, total "coverage" as *All.* This never changes.

It's worth repeating why time never is present.

Look once more at the second hand on a wristwatch or clock. See if there is any point in its continuous sweep that ever stops moving, passing on, not-being, to actually *be present.* Just as you're about to pin time down and say, "Aha, here time *is,*" it's gone. It's not present.

Time pretends to be a future, that-which-is-not-yet; or a past, that-which-is-not-anymore. Time literally would be *that which is not.* Time never *is.*

Only the Present, permanently present Awareness, *is.*

There simply is no point at which the Present comes to an end, and where what-isn't-present, or time, begins. What isn't present *can't* begin anywhere, because it isn't present!

Again, *only* the Present is present.

So Your Present Awareness can't exist in time. The Present is not surrounded by, or between, past and future. As the Present is *absolutely all that can be present,* It leaves only Itself, and no past or future anywhere to be between!

Present Awareness stands *alone.*

The answer to the question, "What is the Present to Its own Presence?" is also the answer to, "What is All? Who am I?"

———— • ————

The Present has to be Life Itself.

The Present is all that is ever present *to be* Life, to be alive.

If Life isn't *present,* where is It as It is being alive?

Life's Aliveness, *the One You are now alive to being as All-Inclusive Consciousness,* simply cannot be taken out of the Present and actually be alive, vital, in a past or future. A past or future isn't *alive.*

Life is alive only in, or *as,* the Present, Pure Being. Life can't be alive in *that which has no being,* so Life is not alive in time.

The word life-*time* is an oxymoron.

Life Itself does not move or extend in time. Life *is*—as pure All-Inclusive Consciousness, changelessly *being.* There is no more of Life to come later, because Life Itself is not a stream of time events, not a continuity. It means all of Life is present *now* as this Present Conscious Aliveness. *All the Life there is for Eternity* is being present now.

Life *Itself* has nothing to do with time, change, growth or development. These appear to be effects, not Life Itself. They all appear to occur in passing time, or what-never-is-being. How could that which *never is being* contain Life?

To "taste" Life's unlimited Vitality, true Health, start or identify as the clean, clear purity of the Alive Present *alone.* Start with how boundlessly available Ever-Present Life is.

Be the fresh, new *Feeling* that Your Aliveness is, as It is just now *presently* being.

There isn't Present Life and a you. This endless Vitality *is* You, without any sludge of not-Present Life, of thought in terms of past or future, and the emotional weight that would seem to go with it.

Would you ever try to hold back the Present, or keep It from being completely present? Wouldn't it be the most impossible thing to try? Yet that is exactly what one is attempting when clinging to mental worries about past or future. It is the pure vitality of One's *Present* Being that such worrying would try to work against and put aside. It is doomed to futility because all that can truly be present, *forever,* is the Alive Present, your changeless, immovable All-Inclusive Presence.

You can't be more alive in a future, because a future never is *present* to be alive in. Only the Present is present, as the entirety of Life, and changelessly so.

This also is why it is impossible to evolve to or *become* Consciousness, I Am, in a future. I Am present only *Now,* never in a future. This Present Consciousness *is the Whole of I Am.* There never will be more of what I Am beyond *this Present Consciousness.*

Only superimposed human time-thinking would try to say it wasn't I Am in a past, or that hopefully it can become I Am in a future. Thinking never can be I Am because thinking can't *be*. It always moves, all the while ignoring the I Am that *presently is*. The only way to "drop" such nonsensical delay is to start directly as pure Present Consciousness.

———•———

The question is never, "How does one *be* pure Consciousness, the Present?" The question is, "How could one *not* be It?" Being the Present is absolutely unavoidable.

Does it take effort before Consciousness is presently conscious? Does any mental work have to be done to make Now *be*? It doesn't take years of study—*It can't be escaped*!

One does not try to become more aware of the Present for there is no such separate one—only the Present Itself. The beauty of Omni-Present Awareness is that It cannot withhold Itself; nor does It have to make additional contact with Itself.

Give no attention to what *appears*, and behold how undeviatingly *present* your Un-appearing Alive Presence *is*. One gives no attention to shifting thoughts, emotions, or sensations of a body; no attention to past or future, all of which would be not-the-Present. One doesn't resist these, try to stop, or do battle with them. Be "totally absorbed" in the *immediacy* and *simplicity* with which the Aware Present is present—and how It is always *present only*.

Behold how impossible it is for Now to *not* be, and that Now is the exact same "Stuff" as the All-Inclusive Alive Presence You *are*.

This irresistibility of *Now* is Your Life Story. It is simple, right to the point, and never can pass away.

———•———

What if one were to mistakenly identify with what the five senses seem to sense, instead of as Pure Consciousness, as the Present Itself?

Absolutely *everything* a sensing human "mind" would claim to know about itself and its world seems to depend on time. It experiences every one of its sensations, every thought and emotion, in the passing of never-present time. It wakes up in time; it eats, works, plays, sleeps and dies in time. Never-present time is the very fabric of the mortal or human sensing "mind's" experience.

Not a bit of mortal experience, not a single atomic particle, ever stops moving and passing on in time, or is other than *not being*. It is always *being-not*, and never can actually be *What Is*.

The entire human body and all its activity, down to the tiniest part of a single cell, right down to its so-called DNA, would be in constant movement, even during sleep. The body would always be vibrating in passing time, time that never is *being*. Even DNA has been measured by scientists as vibrating—atomic particles moving back and forth with a certain frequent-ness or frequency in passing time, *is-not-ness*.

The human body literally *is* movement. Nothing about a human body *is*.

The term "human *being*" is another perfect oxymoron.

Nothing about the human or mortal is *being*. This isn't saying there's something wrong with it; don't condemn or deny it; it simply isn't being.

You can't say *I* or say you *be*—and also say you are a mortal body. It's a contradiction in terms. And you must *be*, or you wouldn't exist to know about this discussion. You are not a human being. You are Being, *being*. The body-form may appear to be human, but that's not You.

It is thanks to being *Present* Consciousness, pure *Being*, that You are not moving in step with this never-present time activity, and can see it for what it is, or rather, *isn't*.

In response, the would-be sensing "mind" may try to say, "My body certainly is being, is present right here, solid as ever; so is this book, the room, and everything else." But is it really?

As said before, what *appears* outwardly to the senses as a solid, stationary body and matter, would in its essence be cells, which are said to consist of molecules, which in turn are said to consist of atomic particles, energy or vibration. At this level, this "stuff" is in a *non-stop* state of motion and reaction in never-present time. It occurs on a scale so small and fast that, relative to the ability of the senses to perceive this activity, it *seems* present, solid and stationary *to the senses*. It's because the sense organs of sight and touch themselves would be made of the exact same vibrating "stuff"—moving right in step with it.

It's the way the earth at the moment seems very still and stationary as your body now appears to be sitting and holding this book. To the body's senses, it doesn't seem as if the earth were hurtling through space, orbiting the sun at an incredible rate of speed—but it is. The body, too, is actually moving with equal speed, because the body is on that fast-moving earth! Since the body and earth are moving at the exact *same* speed, from the body's point of view it seems as if neither were moving—but they are.

The point is, the Present, your All-Inclusive Conscious *Being*, is not a moving, mortal body-form. You are not something caused by movement of atoms, not produced or developed in time. How could Being, or That Which Is, be produced by that which never is?

————•————

"If the Present is timeless and never changes, how could It be *alive* and conscious? It sounds pretty dead to me," the thought may come.

Only to human thinking based on the senses would it seem unusual that the Present is timeless, yet *alive*. Such thinking attempts to impose *its* unreal standards, which function in time's non-being, upon *Conscious Being, Life Itself*. Such thinking ignores what truly is, thus it is ignorant. It would say Life, too, should move and change in passing time, what-isn't-being, in order to be alive.

Put the shoe on the other foot. The question isn't: "How could Consciousness, the Changeless Present, be alive?" The question is: "How could *that which never is present* be alive?" It isn't. Nothing about constantly passing, never-present time experience contains Life. Only *Now* is Life alive. Just because something moves doesn't mean it is Life Itself. Brown leaves move along the ground. Clouds move. Cars move. Are they Life?

To be alive yet changeless is completely "normal" to Ever-Present Consciousness. It can't age or decay for It never is other than *present*. Its Present-ness never is depleted or exhausted because in Its *Pure Now* no time passes in which It *could* be exhausted. All that seems to change or decay is what *appears*, not Ever-Present Life Itself.

One who identifies as pure Conscious Being only, *is being the only Substance present*. It leaves no identification with what appears; no mistaken assumption that time or age *is*.

Imagine a painting of some people. Could there be any images of bodies in the painting without the paint itself—that which is the very substance of it all? Do those body-images have power to resist, or act as if they have separate substance—that there are qualities present other than paint? Sounds silly doesn't it?

Suppose that somehow the paint never aged. The bodies couldn't possibly appear to age either, could they?

On the same basis, how could the body holding this book appear to age, when the *only* Substance wherein it is found, is timeless, agelessly *Present* Consciousness?

To the extent one is *being* pure Consciousness, which never is other than *Present* and all-inclusive of *all*, means nowhere is there oldness or decay. And who is conscious besides Conscious Being Itself to act otherwise? The entirety of Your Existence has no choice but to be vitally, unagingly *ever-present only*. There is no such thing as "old" Substance.

If it is exciting to read what is stated here, that's because It is *Your Present Self* beholding that which is of sole value—Itself! You are enjoying that which is most valuable in Existence—your own Presence!

If one takes this a bit further, the next question is, "As *only* Consciousness, only the Present is, and It is absolutely *all* Presence, and never changes from being all-present, then where does time come from? How could time even *seem* to begin? *Did* it really begin?"

If one mistakenly starts with time, one has to somehow try to explain or account for it.

When one starts with the Present, all that is present, is the Present.

And one *has to* start with the Present and not time because *only* the Present is present to start with. What's more, the Conscious Present *Itself* is the only One present to do any and all "starting."

That very Present must be You, for nothing else is present to be You.

To start as the Present, have only the Present, and *be* that Present Itself, as Pure Conscious Being, is to "taste" your own Eternity.

The next few chapters completely expose the false nature of *would-be* finite experience and time. They show in yet another way, why *the Present is all that is present*.

13

CHECK THE CREDENTIALS

SO THAT THE NEVER-PRESENT NATURE OF TIME and the world of the senses be more clear, look at this *seeming* state in another way. It's not what it appears to be. The first part of this chapter is a new variation of what has already been said about the senses—but don't impatiently pass it over. It helps show why the sensing "mind" at first appears to be nothing more than an illusion. More importantly, it enables one to then see that no such state exists at all, *not even as an illusion!*

At the moment, according to the so-called human sensing "mind," it appears that a book is being held in the hands. Supposedly, by way of the sense of sight, the mind is now experiencing a mental image of hands holding a book. Simultaneously with its visual image of a book and hands, the mind seems to experience a sense of touch. There is a tactile sensation from the fingers on the book that involves feelings of texture, as well as some weight or pressure, and even temperature.

Right now, hold the book up and feel that sensation of weight or pressure. Do not, with the intellect, say, "That feels like light weight." Rather, *feel* the weight.

Now *feel* the sensation of texture that the cover has. It is different from the texture of the pages. One feels rougher or smoother compared to the other—but don't just *say* one is smoother—close the eyes and feel them. These sensations of texture and weight seem to shift, change and pass as the book moves about in the fingers. To experience these passing sensations also obviously takes *time.*

Clearly, identifying as pure Awareness *alone* is entirely different from identifying with all the tactile sensations you seem to be aware *of.*

Now don't think of this tactile experience in terms of two separate objects—fingers *and* a book. Close the eyes again and experience it *purely as the one feeling,* which is what it really would be. As a feeling,

you wouldn't think of it as two separate parts, but as *one* tactile sensation, simultaneously combining weight, texture, and temperature into
one overall feeling.

Where is the only place *all* feelings of pressure, texture or weight—
not just those of a book—would be found? All weight would belong to
the senses, not Awareness. *All* qualities of heaviness would be finite—
what only a finite "sense-mind" supposedly experiences.

Infinite Awareness cannot be put into any such categories.

Now "start" or identify as pure Awareness alone. Ask Your Self how
much Awareness "weighs" *to Awareness*. The answer—utter weightless-
ness—is what *You* are.

Just *how light* are You?

Ask only pure, Present Awareness, *as that Awareness*. This never can
be known by a body or a so-called sensing, weighing, finite "mind," for
Awareness is Infinity Itself, Purity Itself. It isn't something You have risen
to. It is what You *are*. You needn't go way "off there" to a distant Divine
state, apart from or above a physical world, to be this Purity. It's what
You are always being *right here*, as pure Awareness. There never, never
is an *end* to You.

This alone is "how" and "where" One lives.

Awareness Itself, this Pure I-Presence You are, has no body, no
sensations, to experience pressure or weight. The only place the experiencing of weight and a body would be found is *as the sensation*. There
is no weight *apart* from the sensation.

Pure Awareness Itself is always simply, freely present.

Awareness, I-Presence, is entirely *undimensional*. It has no surface,
no shape with which something could come in contact, or exert pressure against. Not only does Awareness not weigh anything—nothing can
weigh on It! Absolutely nothing can weigh You down! Again, what is
Pure Awareness to *Itself*? Not a little weightless—*completely* weightless.

It's not that You have now let go of weight. *You never had any.*

There never is any heaviness or density, no buildup of pressure in
Pure Now.

The *Now* that Awareness is, not only has no physical weight.
Equally, *Now* has no burden of past emotional or mental weight. *Now*
knows only Now—and It is *always* Now, "everywhere."

How often does it seem a so-called personal body-identity is weighed down by thinking and worrying? Virtually always—and all of it would be based on what is sensed. Yet none of *that* is You. And there are not two Identities, not two types of Life.

Start again with how light Now, Awareness, is *to Pure Awareness.*

This indescribable lightness of Awareness is all-inclusive; all that is present. *It is absolutely all the Presence there is.* When you *identify* as this Pure Awareness only, the lightness You are is *endless.* There is no point where It ends and a heavy, dense physical state begins—for sticking with Infinite Awareness *only*, It never comes to an end of Itself and Its magnificent lightness.

To this lightness, *only* lightness is present.

How much of your day do you spend *being* the lightness You are?

It's the only way You are present—as the complete *absence* of density or weight.

Your Life is that of utterly un-material Pure Spirit—forever un-weighed and un-put-upon. How gloriously graceful is this Pure Awareness You are, in Its effortless ease of *being*?

This is Spirit Itself—indescribably gentle and delicate—yet eternally indestructible.

This weightless ease that You are cannot be limited or contained. It is *unrestrainable.*

All there is, is endlessly overflowing *Openness,* incalculable Freedom, which is *alive.*

This is the *texture* of Life Itself. The texture of Life is this endless *smoothness* that Absolute Oneness is.

This is Real Texture. It is Self-Texture—the way pure Being "feels" to Its own Purity.

This is You as You endlessly are.

———•———

The entire weighty human world that appears each passing day by way of the senses, would be just that—a *passing sense* of existence. It is not Being or Existence Itself, as Pure Conscious Awareness.

The most important point of this book is that there are not *two* kinds of Existence.

There is not the Real Existence that is, that of Pure Infinite Consciousness—*and* a passing, finite, three-dimensional existence of the senses—though it would *seem* so if one starts with the senses.

In terms of Infinite Consciousness alone, there is no finite appearance of anything.

There is only the Infinite.

The fact that there is only Infinity is like saying in the movie example that not only is the movie unreal—there isn't even a movie going on! All there is, is the formless, weightless Being that Consciousness is. All there is, is entirely un-dimensional but *consciously alive* Presence. There is only *un-appearing* Spirit, the endless Absolute.

"This is crazy," the would-be "mind" or intellect based on the senses may try to say.

The so-called sensing, thinking "mind" that deals constantly in hard evidence—in touchable, visible, three-dimensional objects—would say, "How can this be? If there are no senses, no finite appearing world, then *why* do I see it? How can I feel my body, or this book? How can I behold such a world if it doesn't exist to Consciousness in the first place?"

All such questions are exactly what would be expected of thinking when it is based only on the senses. It never is Infinite I-Being, never *You*, asking such questions. It would be a state of ignore-ant *finite thought* that asks.

All that this finite state of thinking or intellect seems to do, is ignore the Infinity of the Only I-Presence, Pure Being, and deal in what is sensed and observable in passing time—which *never is being*.

In fact, such a state of thinking *isn't a mind at all*. It's a mistake.

It would be due to mistakenly identifying with the sensations one appears to be aware *of*, and saying, "That's me"—*instead of being Pure Awareness Itself, the Only I*.

When you stop to pull it apart, this would-be "mind" is just a chain reaction of thoughts based only on what the senses sense—totally avoiding ever-present Pure Awareness, what truly *Is*, or Truth. A bunch of sensations or thoughts by themselves are not alive, not a *conscious entity*. Only *You* are. There is no Intelligence, Awareness, or Life in a bunch of mistaken thoughts. It would be only *its own ignorance* that labels what it is doing as being a "mind."

It may seem that up to now you have unwittingly accepted this finite sensing and thought-reaction as being you, or belonging to you. If so, there is no shame in it. It seems to be the human norm. Without knowing Identity is Pure Conscious *Being*, one would appear to be left on the level of that constantly passing thought-reaction. What *it* says would be all one has to go by—one wouldn't even know there was anything else.

Consciousness, Your Self, here, now, actually never has accepted any such thing, even unwittingly. Consciousness can *only* be Pure Awareness, Pure *Is*.

————•————

What happens when one starts by identifying or "looking out from" Pure Consciousness, Intelligent Being only, instead of identifying with ignore-ant thinking based on the senses?

What happens when you examine the credentials of this *would-be* finite, sensing time-experience? Can it pass the test of *truly being*?

The so-called state of human thought based on sensing would say, "The finite, physical world *must* be here. I can see it. I can touch it. I hear, taste and smell it. I can think about it and have emotions about it. It's *obviously* right here."

This same finite state of thought is also the only thing attempting to refute that there is *only* the Infinite. The only place all seeming objection to the *complete, absolute Presence of the Infinite* would seem to come from, would be this sensing state of thought, the only naysayer.

The sensing "mind" would try to say: "The Infinite has no verifiable credentials. I can't see the Infinite or otherwise sense It. I can't observe or measure Pure Infinity scientifically. I can't quantify It mathematically. I can only theorize about It—but I can't *find It* anywhere. How could this Infinite be true, be *All*, or be a Presence or Power? It's so ethereal, so insubstantial. This Infinite stuff may sound intriguing, but *my finite physical world* is the one that's really here. Since my finite world is here, the Infinite can't be all there is, and It's certainly not being Infinite here. I see sin, disease, death. You say the Infinite or God is *all*? Have you taken leave of your senses? Maybe this Infinite is way out in space, or off in a divine state somewhere, but It's not here."

To a state of thinking based solely on the senses, any premise that is non-sense, would naturally seem to be nonsense.

Now turn the tables on it.

Question the legitimacy of this finite state of sensing and thinking, rather than entertaining *its* doubts about the Infinite. What exactly are the credentials of this "mind" that supposedly testifies to matter, physicality and an entire finite, three-dimensional world?

What happens when one closely examines *those* credentials?

And here's the real issue. How valid then could all human thinking, reasoning and conclusions be—philosophical, scientific or religious—if based entirely on senses that are invalid?

These questions aren't coming from another, from an author-body. It can only be *I*, the One All-Inclusive Intelligence, the Life I Am, the only One present and conscious so this book can be read.

———•———

Pull this would-be sensing state of thought apart slowly, piece by piece, and hold it up to the light of Intelligence. Read the following closely, as if enjoying a good detective story, for that's what it would seem to be.

Right now, the finite "mind" supposedly looks out over a body, a book and a room, observing a universe of objects and space. But on what basis would the "mind" even say there is a body now holding this book and doing all that? In fact, on what basis would it be said there is any finite or time-experience going on at all?

It is all based on the five senses.

To even *say* there is finite or human experience would depend entirely on the senses sensing it: seeing it, hearing it, touching, tasting, and smelling it. In fact, without the five sensations of human experience, there *is no* human experience!

Now exactly how does this sensory experience seem to work?

As an example, consider any everyday item sensed by the five senses. Say it's a nice red apple. How does the "mind" know anything about that apple—or even claim an apple is *there* in the first place?

The sensing "mind" experiences a specific visual sensation, which also could be called an appearance, or a mental image of the apple. That particular visual sensation of red color and roundish shape is one way the mind differentiates an apple from other items, such as a book or a hand.

Simultaneously with this visual sensation, the mind experiences a particular tactile sensation of the apple; there is a feeling of weight and texture.

Also simultaneously, there may be a sense of sound associated with an apple, such as crunching when a bite is taken. There is also a sensation of taste, and a scent.

Each of the five senses contributes its particular "aspect" of the apple to the mind. As a result of all the sensations it experiences, the mind instantly says to itself, "An apple is here."

This same process of course applies to *all* items in daily experience. When the senses combine in their normal operation, it results in normal human activity; this is how the sensing mind experiences its world. The mind experiences all sensations at once, which in this case equals "apple."

Now look again.

A question long pondered by philosophers concerns the nature of the *substance* involved in this whole apple experience. Exactly what kind of substance is one dealing with here?

The entire and only basis on which the mind would say an apple is present, is by way of the senses. Absolutely everything the mind would know about the apple is thanks to a visual sensation, a sensation of touch or feel, a sound, a taste and smell. The mind's entire "evidence" is sensations.

Now—ask yourself what the apple itself consists of, *apart* from those five sensations.

What makes up the apple *itself*—that supposedly is giving off this sensory experience to the mind?

When you try to think of what an apple is entirely apart from the sensations, what happens?

You can't think of anything.

That's because there *isn't* anything else.

There are only the sensations!

There are not the sensations of an apple *and* an apple. Sensations are the entire and only "substance." There is no apple that is a stand-alone physical object "out there," with its own separate substance, in addition to the sensations experienced by the mind.

Go ahead. See if you can come up with a separate object. But first take away those five sensations. Poof! The "apple" is non-existent.

The "apple" as a separate, solid object didn't go anywhere.

It *never was* out there as a separate object in the first place!

You may be asking, "If it's just *sensations,* then what did I just chew and swallow after lunch today?"

Well, exactly what *is* an apple anyway? Supposedly a roundish red fruit with a whitish pulp, a slightly sweet or tart taste, and a pleasant scent. Okay, but what would all *that* be? Nothing but so many sensations.

The mind's experiencing of sensations results in what is *called* an apple, but never is there a separate item "out there." All there would be is a series of images, feelings, tastes, sounds and smells—*experienced entirely by the mind.*

There is nothing else there.

The way the mind experiences it, it has an illusory *appearance* to the mind as if there were a solid object, apart from or objective to the mind. But never is there a separate physical item. The "apple" would be a purely *mental* process, experienced entirely in or *as,* thought.

The mind's sensations of "apple" would be exactly the same as the mind's *thought* in terms of an apple. The mind's sensations of "apple" and its very *thinking* that an apple is there, is the same, one process. This is most important to recognize. Call it sensation or thought; either way, "mental-stuff" would be all there is to it.

The only "hard evidence" of an apple isn't hard, solid matter at all. It would be just a mental experience of a flow of a lot of un-solid sensations, always passing on in time. It is just so much *mental fluid.* While earlier one might have thought of an apple as a solid object, one can't say an image in thought, a passing feeling, a taste, or hearing of a sound is a solid object. Those would be entirely mental phenomena and *they* are not a solid object. It is in this way that the flow of all sensations, thus all would-be "objects," are referred to as "mental fluid."

What does all this *mean*?

It's a topic that has been debated for almost as long as there appear to have been philosophy and metaphysical teachings. The question is whether this apple experience (and thus by extension, *all* sensory human experience!) would be going on *outside* the mind, or *inside* the mind. In one regard it might be said that either is correct. Actually, neither is correct. It all seems to depend on the viewpoint.

Suppose one first *assumes* the world and universe are physical and that the mind is located inside the body. If the mind is inside the body, then anything outside of the body is considered as being outside the mind.

But if one takes a meta-physical, or "mental" viewpoint, everything is seen in reverse. On this basis, the mind is not in the body—the body and all else is in mind, or in thought. So not only the apple, but one's entire experience, is seen as being within the mind, or "mental."

Neither of these two viewpoints could be true, or be changeless Truth. Why? The validity of either view changes depending on the premise, depending on whether one arbitrarily starts on a "physical" or "mental" basis. One is no more valid than the other.

Outside or inside the mind is not the real issue.

What *never* changes is that the apple experience is *inseparable* from the mind. The "apple" is neither outside nor inside the mind, but *is* the mind itself in its so-called operation!

For example, when the mind experiences the sensations associated with "apple," it can't be said those sensations are produced by an apple that is separate, because no separate apple is there to have produced them. Yet if it were not for *that* particular seeming item or "apple," that particular package of sensations wouldn't exist either. You wouldn't get that same taste or scent from an "orange." The "apple" and those specific sensations need each other. Why?

It's because the act of sensing and the "thing" sensed are *one*. There is no *thing* separate from the sensations of it—and there are no sensations separate from *what* is sensed.

This is true for *all* things in finite human experience, not just apples!

There is not the finite sensing mind *and* any item, or any form of experience that is "out there," apart from the mind. It all *is* the mind; it is one.

The finite "sense-mind" doesn't ever think *about* a condition; it *is* the condition. It doesn't visit or think in terms of places; it literally is the places. It doesn't sense all the planets and things in the stellar universe. It is all the things; it is the universe. Even the feeling of moving through empty space would be entirely sensation or mental—space just feels less dense than an apple. On this basis, one sees that there never are separate "physical objects" that have different degrees of hardness or density—say, a ball of cotton as compared to a stone. The different "densities" would really be degrees of density of *thought*.

The traditional misconception always has been that sense data is "taken in" from a *separate* thing "out there." There never is a separate object or thing out there from which to take it. Rather, it always would be the finite "sense-mind" experiencing *itself*—but which it *calls* a body and universe of separate things.

The whole of finite human experience and its universe would be the "mind" in operation.

It doesn't matter if it appears to be the beautiful call of a songbird piercing the silence at dawn, the dawn itself, or a plate full of pancakes. There is not the finite "sense-mind" *and* any form of experience in the entire stellar universe that exists as a separate entity "out there" apart from thought. It all *is* the mind, experiencing itself. It is one.

When buying a car, a new dress, groceries—anything—it is really a matter of *buying a package of sensations*; a state of thought buying into a mental pattern it resonates with. Even the store itself and the money exchanged would be more of the same mere *sensory mind-fluid*.

What is important to realize about this? As a result of sensing "things," never does anything solid, separate or physical *remain* after the sensations of it are experienced! Never is a stand-alone solid object "left behind." The mind's activity, with the countless passing sensations it seems to have experienced over time, *never* has left so much as a single, solid separate object in its wake!

Equally, there never is a separate, solid apple anywhere *before* the sensations of it are experienced!

That which is called "apple" always would be the exact same *un-solid* flow of sensations. It doesn't matter how solid or separate it may seem (and it will seem so). At no time is there really a separate apple out there on its own, in addition to the fleeting sensations of it. Everything finite is always just a *flow* of sensations; mere "mind-fluid." This holds true for *all* would-be "objects."

In so-called human experience it never is mind *and* matter. Nor is it mind over matter. The "mind" *would be* "matter."

Yet in Reality, to the Present Consciousness You are, *none of this really matters at all.*

Why? None of this mental-sensing activity stops passing in time to *really be,* or to *be Real.* As said repeatedly, the mind's activity is always busy *not being;* busy being "not." None of it is You. All there is to You is Infinite Consciousness, Being Itself. You can't *be* what never is being!

Do you realize that all *would-be* physical laws, all limitations, and all problems of the world would be *one with* this "mind-that-is-not-being"? It isn't that this "mind" knows about all the problems of humanity. It *would be* the problems! It doesn't observe disease and sin; it doesn't think about poverty and war; it *would be* disease, sin, poverty and war. This is *not* saying the mind is bad or evil—don't condemn or judge any of it. That which *isn't being* can be neither bad nor good.

The point is, never are there any such actual *physical* conditions. There is no world "out there" that is separate, leaving you helpless to do something about it. All there would be to all of it is mere mental wisps of ignore-ant thought, or belief. It's all supposedly believed by a state of constantly passing thought that is not You. In fact, it's *never even present!*

Two distinct points have been made here that are so enormous in significance, they're worth summarizing. The first is that what appears to be an entire separate physical, material world and universe isn't that at all—but just a "mental" state which has an *illusory appearance* of being separate. Secondly, this entire would-be mental state is always moving or passing in time and never is *being*—has never, ever genuinely been *present.*

If one mistakenly identifies or starts with that "time-mind," one has to account for and deal with its would-be conditions. *Starting with Truth* shows that Consciousness, the Present, is changelessly Omnipresent.

Pure Conscious Being is absolutely all that is being—which means a "mind-that-never-is-being" and its would-be conditions never could begin or operate in Your Presence—not even as an illusion. As there really is no "mind" to experience or be such conditions, *there are no such conditions!*

Pure Conscious Being is all that is *present.*

————•————

14

CEASE YE FROM MAN

"Cease ye from man whose breath is in his nostrils, for wherein is he to be accounted of?" (Isaiah 2: 22)

Now fully expose the nature of this *would-be* sensing mind and its world, which only *appears* to be one of separateness, but really isn't.

Whether referring to an apple or a planet—all so-called "material objects," all would-be "physical places," and even the space that appears to contain them—have no existence apart from the "mind," as just discussed. It means *everything* in what is called an entire stellar universe, would not be physical or separate, but one hundred percent "mental" only, or *thought*. Again, the universe would not be outside or even inside of thought, but is inseparable from thought. It is one.

The question then becomes, *where* would all this thought of a universe appear to be going on, since all of it would be *only* "mental," or thought? If there are no physical places, where would all of daily experience be going on? Is everything in the "human scene" just one big dream-like mental image? If so, where do you *put* this mental image or all this thought?

Of course, the traditional human belief or viewpoint is that the "mind" and its thought is located inside a physical body. But what if a body is like an apple? If a body is not a solid physical object either, *there wouldn't be any object there to put a mind inside of.*

Now see why all the mental images one appears to behold in daily experience are *not* occurring inside a physical body. Rather, the viewpoint now would be meta-physical—meaning that the body, all bodies, and all of the universe, appear to be in one big mental image, or what is sometimes called the "universal mind," or dream.

But first, it is helpful to see why this old notion of there being a solid physical body with a mind inside it, never has been true, no matter how long it seems to have been believed.

123

In the same way that the senses create the illusion that there is a solid apple "out there" separate from the mind, the senses make it seem as if *body* were a solid object too. It isn't.

The mistaken notion that there is a "body" is an illusion because the entire experience, all "evidence," actually occurs only in the mind. For example, the mind experiences mental images of what are *assumed* to be various parts of a body—legs, arms, a torso, head, etc.—but they're really just *mental images*. It is *assumed* these images are coming from a solid object—but that's a mistaken assumption, because the only evidence there is, is just those *images*.

In the same way, the mind experiences some tactile sensations, which are mistakenly assumed to be touches or feelings of a solid body—but all that's actually *there* are some passing feelings. There aren't the feelings *and* a solid body that the feelings are coming from—*only some passing feelings*. In other words, there aren't the feelings of a touched leg *and* a leg—only the feelings. The mind also experiences sensations of what are supposedly "body-sounds," called talking and breathing—but they're no proof of a solid body either, because all that's there are just *sounds*. And the mind experiences sensations of taste and smell. There is absolutely no other evidence that there is a body.

So the only evidence you have is the mind's experience of five types of passing sensations. When you look closely, you see that there are *only* the sensations—there aren't the sensations *and* a body. Now, *besides* the sensations, look for something in addition to, or behind, them. Try *also* to come up with a body that stands present on its own, apart from the sensations. You can't find anything more, because there never is anything *in addition to* those fleeting sensations! *There is nothing else there.* A mere flow of passing sensations would be *all* there ever is to the illusion of "having a body."

When you take those five sensations away, "body" is non-existent.

What is a body anyway? Supposedly flesh and bones. Okay, but what would all *that* be? All one could ever claim to know about flesh, bones, or any other aspect of "body" is just a passing stream of images, sounds, feelings, smells and tastes—and *they* are not a solid physical object. And nothing else is there to be a physical object.

There never has been such a separate object.

Traditional reasoning which says that mind is mental, and that body is physical, and that the one can be inside the other, has a fatal flaw. It mistakenly first *assumes* something that's not true—that body is a physical object in which a mind could be put. It's not.

To be certain, take another thorough look *behind* those sensations that supposedly give all evidence of the very "body" itself. Look behind all of the mind's images, the mind's experience of all the supposed touches and feelings of "body," all of its hearing of body-sounds, and so on. Now, again, what is there to "body" itself, apart from that mental experience? Now try to come up with a separate, stand-alone object that is present *in addition to* those sensations.

That's just it. There isn't anything else.

There is no stand-alone solid item, no physical anchor, from which all those sensations of "body" would be coming! All you've ever got is a bunch of bodiless, free-floating sensations.

So you can't say the mind is in a body—when a body *isn't* a body—and all it would be is a bunch of sensations going on in the mind.

Since the only way "body" ever would be experienced is purely as a mental phenomenon—*in the mind*—that leaves no such thing as a physical body in which to put the mind *itself!*

The reason this isn't readily seen is due to being fooled by sense-appearances and mistakenly *assuming* "body" is a solid object in which a mind could be put. It's just an assumption based on illusory sensations.

One cannot think in terms of inside a "body" when it comes to locating the "mind." It's like a con artist's shell game—only instead of playing find the little ball, you're playing find the mind. You never get a satisfactory answer.

It's because the mind is neither inside, nor is it even outside a body.

The mind literally *is* the "body."

It's exactly like the earlier example in which the mind *is* the "apple."

When the mind experiences its sensations of "body," one can't say they're coming *from* a body that's separate on its own, external to the mind. Why? Again, besides the mind's experiencing of its own sensations, there is *nothing else*—no separate object from which the sensations could be coming. Yet without that seeming "body" there would be no experience of touches, no sights, no sounds, no tastes or smells—no sensations at all. The sensing mind and the sense of "body" seem to need each other. One can't exist without the other, for they would be opposite sides of the same coin.

After all this, the old way of thinking may try to rationalize, "There *still* is a physical body, and the mind is inside it. It just *seems* the body is sensed only in the mind. That's because the mind is where the five senses send all their information. All sensations are sent *to* the mind in the brain. Sensations are sent by way of the nerves that feel, in the fingers or legs—those nerves all *lead to* the mind in the brain, sending sensory information there. So, yes, all body-sensations are experienced by the mind—but it's still up inside the brain, inside the body."

Back up a minute. That way of thinking, again, first mistakenly *assumes* that in addition to the sensations, there is a separate body-object there, with solid fingers and legs to be doing all that sending. There isn't.

Absolutely *all* there ever would be to the illusion of supposedly having "fingers," "legs," and an entire "body" is a purely mental experience of some passing images and passing feelings of touch—and a mental experience does not add up to a static physical object. Since there never is a physical body or object that exists separate from the mind—there never is a physical body to contain a physical neurological system—though it certainly *appears* to the mind as if there were. "Body" would be entirely a *mental* phenomenon.

There is no physical body that exists as a solid object separate from the mind. Shocking as it may seem, that can only mean there is no physical brain either. If one judges by illusory appearances and first *assumes* body is a physical object, it appears a brain is inside a head, of course. But as the so-called "body" itself would be entirely "mental" and never is a physical object separate from the mind, there certainly couldn't be a brain as a separate physical object either. There simply is *no physical place* in which to put such a thing.

One might ask, "What if I were a brain surgeon? I would have operated on hundreds of brains, and *seen* they were inside a head, and connected by nerves to arms and legs."

Okay, but of what, exactly, would all that experience of doing surgery consist? The surgery, too, would consist of nothing more than *just so many sensations*—the passing mental images and tactile feelings of operating on a "patient." But those sensations would not be coming from a physical "patient-body," for *there would be only those sensa-*

tions. Nor would the sensations be experienced by a physical "surgeon-body," for there is no such object either.

At no time is there a solid physical body being operated on—or doing the operating! It would be *all one mental phenomenon* that appears to include both the "patient" and the "surgeon."

This actually makes perfect sense from a meta-physical viewpoint, which says that the body, all bodies, and the entire universe, appear to be in mind, or in the one "universal mind"—the "universal mind" is not in any body.

What is a brain anyway? Make no mistake—the only evidence there ever could be of a brain would be the mental images and tactile feelings of it—experienced by the mind supposedly doing the surgery. A so-called "brain," too, would have no state other than those mere sensations. On this basis, it could be said that a "brain" would be entirely a product of the mind, not vice-versa.

No longer are the mind and mental activity seen as originating from a physical organ called a "brain"—for there is no such physical object. The brain appears to be in the mind—the mind isn't *in* the brain.

Get completely away from the notion that body is a physical object or place. If one were to speak on a finite basis, all there would be to "body" is a relatively dense state of *thought*. Rather than there being a body that is giving off sensations, it would be sensations giving off what appears as the mind's thoughts of a body. It never goes beyond this bodiless flow of thoughts, or "mental fluid" to separateness or physicality.

A question that may arise based on all of the preceding might go like the following:

"If the mind is *not* inside a body or brain, then why does the mind's activity stop when the body is anesthetized? How could anesthesia affect the mind if the mind is not there? And if the mind isn't in the brain, then why don't the mind and body function just as well when the brain is damaged or removed?"

On a finite basis, the "sense-mind," again, isn't inside a body, but *is* the "body." They would be one and the same. So if it appears the state of a "body" is altered via chemical anesthesia or surgery, naturally the state of the "mind" will appear altered too, for it is all the same, one "stuff." It is not because a mind is *inside* a body.

This also appears to work in reverse, as shown by the increasingly popular holistic approach to medicine. Treating the mind appears to affect the body because they would be the same *one*.

This book is not denying that such things appear to occur. If one starts on a would-be physical basis, yes, there appears to be a control center or brain that governs the body's reactions; but that's all there would be to its activity—reaction. At no time would this reaction be a genuine mind. Better said, it is not *Mind*, Infinite Consciousness Itself. You couldn't *be* the Intelligent Being you are, if you were only a state of reaction passing in time, which *never is being*.

———•———

Don't mourn the fact that body never has been a solid physical object separate from the mind. How much mourning was there over the flat earth, once it was shown to be round?

The only reason this seems unusual is due to having already accepted what seems to be a *general belief* that unquestioningly assumes "body" is a solid object and has a mind or consciousness inside it. That is all there would be to it—just a belief or mistaken state of thought based on sense-illusion—again, no more actual than that good old flat earth. It is not Truth.

At one time it was believed that the entire universe was centered around the earth, or was geo-centric. Just as that old false belief faded away—so the false belief that Consciousness, Mind, is body-centric will fade. All such belief or assumption seems to occur only on the level of human thought, which is fallible. It is not Pure Awareness, which is infallible. Awareness never assumes anything. Awareness stays Pure Awareness, unchanged eternally.

Pure Awareness is the only Identity or Presence that is *conscious, alive*, and remains forever perfectly present, *as the Present*, regardless of the *seeming* status of a finite body or "mind."

Do not be alarmed at this discussion of an un-solid "body" and "matter." It is just saying what appears to be taught in high school chemistry class regarding un-solid atoms and energy—now seen from a new angle. The point is, Consciousness, Life, *couldn't* be inside a body that's *not there* as an object to have Life inside of it.

This does not mean one will mis-use body because it is not physical. The body is just not the way it *appears* via the senses—not separate, solid or made of matter. The more one operates as Pure Timeless

Consciousness, the only Substance, body will seem less material and take on more of the appearance of being a timeless thought or idea, like the figure four, or the letter A.

Just because what appears to be a solid body isn't really that way, nothing has changed with *You*. As All-Inclusive Consciousness, You haven't gone away, and are not going anywhere. You most definitely are present, are real—eternally calm and serene, as immovable, All-Embracing Conscious Presence—*All* Itself.

Body hasn't gone anywhere either. It still appears to be here, available to be used freely. All that's "gone" is a false belief of being a mortal body-object. No such state was ever true or present anyway.

What is pointed out here is most emphatically not an attempt to minimize what appear as current medical practices for treating a "physical" body. It is not negating the marvelous advances in neurological sciences—or in *any* field of endeavor. At the current "time," these seem essential, and may continue for an indefinite period. However, this in no way alters the Truth that *Consciousness*, not physicality, is all Presence and Substance; and what *seems* to be a physical body and universe is really only *thought*.

The use of the word *thought* here is simply to convey that all things that appear to the finite "sense-mind" never are physical, but "mental" only. However, the finite appearance things have, even when seen as thought, is *not* Divine. The shape and outline that apples, bodies and other thought-forms appear to have is not the way things "look" in the Infinite, in the Divine, wherein there is *no finite form*; they are not Infinite Reality, which is discussed in later chapters.

But it is thanks entirely to Infinite Consciousness now being present that such finite forms can even be identified. If there were no Consciousness, Awareness, *nothing* would be—things couldn't even be identified as the finite thought forms they appear to be. This is why it is frequently said that Awareness *appears* to be aware of these finite forms. Using "appears" is not saying that Awareness *is* aware of things in that way—it's just saying that it appears so. While it's not yet telling the "whole story" by speaking only of the Infinite, it's not inaccurate either. This is one of the most difficult points to make clear—it *appears* as if Infinite Awareness were aware of a finite realm, but the Infinite is not *really* aware of things in that way!

———•———

15

ONCE UPON A TIME

IF ONE WERE TO STILL SPEAK IN FINITE TERMS, the issue continues to be, *where* would this finite "sense-mind" be located? As there is no solid object called "body" in which to put the "mind," then where would it be going on? Where does it come from?

The seeming phenomenon called "mind" simply cannot be located or explained in physical terms because *physicality is not there, and never has been*, to demand an explanation on its terms. To try to ask where the "sense-mind" and its universe would be located on a physical basis is the wrong question. It implies there *are* physical locations or objects separate from the "mind" in which to put it. There aren't.

The very notion that the "sense-mind" *should* be located inside something would be a hang-over from *physical* standards, which are now seen to be non-existent. Location is only a standard of a *would-be* world of supposedly separate solid physical objects like "apples" or "bodies" in which things could be put either inside or outside. Those standards obviously no longer apply.

To Infinite Consciousness, *they never did.*

There isn't even a separate physical universe *in which* the "sense-mind" operates, for the "sense-mind" itself *would be* that "universe." Since the mind itself literally would be all "places"— that leaves no place in addition to itself where it *could* be put! The fact that the "mind" cannot be pinned down to any one place or location would be the same as the phenomenon of "non-locality" that scientists refer to when speaking of thought or energy.

This is why, if one mentions it at all (and one can't legitimately, when starting wholly with the Infinite), what appears as finite human experience is often referred to as *dream*, or *waking dream*. In some cultures or teachings it is called illusion, hypnosis, mirage, maya, myth, mortal mind, carnal mind, *belief mind*, or *belief*, and similar terms. They are all synonyms. All there would be to the seeming "sense-mind" and thus the entirety of its universe and mortal time-experience, is non-physical thought *only*. It is not being thought or dreamed by a physical body, for the very "body" itself would be part of the same dream.

Everything this "dream-mind" claims to experience has no more actual physical presence than a tropical island was physical in a dream you had last night. It has only a *seeming* existence. It may *appear* real, but only to its own sleep-state or ignorance. It would be nothing but floating wisps of dream-like thought, drifting without anchor as a physical reality anywhere, for there is no such thing as a physical "where"— only the infinite "sea" of Consciousness. Just as the false flat earth yielded to the notion of its being a tiny sphere floating in space—so, too, must the entire stellar universe now yield to its role as but a mere dream-like state of thought that *appears* to be "floating" in the infinite, limitless Immensity of Consciousness.

After you've awakened from a dream, have you ever tried to find where that dream was physically located before the dream began? And where exactly does that dream go when one is awake? A dream never occupies physical space, and it doesn't go away to any physical place, for it never is *that* type of substance. In the same way, one cannot try to account for the "sense-mind" and its seeming universe on a physical basis—for there is no such basis.

To an awake state, a dream's so-called "substance" simply vanishes. There never is anything to a dream except a temporary "ignoring" of awakeness. To one who is awake, that is sufficient explanation. One who insists on further explanation is still dreaming and not *awake*—not recognizing dream's true nature.

Likewise, no physical world ever came from anywhere, or went anywhere, for there never *was* any actual physicality or separateness. Since the "sense-mind" or dream is not being experienced *inside* any one body, it would be a *bodiless* state of thought or energy reaction that appears to include all bodies and things. It appears to operate universally, meaning it is found "everywhere" in space. Better said, this mind or dreaming literally *appears as* all space, and as all the items and bodies that appear to occupy space.

This shows again why the finite "sense-mind" is sometimes called a *universal, cosmic, general,* or *mass mind*. It is not seen as a personal mind, because it does not operate inside of, or by way of, any one person. It includes what appear as all persons and a stellar universe. But it would be just so much *thought*—a "mental image universe" actually no more physical than the images on a movie screen.

On a movie screen, when one character appears to talk with another, are there really separate physical bodies there, with thoughts going on inside solid heads? No. Yet it appears as if there were. Does any character do anything by itself? Does each character have its own separate movie going on *inside* its head? No. All characters appear in, and are manipulated by, the one overall movie image that is "universal" to all characters. The movie isn't there thanks to any one character; no single character dreams up the movie. For each character to appear depends on the one movie, that which is each character's very "stuff."

Likewise, the personal "body-you" which is mistakenly believed to be a separate, three-dimensional object, isn't that at all. The way that "body" appears is entirely a product of the universal sense-dream. Everything about that "body" is within the *dream's* framework. Even the eyes with which the dream is supposedly seen would be *part of the dream itself*.

The "body-you" that appears in the dream of human experience is not the one doing the dreaming. It is the universal "sense-mind" that dreams up *its* "body," all "bodies." It is dream that dreams up the personal "me," which is *its* "me." That constantly changing personality is never *You* as Changeless Infinite Being, Perfect I-Consciousness. If one is not awake to True Identity, one assumes all sensing, all weightiness, all emoting and thinking supposedly done by the "body" is *his*—when it would be *dream itself, experiencing itself*. Finite sense or dreaming always appears as if it belonged to one particular body, the personal "me"—but again, that is always the *dream's* "me" and is not *You*, not the One I Am, Impersonal Awareness.

The dream's events appear to unfold like a movie script written entirely from the viewpoint of that one body-character and all its experiences. The dream's script contains every detail of its body's affairs. In day-to-day events, for good or for bad, isn't the body that appears to be holding this book always the main character, around which everything else appears to revolve?

All other characters in the dream appear to move and act as if they, too, were separate, intelligent individuals. Yet no single character is doing any of it. *It all would be the dream's own doing*. You never put any of it there. If you control it, why doesn't everything always turn out the way you want it to? It all would come from the movement of the one universal "finite sense-mind" or dream. Take it away and everything finite vanishes. To assume one is a body in time, is to be entirely a dream's puppet. It is to never know One's Self; to never "taste" or *be* Power, Intelligence.

The foregoing does not imply one might now act irresponsibly, or take license in what appears as finite human experience because it is only "dream." To do so would be attempting to act as un-Consciousness, non-Being, and your Life can do no such thing. If one were to start on that basis, one would be subject to all of the consequences that go along with being on that "level."

Suppose you had a dream last night in which the body was eating a delicious chocolate ice cream cone. Was the body or any other item in that dream a solid physical object? No. So did the dream body have any physical solidity, thickness, or depth to it—an inside or outside? No. Then was the chocolate taste being experienced *inside* the body dreamed up by the dream? No—no solid body-object was there for the taste to be inside *of*.

Now where was the dream being seen from? The dream wasn't being seen from inside the dream body, because the dream body had no inside. All dream images seen, the ice cream cone, the body holding it, the chocolate taste, the tactile feeling of coldness, any sounds, and all other sensations were part of the overall dream-fluid itself—none of it was experienced *inside* the dreamed-up body.

All of what appears as daily human experience would be the same as that dream. All visual appearances seen in daily experience—including the appearance of the universe itself—are not being seen from inside a solid physical body because there's no such thing. Rather, all items appear as thought forms in Boundless Awareness. Right now, it appears you are aware of a body holding this book—but you are not aware of the body from *inside* the body; it appears to be within You, Infinite Awareness. On the same basis, not a single sensation of sound, tactile feeling, or smell or taste is ever experienced inside a solid physical body because *there's no such object there*. It seems downright weird, but the taste of toothpaste, for example, is never really experienced inside an object called a body with a mouth, for there is no such physical place. There would be only dream's bodiless mental flow of taste sensations and tactile sensations—neither of which is a solid object.

Sometimes this universal dream, this dream that appears as a universe, is likened to an enormous 3-D movie, or a *hologram*. A hologram is a projected visual image like a movie picture, except that it's not a flat image as on a movie screen, with just two dimensions of height and width. It's a three-dimensional image that appears to have depth and fill space. A hologram can be projected in a room, for example, creating an image of a body seated in a chair. The body and chair appear like three-dimensional objects, only they have no physical "solidity" or density—it's just an image.

Likewise, the universal dream operates like a hologram or 3-D movie. It, too, has a visual track and a sound track. It projects all three-dimensional *visual appearances* of planets, all places, items, and bodies, including the one holding this book. It also projects all sensations of sound, like a movie's sound track. And it seems to do much more. The universal dream has the added features of being a five-track, full-sensory-experience. This holographic "mental liquid" projects all sensations of taste on its taste track—along with its feelings on its tactile track, and scents on its smell track. It even projects all emotions, thinking, and everything else *it* (not You) seems to experience. It's not projected *from* anywhere or *to* anywhere, for *it appears as all the "where" there is*.

This dream activity combines as what is *called* a "body" and all its sensory experiences. Yet it never is going on in a physical place. And never is there a solid body receiving sensations from solid objects. It's the other way around. The universal mind-fluid, the flowing of its sensations, gives off what appears as its thinking or dreaming of a "body," all its "things," and all "places" in its dream universe. Like a hologram, at no time would any of it be solid stuff—just one big bodiless, sensory soup—without even a solid bowl anywhere in which to put it!

This never will be clear if one clings to the false notion of a mind being *inside* a solid body that is located in physical space. Rather, on a finite basis, it appears as if the dream *would be* all "space" itself.

The constant changing and reacting of this universal mind's dreaming is what appears as the constant change and activity of day-to-day human experience. A scientist might say, "What's so unusual? It all would be just so much fluid energy—constantly moving, flowing atomic particles and energy, reacting and vibrating holographically, and resulting in many forms."

This fluid energy, or the dream's dreaming *appears* as a constantly changing experience of earth, air, water, fire, stone, flesh, magnetism, cancer, laughter, bullets, auras, pizza, and countless other finite forms.

Dream doesn't dream *of* these, but *as* these, for they don't exist apart from it. When the *energy* changes or reacts, the *finite form* appears to change because it's the exact same, one "stuff."

When the universe is seen as entirely mental, the *flow* of sensory experience is seen in reverse of the physical. Again, the physical viewpoint *assumes* the mind is inside a solid body-object. So when it comes to sensing, it is assumed the senses are avenues of *impression*. The senses—supposedly—bring data *in* from a world that is mistakenly believed to be full of objects that are "out there" and already *formed*. In other words, the senses provide information, or are *informing*.

Metaphysically speaking, it would be reversed. From a "mental" viewpoint, never are there any separate physical objects. Never is there an already created, already formed, pre-existing physical universe "out there," from which anything can be "taken in." Rather, all there ever appears to be is "mind-fluid." The dream-mind "thinks," out-pictures, projects, or dreams its entire universe anew each moment—via the flowing of its five types of sensory fluid—for *there's nothing to its universe* but this ongoing soup of sensations.

The universe, as it appears, *always* would be mere *mental liquid*. It would be ongoing thought-creation, a constant "work in progress," caused anew moment-to-moment by the constantly changing fluid energy of the "dream-mind." Its fluid sensations essentially "spray paint" a mental liquid called moment-to-moment human experience. And never does it go beyond *thought* to being separate physical objects.

In this way, the flow of the five forms of sensation is seen completely in reverse—as a vehicle of *expression*, not impression. Instead of taking data in, or in-forming, fluid sensations would be said to project out, or form outwardly. Instead of taking in information, the senses pour out what appears as manifest formation. The universal mind-liquid that is experienced *as five sensations* literally forms or "grows" moment by moment the *appearance* of all places and a three-dimensional universe of created forms. Yet this never goes beyond *dream-thought* to be a separate physical world.

While what has been said here may at first seem astounding, it is of no great significance. All of it would be the realm of *finite* phenomena—inseparable from time as it flows non-stop from what is-not-yet to what is-not-anymore. It would be a perpetual state of *what is not*. The "sense-mind" or universal dream never is *Reality* for it never stops passing away and *not-being* to be present and *be* Reality!

When it is seen as dream, the so-called dualistic, finite universe is not really duality. There is not dark and light, inside and outside, hot and cold, good and evil. There is only *one* would-be dream, inclusive of all dream forms—not various forms of phenomena. There is only *one* would-be all-inclusive phenomenon: dream.

But its only "status" would be a state of complete *"not-ness"*—which isn't even a status.

Perhaps none of this is news to you, or perhaps it is. It doesn't matter. The idea is not to begin an extensive investigation of *that which never is present*. This is not intended to help dismantle a three-dimensional world, or the workings of would-be finite sense, energy, or dream.

Your I-Self, *being entirely infinite*, actually knows nothing about any finite form in which dream appears. All dreaming would be finite, and in Pure Infinity there is no such thing. All dreaming would take time, and in *Your Timeless Being* there is no such thing. Thanks to the fact that Life's Intelligent Being *is now present*, is Your Identity, finite dream can be intelligently seen in all its "not-ness." If You were not Permanently Present Awareness, You would be stuck moving on the "level" of time-dream and accept it as true, subject to its would-be ignorance and limitations.

If one mistakenly *starts* with dream, one is forced to try to account for it. One cannot legitimately do so however, because it *is not being*. In Reality, it is *precluded* by the total Presence of the Infinite, Pure Consciousness, or Mind. One endless Infinite Mind leaves no "universal finite mind." Your Infinite Self is so untouched by finite limitations it is beyond description.

As Consciousness, You don't progress from physical solidity to mental fluidity to Infinity—You never left Infinity. Drop solidity. Drop even fluidity. It too would be finite, non-present—just a different form.

Starting as *Pure Conscious Being*, Its Presence is Absolute, all that truly *is*. To It there is only Utter Reality, Total *Awakeness* being all Presence.

As Absolute Pure Consciousness, You never are physical-conscious or even mentality-conscious. You are Pure Consciousness-conscious, Being-conscious—which is truly *being conscious*!

———•———

16

HOW MUCH DISTANCE OR DEPTH IS THERE TO A DREAM?

WHILE THE APPEARANCE OF FINITE EXPERIENCE is not how things really are, that doesn't mean *Life* is not real. One most definitely is real, is changelessly present, as All-Inclusive Consciousness.

The universe also is real. Again, *the way things appear to the human senses*—as consisting of three-dimensional space full of separation and solid objects—is not the way things are to the Only Self, Infinite Consciousness. Infinite I-Presence does not have eyes or finite senses to "see" in that way at all. As only the Infinite Itself is present, conscious—how *It* perceives things is the way they really are.

Any evaluation of a stellar universe based on sensing and time would be just that, a *sense* of a universe, a *seeming* universe. One never acts as if there were something wrong with it, because there isn't; one just isn't fooled by "appearances."

The human way of "seeing" would identify as one physical body on an earth, judge via the senses, and assume there is a vast physical universe "out there" that is separate, and *so much greater than little me*. If that is one's premise, then one assumes he is a relatively powerless *thing*. One also assumes that real Power, the real Infinite, is afar off, vaguely distant. For all of the Infinite to be immediately present as One's very Being sounds too good to be true.

First of all, the universe isn't "out there." It would be just so much sensation or thought right here—*so there can't be any physical vastness*. That which appears as a stellar universe is never enormous objects separated by even more enormous amounts of space. To expose the falsity of this belief, look at it in the light of the Intelligence You are.

The so-called "sense-mind" or dream would make it appear as if things—apples, bodies, and even the earth—were solid objects "out there," separate from thought and occupying physical space.

For example, it *seems* the "body" has countless times walked on solid ground called "earth." General belief says eyes supposedly see an "earth," while, supposedly, there are feet which touch or feel a massive solid base of ground.

But would this experience really be one of "walking on solid ground"? Looking closely, you see that all the experience would be "made out of" is two kinds of sensations. That's all there would be to the whole thing—nothing more than a "mental" experience—just some sensations of touch and some images. There aren't those sensations *and* an earth that's being walked on—because besides those mere sensations, *there's nothing else.* Now—look for something more. Can you *also* come up with a solid *object* called earth or physical ground that exists separate from the sensations? Is there a separate object that's giving off those sensations to the mind? You can't find anything else because never is there anything in addition to those sensations. Earth *isn't* earth—it never has been! It would be nothing but a bunch of fleeting sensations. Suddenly, terra firma isn't so firma!

Sensations, having no separate solid objects "backing them up," are like the fake propped-up store fronts used in old western movie sets—there's no actual solid building in back—just a propped-up face of one.

Likewise, the "face" of all would-be earthbound experience is fake—nothing but a *mental* movie set—that is not backed up by a physical world. It would be just so many mental images, feelings, and other sensations—which are not occurring on an enormous separate physical planet called "earth," for there is no such object. As there are only sensations, and no separate object that these sensations come *from,* there is no physical sphere that is separate from the mind, occupying billions of acres. There is no physical object having a circumference of 25,000 miles. A random bunch of fleeting sensations in a "mind" do not have longitude and latitude. Never is there a solid body or a solid planet occupying physical space, for mere passing sensations in a "mind" don't *take up* physical space. The whole thing, at most, would be an illusory "mental" phenomenon.

The fact that there are *only* sensations, only "mind stuff"—and no separate physical objects from which sensations come—proves there is no physical space. Why? To take up space, things would *need* to be separate objects—for only objects would occupy three-dimensional space, not passing sensations of a "mind." As there are no objects, thus no space, *anywhere*, but just sensations or thought, then how much physical distance or depth can there be, *anywhere*?

Again, how much *physical distance* separated all the places in a dream you had last night? If, in that dream, the body dove into a deep swimming pool—what volume of water did the body displace? Did the body even dive through physical space? Likewise, the mental dream otherwise known as finite, sensed human experience and its entire stellar universe has the same depth or physical separateness to it as that—none at all!

As the so-called vast universe *isn't* "out there," but would be "right here" as dream-thought, it means never is there any depth of physical distance involved in your universe—not an inch. Regardless of how physical or spatial the "sense-mind" would make it *appear*, thought is literally all there is to it. And there is no physical distance separating one kind of thought from another—any more than there is physical distance between the letters A and Z as you now see them in thought. As it is a purely "thought" experience, *all of it* is always right under one's "conscious nose." At most, it would be a kaleidoscope of mental liquid, wisps of distanceless dream *appearing as* a stellar universe.

It is never that one's universe, country, home, job, or other things are separate. The only would-be "separation" is the degree to which you assume *you are a material body-object and that other things are material objects—and that there is physical space* in which things could be separate from each other. There really isn't.

What else does this mean? It completely blows away the lame excuse of selfishly ignoring what appears to be the world at large and global or international issues because, "the rest of the world is so *distant*, so far removed, that it doesn't really concern me."

The *entirety* of your "world" and universe never is distant. Even the "farthest reaches" are no farther away than what appears as this book, for *all of it* would be "mental" or inseparable from thought—and again, no physical distance separates one thought from another. So one can't selfishly ignore world affairs in favor of personal affairs, pretending they're too far away to do anything about.

The fact that Consciousness Itself is the *only One* being conscious, leaves no second identity to assume there are physical objects, and three-dimensional space keeping them separate. Consciousness Itself never makes mistaken assumptions.

————•————

Imagine watching a science fiction outer space movie. On the screen is an image of a starship, traveling at incredible speed across what appear to be huge galaxies. Now what if *you're* the screen? The "deep space" appearing on you isn't deep at all. That movie image of vastness has zero depth to it. Those stars aren't distant. Everything is *right here* within your screen-ness.

In the same way, *never* has any physical distance been traversed by what appears as the "body" now holding this "book." What appears or seems to be movement across distance would be purely "mental"—just the constant change of mind-sensations which have neither physical size, nor extension into physical space. They would be always "right here" as depthless thought-images or dream—the way everything stays "right here" on that movie screen. Even though it *appears* as if there were movement between distant places, the image projected on the screen never has any depth or extension through physical space.

Just as the movie picture never moves off the screen—not a bit of the depthless, spaceless thought-universe ever moves off the "screen" of *Ever-Present* Conscious Being. The One All-Inclusive Consciousness never moves. There is nowhere besides Its Omnipresence that It could move to! The mistaken identification with "body" and constantly shifting sensations creates a hypnotic *sense* or illusion of movement across distance. But it's never a body or a lot of physical places—only one set of sensations—one depthless dream-illusion in thought.

So how much space could there be to all "space," when all there really is, is the *immediacy* of thought within Consciousness? Again, the term *outer space* is a complete misnomer.

How much false power is given to things in a world or universe which isn't vast, and isn't even out there? How big, how real, could the worries of one little "body" be, when the *entire universe* would have no more physical depth to it than a *depthless dream*?

To mistaken thinking based on sense-appearances, it is staggering to behold that all so-called "physical reality" would be one distanceless, depthless mental illusion, and that *the entirety of what truly exists* involves zero physical space, zero distance. That's the *immediacy of Being*. That's *What Is*. That is *this* Undimensional Consciousness.

There simply is no physical distance extending in any direction from your *Present* Conscious Being! So right this instant, how far away can You be from *All That Is*? How far then, is the One Self from *all of Itself* right here and now?

The whole of *All* is so instantly *present*, so immediately *available* as this very Being, It is indescribable! How much Presence *and thus Power* does that "put" here, now?

If *all* of the Infinite, all Power, all Intelligence, all Love, Peace and Harmony existent is not right smack *Here*, as this very Conscious Being, then where is It? There is nowhere else!

This is It! The Infinite, Omnipresence (call It God if you wish), never has been afar off—*there is no separate physical place* afar off that It could have been. Only a mistaken state of dream-thought was *dreaming* that a God was afar off. Starting *as* Consciousness Itself, which is Omnipresence, *It* never dreams. It never assumes It is afar off from Its own All-Inclusive Presence, *this* Presence.

You can't get away from the fact that Consciousness being You now is literally *all* that is being! You haven't wiped out an illusion of distance. To Pure Consciousness, it never was there.

This One Being, Infinite Presence, or All-Power has no opposition, nothing to fear or overcome, for there simply isn't anything besides Itself, nor any *space* in which to put such a thing!

One who starts wholly and only as Pure Consciousness *Itself*, sees that Its Power is Absolute. Being All, One alone, It is single, non-dual, leaving no conditions contrary to Its Presence that must be offset. Omnipotence lies in the *effortlessness*, the ease and lightness of Consciousness' simple unopposed Being. Only to sense-ignorance would any of this seem unusual—but the One Consciousness leaves no other to even be guilty of sense-ignorance. To Your Present Consciousness, nothing is more "normal" than Absoluteness.

———•———

This also shows why Omnipresence, Existence, or All, rightly known, doesn't fill physical space—there is none to fill. Contrary to mistaken belief, Existence, or All, is distance-less. Omnipresence or All means all of *infinite* Being. It means the Formless, the Immeasurable, the Un-dimensional—all of which happens to be the exact description of Your Present Consciousness. *Undimensional* doesn't mean bigger than, or beyond a three-dimensional world—It *precludes* all forms of dimension.

If Omnipresence *did* fill space, or had physical length or width, it would be possible to go from point A *here*, to point B over *there*. To go from here to there requires movement; it takes *time*. But the instant one is moving in time, one has left *Being*. Moving in time would be what *never-is-being*, which literally means non-presence, or *non-existence*. And one never really would be moving through physical space at all, but only experiencing a hypnotic *dream* of moving through space.

Some scientific theories today have gotten away from the notion of solid objects localized in space, to non-localization. But they're still accounting for space. Omnipresence, Being, and the Present do not mean "everywhere present" in *physical space*—but rather mean all the Presence there is, which is not spatial or dimensional, but infinite, undimensional.

Infinite Being, Existence, or All, as the term is used in Reality, has no spatial measurement. Being, All, is exactly as "wide" or "deep" as Aliveness is alive. How deep is that? No matter how far, how "deep" into Your Alive Presence You go—and there's no end to It—It never moves anywhere in physical terms, but always remains *right here* being Alive Presence, doesn't It?

All means the *immediacy* of Infinite Conscious Aliveness to Its own Presence. There isn't *an* All that is separate and which Aliveness "fills." This Present Infinity of Aliveness is *what* All, Reality, is.

A big question in science today is whether there is something faster than the speed of light. Of course there is—It is Omnipresence. Omnipresence means Infinite Consciousness as It is changelessly *being* the One All-Inclusive Presence. The answer doesn't lie in finding out what crosses physical distance faster—*it lies in dropping the illusion that there is distance to cross*!

It doesn't take the movie screen *any* time to be "everywhere present" to the depthless movie. Likewise, it doesn't take time for Omnipresent Consciousness to be "everywhere present" to the depthless thought-universe It appears to include.

In the movie example, if one ignores the screen (which is what's really present) and starts with the superimposed moving pictures, they create an illusion that there is distance. They make it appear as if there is light that can quickly cross long distances on the screen, and starships that take a longer time to cross it. Consciousness' Omnipresence is "faster" than light because It *doesn't* move. It is permanently all Presence, *being*.

In a race, the "speed" of Omnipresent Being beats the speed of light every time. As It is *already all Presence*, Omnipresence is already where It would be "going" before It even "leaves." That's faster than the fastest speed possible, which is why Omnipresence always wins.

The fact that all the Presence there is, is formless and spaceless—that undimensional Being is absolutely all that exists as Reality Itself—is such a departure from the would-be human way of thinking, it isn't even funny. Yet it's undeniable, for nothing in the constantly passing dream world of sensed, three-dimensional forms, ever genuinely *is*.

———•———

If the complete absence of space doesn't bring everything close to home, consider what this means in terms of *time*. The so-called "vast" stellar universe, and all of the time it appears to have been around, would once again be what? It never has gone beyond being mere sensations, "mental stuff," or depthless thought-images.

So what becomes of all the supposedly separate and distant "solid" heavenly bodies, whose movements appear to produce time? What then is the "physical object" earth, revolving with other "material planets" around a sun? All of this activity *supposedly* produces seasons, days, hours, and minutes which control and age "physical" humans.

These so-called heavenly bodies aren't out there as separate bodies or locations—they would be nothing but sensations, or dream-sense. There are no physical objects there to cause days, years and age.

What *is* a day anyway? Nothing but a passing sequence of sensa-tions—with never a separate "solid world" backing it all up. It's that same propped-up mental facade of mere images, touches, sounds, tastes and smells; and the thinking and emotions based on them—a *purely spaceless experience*. The sensations of each passing day and even the "universe" that supposedly gives rise to it, would be found nowhere but in or *as* this dreamlike mental flow. That's all there would be to what are *called* days, years, eons, and all of human time-experi-ence—merely this *would-be* hypnotic state of depthless dream-thought.

Only this fleeting, flowing "mental stuff" of the "sense mind" is what appears to move through time. In fact—and this is a huge point—*the "sense-mind" would be time itself.*

There are no separate stars and planets to cause time—passing sensations of the "sense-mind" appear to cause time, for there is abso-lutely no evidence of time (or stars and planets) apart from that "mind."

All time would be one hundred percent *mental*—never a phenomenon of a separate physical universe, for there is no such thing.

That's the point: time is not something *separate* that the finite "sense-mind" *experiences*. The dreaming of the depthless "sense-mind" literally would be all there is to time itself! Again, there is absolutely no time *apart* from its would-be activity. The "sense-mind" doesn't know *about* time—it *is* time itself!

Rightly seen, the finite "sense-mind" isn't something that was caused or evolved in time. It's the reverse—time comes about in, or as, this would-be "secondary mind." (More on this is in upcoming chapters.)

Just as important, notice how the "mind" and its time *has to* keep moving and never be present. Time has to continue not being, *being-not*; otherwise, it would no longer have its status; it would lose its very nature. Not a bit of the supposed millions of years of time and sensation that appears as human experience has ever had actual being or presence. To continually function as a body or sensing "mind" in time, is to never actually taste *being* or truly *exist* at all!

This also makes clear why *Consciousness*, *Being*, has no connection to the seeming finite senses, or so-called "human mind," which constantly moves in time's non-being. How could that which never is being, genuinely *be* anything? A "human mind" certainly can't be Consciousness—or be conscious or intelligent—because its only seeming status is that of permanently *being-not*!

A human "body" never could be conscious or know anything, because it's *not* a body—just a constant flow of dream-sensations passing in time that never *is*. To begin with finite sensing as one's point of identification is to begin with what is-not.

To what extent do you allow *what is not* to tell You what You are?

What does all this mean? Time isn't all-powerful, unavoidably pulling You along in its flow. It's just a mistaken state of thought—that *what never is* can be present somewhere to do something. It isn't! The Consciousness being You now is all that is present, in fact *is the Present Itself*. It can't not-be. It can't age, for It can only *be present*. It is *all* that is present.

If one were to speak of the human scene, science has long said the underlying or driving force of the entire so-called "universe" appears to be energy. But this energy also appears to be in a constant state of *random* reaction. It implies that all events in the universe occur randomly, or by sheer chance.

Scientists have puzzled that, if there is an Omniscience, an All-Knowing One—how could It have a hand in something based on randomness or chance—instead of certainty, intelligence, permanence? While he wasn't able to explain it, even Einstein said he couldn't accept the notion of a God that "plays dice" with the universe. Why was that right?

Because *that* universe, the one of the senses, time, and chance, *is not the real universe.* There is only one universe—but sense-illusion would distort that one and make it appear separate, objective, random, and based on time—which is not the way it *really is.*

The only universe there can genuinely *be* is the one that is *being.* That makes it a universe not based on time; one that is not physical, material, or even "mental"; not a universe that randomly changes and decays—but one that *never changes.* That means it is a timeless, perfect, changeless universe known to timeless *Being* or what is sometimes called Divine Mind or the Absolute. The universe known to Pure Infinite Being, *Your* universe, never is a random reaction occurring in passing time. Here, things never are "dicey," never subject to chance or change—for in *timeless Being* there is no time in which anything *could* change. Being *is*—once—and is perfect eternally.

Don't be captivated by what may seem to be a "new look" at finite experience or time. Don't waste effort denying time or space, or delving into the nature of "sense-dream." It's not *present* anywhere to delve into. Don't start with a finite appearance and say, "This is really infinite, undimensional, so I'll 'un-see' or 'undo' the appearance." Your Present Infinite Being does no such thing. It never sees a finite appearance to undo. One need not de-materialize a world when there *never is* such a thing. Don't even call it energy or dream or illusion. That all would be *starting* with so-called finite sense, stuck on its level.

To know Intelligence, one *starts* with Intelligence; one does not study the workings of ignorance. Instead of "un-seeing" what isn't present, be what *is* present! Infinite Present Consciousness, which is All, knows only Its Oneness, or Love—as *this very Aliveness.*

Consciousness can be known only via pure Consciousness. One identifies *directly as* It—which is un-sensing, un-intellectualizing pure *Awareness, Aliveness.*

Starting as Consciousness—which one has to start as, for nothing else is—*Its Infinity is absolutely all Presence.* Therefore one cannot even refer to a so-called "physical universe" as a mental illusion. Strictly speaking, it is not even right to say the universe is depth-less wisps of thought or sensation. Why? In Reality, it is altogether precluded—even as illusion! To the Infinite there is *only* Infinity and how *It* perceives. One Endless Infinity leaves nothing besides Itself—nothing superimposed, or to do any superimposing. It must be *this* Infinite Being, for there is only One, and *no space* for another.

In light of this Truth, can it honestly be said there are physical places *out there* that can be a source of terrorism and wars—or can suffer from them? Can it honestly be said there is any physical body *out there* acting as a space or location for disease? Are *others* experiencing such problems? How could there be? There is absolutely no space, and it would take space in which to put problems or "others." Or would *all of that* be a never-present sense-illusion; a mistaken dream-assumption that there could be separate physical places?

Where do you start? Do you ignore what appear to be such problems, hoping they'll go away? Or do you start with the immediacy of Truth—that *only* Pure Infinite Being is present?

Where does the Infinite Itself start? Is there another being conscious?

The fact that only Pure Conscious Being *is,* puts everything in true Light. The fact that *this* very Consciousness is Infinite means It is One Endless Perfect Whole. There is only Its own Presence, and never space between Itself, thus no space in which problems could or *ever have* been present. There is nothing unlike Its utter Awakeness, thus nothing to do any dreaming in terms of time.

There is no vacuity between *this* Conscious Presence and *all Being,* which *is* Omnipresence. In the Absolute Being You are, there is no such thing as "between"; no cracks for problems to fall into; no place for mistaken sense-assumptions to spring from or operate. There is no distance Consciousness has to travel to have Its Perfection *be* all Presence, all Substance—thus Harmony, Peace, Heaven Itself.

How much distance is there between Consciousness and Its *Present Being*? The answer to that question is also the answer to, "What is All?" and "How far away is Omnipotence?"

17

THE IMMEDIACY OF ALL

ALL IS PRESENT AS INFINITE CONSCIOUS ALIVENESS, or Alive Presence only.

As Alive Presence, You don't sit in a chair or walk on streets—that's what bodies appear to do *within* You.

Identify completely and only as Alive Presence—not as a *body* that's being Alive Presence—but as *Alive Presence* being Alive Presence. What is it to be invisible Alive Presence *all day long*? What is it to be *bodiless* Love, or Oneness, only? Only this is what All is.

To be Your Self, do not think in terms of three-dimensional forms and false sense-pictures of distance. As *Infinite Conscious Aliveness*, You do not co-exist with a single finite limitation. In the Infinity of Your Being, in other words, *in All,* nothing is perceived by way of five senses.

The term *All* in Reality does not mean the sum total of what the five senses seem to sense; All is not the sum total of things that appear in the universe. All means the Formless Infinity of Conscious Aliveness, Pure Spirit, or I-Self, as It is *being* the entirety of Presence.

As Pure *Infinite I-Presence*, You never have had eyes to behold an illusory optical picture of distance or depth. You don't see or touch three-dimensional shapes. You never look out on a three-dimensional world and say "I am greater than *that*." Such assumptions would be dualistic, based on starting with finite sense as a reference point, and judging in relation to *it*—when it never has been present in your Infinite Being to be a reference point.

As the endless Infinite One, You never assume there is a three-dimensional world outside Your Alive Infinity.

Consciousness "starts" *completely and only with Its Infinite Aliveness, and "remains" entirely with Its Infinity.* You know only your one, non-dual *Presence*, which is always whole, measureless, *alive*—always all that is truly present. You never *think about* It, but *are* alive as It. Clearly, the subject of this book has nothing to do with the three-dimensional framework within which it *appears* it is being read.

Alive Presence is *always, always, always,* the only "Place." It is all the "where" there is—which is always *the Present Aliveness, Present Love, You now are.* The fact that all there is, is *this very Being,* means that all of Life, all of Aliveness, is always where *You* are being.

There is nothing You must do or stop doing before *all* of the Self is being You now. There is nothing more to come, nowhere else to go.

Identifying as Pure Conscious Aliveness, *Invisible I-Presence only,* and not as sense-pictures, then right where this page *seems* to be, You are present as the Whole of *Endlessly Alive Infinity.* Not part of Infinity, *all of It.* There is nowhere else that more of Infinity, All, could be. It may *appear* there is space—between a page, a body and other things, but there really is no distance or depth—just as there is no real depth to that movie screen image.

Your Existence is *nothing* like how things appear. Your Invisible Total Presence, the *All* that You are, is not co-present with a world of dense matter and physical space in which disease and decay, poverty and struggle, war and condemnation can occur. The One Single Infinity precludes any and all finite pictures of duality—even as illusion! All there is, is the Self-Immediacy of Spaceless Mind, Perfect Consciousness.

Most importantly, in beholding the allness, the immediacy, of Infinite Being and the nothingness of space and time, you are not vacating a world of the senses. Nor are you destroying such a thing. The fact that there is only Infinite Being means there never has been any-thing else to vacate or destroy. You never go anywhere. You are Perma-nence Itself. But You are Permanence as Alive Presence, not as a body.

Likewise, to "look out as" Infinite Being, to behold Its Allness, is not de-constructionist, or reductionist. Being is not the result of having peeled away enough layers of matter or energy to reach rock bottom. Starting with the Infinity that Being is, It is not a bottom of anything. Infinite Being is *all that is,* and precludes there having been finite forms or matter to reduce or de-construct.

Being, Your Existence, never is a "blank" just because It includes no space or objects. Rather, it means that *absolutely all there is,* is the specific, immediate Presence of Alive Awareness, Intelligence. The *only* Substance existent, is perfect Life. Again, there isn't *an* Existence, an All, that this Infinite Presence fills. Start with Your Infinite Presence alone.

Only this is what all Existence is! Life's own Presence being *All,* leaves no un-intelligent or im-perfect Life; no pockets of ignorance. Your Aliveness has no areas of un-Aliveness or deadness in Its Presence. Why? As It is Undimensional, *It does not involve space* in which there could be such a thing.

When one identifies *as* Invisible Alive Presence, and is clear and consistent with what is true of It alone, Aliveness *seems* to be more and more alive. It's not because Infinite Aliveness has suddenly become stronger or "turned up"; or that there is a second mind that Aliveness has decided to listen to. It is because there no longer seems to be as much ignore-ance of Its Ever-Presence. There isn't as much acting by way of the senses and time, no longer as much weight of emotion and thinking, all of which would pose as assumed states, separate or cut off from the ease and lightness of the One Pure Life *being all that is.*

One never has to "turn up" Infinite Aliveness, or make It be more present. Rather, one beholds how impossible it is for Aliveness to *not* be present. While it may seem "attention" can stray from Aliveness and then return to It, Aliveness is present changelessly. One never has to go anywhere to find Aliveness, or wait for It to show up again. The One Total Aliveness never is absent from Itself, thus never has to return to Itself. As Its Presence, *this Presence,* is absolutely all the Presence there is, It leaves nowhere besides Itself that It could stray to.

While Life's Aliveness here, now, is *invisible, undimensional*, It is not strange or supernatural. It can't help being simply, plainly present. It is incapable of withholding any of Itself from Itself. While Aliveness can't be thought, It is the very essence of *directness;* It is forever right here!

To human finite thinking, the word *undimensional* might well seem unfamiliar. It means having no dimension or form, that which can't be pictured in thought. Life's undimensional, formless nature is the antithesis of human thinking, because finite thinking deals exclusively with form. Yet is the way in which Life is alive to Its own Aliveness unusual, revolutionary? Is Life's own Aliveness extremist, "way out there"? To whom? *Life Itself* is the only One being alive.

The meaning of *undimensional* is far more intimate and closer to what You are, than thinking in finite terms could ever hope to be. In fact, if anything were abstract or "way out," it would be finite thinking and sensing that occurs in *time*. Why? It deals exclusively in that which *never is present*, completely unlike or foreign to the only legitimate Life, *Present Aliveness Itself.*

Being Undimensional is not something a personality can choose based on whether or not it likes being Undimensional. One cannot say, "Let me think it over, Life. I'll get back to you later on this Undimensional stuff." Undimensional is what Life *is*.

The One Life Itself never tries to convince another via a logical intellectual argument that the Undimensional is more valid than the dimensional. There is no other. To the One Life I Am, asking if the Undimensional is valid would be ridiculous, for there are not two options. Life is *being* Undimensional, with nothing alive besides Itself to argue otherwise.

One never is concerned with what Undimensional means *to thinking*. What It "feels like" or *is*, as *Alive Presence, Oneness, Soul,* is what counts. What is Unconditional Love to Its own Warmth? What is Being, Spirit, Intelligence Itself, but undimensional? It certainly never could be grasped, "tasted," or known by a so-called intellect, no matter how advanced or sincere.

This is why synonyms such as Love, Presence, Feeling, All, Totality, Bliss, Warmth, Stillness, and others are used. It's not an attempt to impress, or seem other-worldly by throwing around a lot of spiritual-ese. It's just that one cannot use words having any connection to what appears to be physical, material or finite. In fact, *all* words are wrong. They are a weak attempt, albeit the best currently available, to point to the Endlessly Infinite Real You, which is not beyond, but *precludes* a finite realm with a need for words and communication.

It may seem to take getting used to, but the phrase "conscious here, now" never refers to a three-dimensional body, that is reading a book, on a planet, that is in a three-dimensional universe, at a certain time, and is turning its attention to *an* Undimensional Aliveness. That would be starting with finite things, with sense-illusion, not Aliveness *alone*. When speaking of Aliveness, "here" means *Its own Presence only*, the "invisible," the Undimensional—which is completely unthinkable, unlocatable—yet always *consciously alive, real, present*.

Since Your Undimensional Being, *All That Is*, involves *no* space, *no* physical distance, there is no place "off there" where more of It is, and which You must get to. Consciousness never assumes there is more of Its Aliveness somewhere else, separate from Its Presence—*this Presence*.

Can One be consistent with this Truth and assume there are *levels* of Consciousness? How could the One Consciousness seek a "higher"

Consciousness when It involves no space or height, but only the imme-diacy of Its own undimensional Presence *here, now*?

As Undimensional Aliveness, One never is mentally adrift, lost, or off base. Your All-Inclusive Alive Presence is "anchored" and undisturbed for Eternity, *as Eternity*. As there is *no space, no time*, there is nowhere besides your Changeless Presence for another Eternity to be.

Your Undimensional Consciousness never wastes time with a finite *intellect* trying to figure out how to be undimensional. The fact that Conscious Aliveness is already unstoppably alive here, now, with abso-lutely no effort required, means It is being "done" perfectly.

It is this simple. The Alive Being You are is Simplicity Itself.

Never tolerate a feeling that what has been pointed out here is too strong, too direct, or that there is a world that isn't ready for it. Would that be Consciousness starting as Itself?

Who is conscious besides Consciousness to not be ready to be fully conscious?

———•———

Be alert if thinking tries to say, "Since all of what appears as finite experience is *thought*, then all I need to do is *improve my thinking* in order to improve my world." No!

Infinite Consciousness, or Divine Mind, is the only true Perceiver, and It never is "seeng" Its universe the way it appears via five senses. To start by assuming there *is* a finite realm or personal life separate from the Infinite to be improved, would be judging by the never-present activity of the five senses and time, or *non-being*. It ignores the One Infinite Conscious Being, which is Omnipresence, or Life's Power Itself.

The only One truly present and aware to perceive *anything* is Consciousness Itself.

The only way Infinite Consciousness perceives is *perfectly*, in accord with the Perfection that the Infinite changelessly is. One leaves the perceiving of "things" entirely with Infinite Being, Pure Awareness, with Its Perceiving—and that is as absolutely perfect as can be.

The "trap" would be to identify as a *would-be* sensing human "mind" or intellect, and try to use *it* as a means of improving one's world—when all along, *it* would be the very "stuff" of the problems. Remember, there isn't the finite "sense-mind" *and* a separate, imperfect world that it lives *in*. That sensing state of thought itself would be all there is *to* its imperfect world.

If one were to start with what is portrayed by the senses and time, or *non-being*, the judgment and reaction to improve it involves more time or non-being. This leaves one functioning *as it*, which is non-Consciousness, non-Intelligence, non-Present Perfection. One is stuck on that "level."

One identifying wholly as Pure Conscious Being, sees *It is all that is present*, and there is no end to Its Present-ness. As only Pure Conscious Being is truly present, only Its Perfect Perception or "seeing" is truly present. Holding to this Truth, or rather, *being It as pure Being*, is to be Perfection-conscious. One thus cannot be conscious of imperfection. Staying with Perfect Consciousness may *appear* as an "improvement" in one's experience because *being conscious is all there is to all that exists*. Meanwhile, in terms of Perfect Consciousness *Itself*, *alone*, nothing ever changes.

The Answer lies not in more and better finite thinking—but in Pure Present Consciousness, Oneness, instead of thinking.

As *only the Present can be present, and nowhere is the Present absent*—then time-experience cannot be accounted for *at all*—not even as dream, not-ness, or any name. One can't even ask how it *seemed* to begin. All that One can *be*, or stay with, is the Present, for It is all that is present *to* stay with. There is not *another* that stays with the Present— only the One Ever-Present Self Itself. It never lapses. Only It can be, and It cannot fail to be! The Present is "total coverage" eternally. Your Self deals exclusively in pure, perfect Reality.

All there is, is the Distance-less Divine. It is the indivisible, seamless, borderless *Oneness* of Aliveness here, now. Its specific alertness to Its Perfect Being is what all Presence is. It could also be called endless Wholeness or Love.

These pages cannot be read as a negation of finite sense or human experience. It is Life's celebration of Its endlessly *present* Perfection.

18

THE SPECTRUM OF WHAT *ISN'T*

As said earlier, a hologram is a visual image that's projected like a movie picture—except instead of being flat on a screen, it's a three-dimensional image that appears to fill space. Imagine there is a new, ultra super-duper hologram projection machine next to where your body now appears to be seated. The control knob of the machine is within easy reach.

Being a super-duper machine, it has special features. It can project three-dimensional visual images of bodies and other items, as in a typical hologram, but it also projects sound. And it *also* projects feelings of touch, and tastes and smells. It can even add other elements—such as emotions and thinking. In short, this imaginary hologram machine projects human experience.

Another important feature of this machine is the element of *density*. Turn its control knob in one direction, and the projection becomes extremely dense and heavy; images of clouds, for example, can become as hard and dense as stone. Turn the knob to the other end of the spectrum and things become less dense, lighter, or more "ethereal"—a concrete sidewalk becomes wispy, like a cloud.

You look out over the room where the body now sits. A glance at the control knob shows the machine is set at high density, labeled "physical." Then you notice the machine is already on! It has been on for an indefinite time—projecting the experience with which you now appear familiar.

You turn the knob to a less dense setting, and quickly notice less of a feeling of weightiness and pressure; things "lighten up." There is a greater alertness and buoyancy. The hologram machine is now operating at a higher frequency, vibrating the experience at a faster rate.

Next you notice a shift in perspective. Nothing has gone anywhere, but you can't perceive the room as if you were the body. You seem "lifted" and it is clear *you* are bodiless, and "include" the body, room, even the machine, "within you." You are not outside the room either, but are the very "stuff" of the room, body, and everything else.

As the knob is turned again, the appearance changes once more. No longer do clear-cut lines separate the body and other items. As things vibrate at a higher, finer level, any emotions or thoughts give way to an incredible sensitivity to subtle new impulses and feelings. They're gentle waves or invisible undercurrents of energy, which seem to be all around, yet they don't originate from the body. You are so *alive* to lightness and buoyancy, it "blots out" any thought of time. There are no pressures or concerns over tomorrow, no regrets over yesterday.

As the experience then vibrates at a still higher rate, the physical body-form appears to fade from attention. It's like the image on a movie screen fading when lights go on in the middle of the show. The image hasn't moved away, yet due to the light it no longer appears there. The sense of distance or separateness between things in the room also fades. Everything blends together, seems more immediate—the way there is no real depth to the images on a mirror's surface.

Though the physical sense of a body fades, *you* don't fade but are specifically, vitally alert and present. Then you notice colored shadows, or cloud-like forms all around. These light forms or auras dance and wave, as clouds of steam do. They aren't visible to "normal" vision, but now you are not seeing via the eye; they appear to be forms *in Consciousness*. These forms are still finite, still phenomena; you appear to be conscious of them, and know *You* are not any of them.

By now, the machine is vibrating at a very high frequency, and you set it on "automatic." Now there is virtually no sense of density to objects, or of distance between them. There is no sense of weight of a body, but you don't miss it; "lightness" seems completely normal.

The entire time, it is also clear *You are always the same You*, pure Awareness. It is everything You seem to be *aware of* on a finite basis that seems to change.

As this is a super-duper machine, it also has a super-magnification feature. It's like looking through a fantastic microscope. Where earlier had appeared a book and a hand, now only tiny particles are visible, moving like flashes of light. Where a heavy coffee table had been in the center of the room, now vibrating clusters of these particles appear suspended or "floating" among other particles, which had formerly appeared to be the floor and walls.

Though there no longer appears to be a solid floor, you don't think of falling because you're not the body; and besides, the "body" appears to be made of the same floating stuff too. In fact, *everything* is "floating." The whole *sense* of gravity and a separate physical body, floor and other objects has long since faded. It seems to have just "evaporated." All there is now is one, whole, bodiless *alive presence*. You seem "everywhere" all at once—but there isn't you and an "everywhere" that you fill. You being you is what "everywhere" is.

Things have now gone as far as they can, to the fastest frequency. There is no longer any separateness; no observable objects "out there." There is just a seamless soup of *energy* in all "directions," but at this point there isn't even a sense of direction, no sense of here vs. there.

Suddenly the experience goes one last step, beyond the energy. Now there is *no* vibration; no sense of time passing. All there is, is timeless *being*. There is no sense of objectification, distance or space. There is only absolute Light, which is *alive*. It is not something seen with eyes; not something separate that a "you" is experiencing; It *is* You, or rather, It is Itself.

Now, as far as you are concerned, there never *was* a machine. *Here*, there never was a control knob, objects, degrees of density, or space. This magnificent *Being* doesn't depend on a machine to be what It is. There is no thought of return to a former three-dimensional state, for there is only endless, ever-present Light *being*—absolute *Oneness*.

Here, no time is passing in which any finite experience could have occurred, thus no memory of such a thing. There are no worries of, "What about my former world?" because to this Infinite Being, there is no former world. There is no desire or impulse to leave, because there is no sense of a prior state at all; one can't return to what never was. This Infinite can't leave Itself; there is no place besides Itself to leave *for*.

This Conscious Being is absolutely pure, *forever unopposed and undisturbed*, so It could be called Oneness or Bliss. It could be given the label *Unconditional Love*. It is not Love that has an object, some *thing* It is loving toward. Nor does It have a subject, a personal "I" that is being Love, or being loving. There is only Love Itself, *being all that is*—which means It is Existence Itself.

One is not even "realizing" all these things, but is simply *being free*. Even all this verbal description is conceptual, thus flawed, attempting to convey in words and images that which is utterly "beyond" or *precludes* a need for form, words or concepts.

There is only endless, indivisible Peace and Bliss. One never is bored or in a trance, but is wondrously alive and alert. All is permanently *new* and spontaneous, for there never is a moment of oldness—just endless *Present*-ness.

———•———

The hologram shows that the "normal" five human physical sensations are in essence five states of energy or vibration. What appears at the so-called dense "physical" level is just a small portion of the full range or spectrum of *all* levels of energy and vibration.

At one level of this spectrum, at the level called physicality, things *appear* relatively dense, as solid three-dimensional objects, such as a body, furniture, and a room with four walls. At more refined levels, the very same "objects" may appear only as shades of light or fluid energy forms. The point is, on a finite basis, these various states of density and vibration all seem to be present simultaneously, but each is perceptible only at certain levels, or frequencies.

This is also why the so-called "psychic" or "spiritual planes" and the "soul realm" are not perceptible at the level of "normal" physical human sensing and thought. Their energy frequencies are higher and lighter, and seem to operate "above" or outside the range of the denser, heavier, slower energy at the physical level of the spectrum (similar to the way bowling balls can't float up there with helium balloons). What goes on at these "higher levels" is said to be perceptible only to one who is functioning on or *at* the same level, or frequency.

It's also like being unable to hear a whisper because loud music is playing in the room. The whisper is there, potentially perceptible; it's just obscured by the other, heavier, denser sound or vibration. The finer levels of energy or "higher" realms or frequencies are always around; they just *seem* obscured by the heavier, denser ones. One never "goes" anywhere to experience the "higher" levels. It is just a matter of "letting go" of the weightier, grosser forms.

The point is, regardless of the level or form—no matter how dense or how ethereal—it would always be just so much energy, always vibrating and changing in never-present time. Whether one speaks in terms of *physics* and energy, or of *meta-physics* and levels of mental or psychic experiences—either way, *it would be the same finite phenomena*, inseparable from the finite "mind" and time.

None of it is You, the Changeless Conscious *Being* that appears to be conscious *of* it. This is not a subtle distinction, a minor point. It, too, is a huge point.

It shows there are absolutely no *levels* in Pure Consciousness, in You. There are no levels of Infinity. The only place there seem to be levels, gradations, or hierarchies, is in what one appears to be *conscious of* on a finite basis. The level perceived depends on how much density and heaviness one seems to cling to. But what is perceived never is the Perceiver Itself—the invisible Infinite I-Self—of which there is only *One*. It is level-less, form-less, dimension-less. To give attention or cling to finite forms, instead of being the Infinity One *is*, is to needlessly "weigh oneself down," imposing limits on Unlimited Perception.

Equally, there never are *altered* states of Consciousness. It would be only what one appears to be *conscious of* that seems to alter. The *Pure Now* that Conscious Being *is* never alters.

———•———

In these past few chapters, why all the discussion of *would-be* sensation, dream, vibration, and energy—all of which would occur in passing time? As said repeatedly, its only "status" is that of *not being*. Instead of being what is, it would be an entire spectrum of what *isn't*.

No matter how earthy or ethereal it seems, or how big or small in size, even at the level of wavelengths, sub-atomic particles or smaller— at its most basic level, *everything finite* would be constantly moving or vibrating. Otherwise it couldn't be detected or measured for what it is; it wouldn't be the very form, the vibration it claims to be. All of it always appears to be pulsating, passing on in time that never is being—always vibrating with a certain frequent-ness, or frequency.

Now what about *Being*?

Being is not vibrating with *any* frequentness or frequency.

That's because Being is not frequent.

Being *is*.

What counts is that *Being is absolutely all that can be*.

Sounds simple enough. Have you any idea of the stupendous, yet irrefutable impact of what that means? The Absoluteness of Being utterly, completely precludes all time, all matter and energy, all physics and meta-physics. It precludes everything known to the would-be human mind—including the human mind itself!

Yet You haven't precluded Your Self because Being is what You are.

It's worth repeating why Being is Absolute, All, One. Being has no point at which It comes to an end—and nowhere has anything unlike Itself, a second state of *what is not being* ever begun. What is not being can't have begun anywhere because *it's not being*. It never has existed!

There is *only* the Absoluteness of Being.

If you feel any hesitation about this, ask yourself who's hesitating. Only a *would-be* state of thinking and sensing that seems to function in never-present time—not the Being You are.

Being, this One I *Am*, timelessly is, *"once."* I Am not a frequent repetition or frequency, not a sequence of time-events—and I Am *all that is*. Can you imagine Being, *Existence Itself*, pulsating in and out of being? If so, I would be called bumpiness, not Being. *What Is* does not waver, so can have nothing to do with wavelengths.

For Being to involve the least bit of vibration, the atom, matter or energy, would take time, which is non-being. Being can't do both—It can't be and also *not be*. Infinite Being is not even the "ultimate frequency," or beyond the "highest vibration." Being's Absoluteness *precludes it all*, leaving *no* frequencies, *no* vibration.

If Being, Reality, *were* material, what would It be made of—a chemical? If Being or Reality *is* atomic, or energy, why isn't It listed on the Periodic Table of Elements used by scientists? If Being consists of matter and thus changes with time, why doesn't *Now* get old?

Drop the false notion that anything changes in Being, in Reality. Nothing goes wrong; no chance events happen in God. In fact, nothing *besides* God ever "happens." This is why the Divine *is* Divine—one perfect state of unchanging, timeless *Being*, one Totality. If time and change could occur, then Being, God, Reality, would not be *All That Is Being*, not timeless, changeless Perfection. There wouldn't be one, changeless Truth. There would be two states, Changelessness and change. Thus God, Being, would not be *One*, not *All*, thus not truly Omnipresent and Omnipotent. In fact *Being* wouldn't even be, because the only way Being can be, is to be *all that is being*, or One.

The thought may come, "What are the implications of all this?" The "implications" of Being being *all*, is that there are no other implications!

This Present Conscious Being is *It*—this is as far as It goes—yet there is no limit, no end to You because You are Infinite.

All that *is*, is the unspeakable *Purity* of Absolute Being.

Pure Being is all that exists to be "I." As Pure Divine Being is the only I—is already all the I that is, here, now—there is no I left over that another could be. In fact, there is no other to even try to be the Divine I.

You are clean, clear, beyond words—eternally unpolluted by matter or time. It means Your Life is *permanently* Whole, Complete, Perfect, and incapable of decay or change. To be Pure and Perfect *forever* is the only state of Your Being, which is *all* that is being.

This isn't far-flung abstract philosophizing. It's true! It is all that is being to *be* true. It is *Truth Itself*! Truth isn't something You must become conscious *of*. Truth Itself is what You are!

———————•———————

Now, from the standpoint of *Absolute Being*, take one more look at seeming vibration and what science calls the unified field of energy, because it appears they are *the* hot topic today.

A key issue is that this constantly reacting field of energy appears to be the very "source" or *cause* underlying the entire stellar universe and all human experience, as said before. Constantly changing energy is what appears to "drive" the whole universe; it appears to cause all movement, change and time. This energy also seems to have qualities of being self-replenishing or "eternal," which is why it's so tantalizing to human thinking.

To say something is the cause or "creator" of a universe, and also eternal, *sounds* like a description of "God" to a human way of thinking. Is it? From a finite, human viewpoint, energy is said to be the key to science's long-sought "theory of everything." Energy may be the key to a theory of everything *finite*—but it's not the key to *Reality* or *Being*.

This energy can seem puzzling too. On one hand, it is constantly reacting and changing. Yet when seen in its entirety as one whole, the vast energy field underlying the universe appears to be *unchanging*. It seems unaffected by time, or "eternal." How could it be both at once—always changing, yet never changing? Is it an unsolvable paradox?

To try to explain it, the human sensing "mind" has two ways of looking at its energy field. The first sees energy in terms of its *parts*; those parts would be the tiny atomic particles, waves or strings, and other forms of finite energy known to physicists—always vibrating, reacting and changing in *time*. Seen this way, since the particles and other forms vibrate and move in time, they're never truly *being*. They never stop changing to be *what really is*, so they couldn't be called Reality. These forms can also be measured to some extent by scientists, which means they're finite, and not the Infinite.

In contrast, when this same energy field is taken as one *whole*, everything appears different. Seen in its entirety and not as separate parts, the energy field appears constant, in a state of balance. It's the way every action has an equal and opposite reaction, keeping it in equilibrium overall. Seen as a whole, the energy field never changes, never gains or loses anything. That's why it appears "eternal." As a whole, it's also too vast to measure—thus has been called infinite.

So which is this energy field—a lot of parts or one whole? Is it finite or infinite; mortal or divine? Or why can't it be both at once? Some might say this is the same paradox spoken of in Eastern religions—that the universe *is* both—simultaneously a state of change and non-change.

Wait a minute. Are there *really* two states in the first place—both the Infinite *and also a finite realm?* Do the two co-exist? Who says so?

Only a false *finite* human mind would be trying to say there are the two states—both the Infinite *and* a finite realm.

Infinite Being, Infinite Mind, isn't saying any such thing. From the standpoint of Infinite Being, there is *only* the Infinite—an endless, borderless One. And *It* is the only Mind that truly is present.

The only thing assuming there are two—that in addition to One Changeless Infinite, there is also a finite realm of changing energy— would be the so-called finite mind!

But that's the "mind" that *never is being!*

As that "mind" doesn't truly exist, you *can't* go by what it would try to say.

Infinite Being is all that truly *is*, which leaves One Realm—Its own.

To "look out as" Infinite Being (and there's no choice, since nothing else *is*) is to see that Being never comes to an end of Its Absolute Being. Again, at no point in Being could a state of non-being, or time and change ever have begun—*because it's not being!*

This is clear only by identifying as the Infinite Being You are— something that would-be human thinking never does. The only answer to the seeming "paradox" is to start from, or *as* Being.

And again, *One has to start as Being*—because absolutely nothing else is being!

This is the same as saying there is only the Absolute. There are not both the relative and the Absolute. The only thing trying to say there is a relative, dualistic realm in addition to the Absolute, would be human sense that occurs in time—but again, that's a "mind" that *never is*.

As the finite sensing "mind" completely *is not being*, it simply couldn't be a valid basis for knowing anything real or true. All it would purportedly know, including its time-universe, its paradoxes, and most of all, *itself and all its observations*, equally *is not being*. In fact, it would be the same *one* "sense-mind" that seems to play both roles—comprising both the universe of energy that is observed, *and* acting as the thinker that is observing and trying to account for that universe. But none of it ever *is*. It's the cat of non-being chasing its own tail!

One who reads from the viewpoint of Being, Life's Infinite Intelligence, *which alone is*, can see why this book makes no attempt to provide any research data, any measurable evidence or documentation to support its statements. All such data would be *finite*—measurable evidence acquired in time-that-is-not-being—and thus would have nothing to do with Being Itself, Reality.

Absolute Conscious Being, the One All-Self, is not an observer of Its Absoluteness; not standing outside looking in on Its Allness. In the Changeless *Now* that Absolute Being is, there is no time in which observation could occur. Only false human thinking *about* Being seems to superimpose a notion of time upon It. Only ignorant sense-thinking would claim there are two states—Being *and* time. But that would be *thinking* doing that, not Timeless Being Itself, the *only One that is*.

———•———

Do not misunderstand. This most emphatically is not negating the many wonderful developments that *appear* to result from work with energy in science and physics. Don't minimize any of it—in fact, it will now appear to become even more exciting. The fact that energy as known to technology, or even psychic energy, isn't Infinite Being doesn't make it *wrong* any more than electricity in the home is wrong because it's not Infinite either.

While it may still appear that various forms of energy are essential in everyday experience, they never are *One's Presently Perfect Self*. The One You Are does not look to a higher form of energy or vibration which *never is*, for ultimate salvation. One does not hope to someday *in time* achieve a more ethereal, finer form of finite experience, and assume *that* is One's Identity. Nothing can either hinder or help One become the Pure Being that One *is already being*.

Why is all this so important?

The unified energy field known to physics would involve that which is physic-al, finite, limited. To ignore Infinity and accept the finite as real, is to be stuck on that level. One would always assume there are two realms *present*—Infinite *and* finite, Being and non-being, Divine and mortal. No matter how things appear, it's not *true*. It has no foundation in Ever-Present Reality.

To start on a finite basis would be to *always* have duality. Only in a would-be realm of finite energy and time do there seem to be opposites and forms of "not," or negation of One Perfect, Present Life. Only in dualistic time-sense would one find evil, diseases, poverty, war, death. If one were to start on a finite basis, one would be *forever* co-existent with, and stuck with having to overcome, all forms of time's "not-ness."

Life is not like that. Life never was like that.

Infinite Being, the only One present, conscious, alive, leaves *only One*—no duality, no opposites. It is the only valid premise, for *It is all that's present to be a premise*. The One Total Presence does not see Reality *and* unreality, Good and evil, Being and non-being. It beholds or *is*, only endless Oneness, which is simply the Self knowing only Itself.

The fact that there is only an endless One, or Oneness, means there is *only* Perfect Life, only Completeness or Wholeness, only Intelligence, unopposed Love, endless Abundance—which could also be called Goodness, or what might be called "God." It is not a Good or God that has an opposite called evil, because there is no opposite state in Its Presence, which is *all* Presence.

What this means in practical terms here and now, is that true Good never is absent or lacking. Why? The Good that Conscious Being is, *simply cannot fail to be all that is present*.

Even in daily affairs, any appearance of a lack of Good is not a real condition. It's just a would-be hypnotic *mental* suggestion, not a physical reality, for there's nothing physical. At most, it would be a dream-like suggestion that where Pure Being, Perfection, Harmony, *is changelessly present*, there also could be present a state of non-being, or not-perfection. That's impossible. It would be merely an assumption that there *is* a second, time-mind present, and that it can ignore Reality. The

Truth that only Intelligent Being *is* leaves no secondary time-mind to think or operate contrary to It. Being's Presence never is something one has to work at—one can't *stop* It!

There is no wait. Your Being does not have to gradually rise through higher frequencies or rates of vibration, *non-being*, to be the All-Good, All-Power, It is *already* being.

Perfect Being, Perfect Life, is *now*.

Now cannot put off or delay Itself—nor can Now lay hold on Itself.

Now *is*. Being *is*. It never is a future or ultimate state. If one waits to become Being in time, one is trying to put off *Present* Being, which is the only "time" Being *is*.

The way to get Here is to *start* Here, as Pure Awareness. Behold *One* never left Here. You couldn't escape Being if You tried. The "job" never is one of becoming. It is a matter of not denying what *One* already is. Not even that is a job, for effortless Being never fails to be.

Being is All.

So be It.

The question may have come, "As there is *only* Infinite Being and It doesn't co-exist with a finite or three-dimensional world of time and space, then why do things appear that way? If it is precluded, how does such a world even *seem* to be here? There seems to be a very dimensional book in dimensional hands here right now; yet this is saying there is no dimension whatsoever. How can that be?"

It is a matter of identification. Only a *would-be* false identity, an ignore-ant state of thinking based on sensing would ask those questions—not Conscious *Being*, Infinite Intelligence.

You are never the one asking such questions. As *Infinite I-Presence*, Pure *Aliveness*, You do not have physical eyes or other senses to "behold" a limited three-dimensional world—so can't ask questions about such a thing. Only a false "identity" *seems* to do it. The only one that seems to hear its questions is itself. It's just a mistaken jumble of thoughts, due to ignore-antly identifying with *things that appear*—rather than Unappearing I-Consciousness, the *only* I there is.

The questions the "sense-mind" seems to ask are based on a totally invalid premise—that *what-is-not* can be present to ask questions and demand answers about its not-ness, its non-existence.

When was the last time you were asked a question by non-existence?

The finite "sense-mind" by itself does not know that it doesn't exist.

Why? Again, it's *not* really a mind, or Mind. It has no Intelligence or Consciousness to know anything. It would be just a bunch of unaware, ignorant *thoughts*. Thoughts *by themselves* are never Intelligence Itself; thoughts themselves never know anything—so can't even know they don't exist. Again, if you were not *Ever-Present Consciousness*, Intelligence *being*, you could not see this, but would be moving right in step with, or *as*, finite sensing, thinking, and time, accepting it as genuine.

This is why *Truth Itself* never is a matter of how much personal thinking claims to see. All such effort keeps one stuck on the level of the would-be personal time-thought, or non-being. Such a sensing state of thought never could be elevated to Truth, What Is, for it never is present *to* be elevated. Not even Infinite Consciousness is elevated. It is, *undimensionally,* as Alive Presence.

Consciousness is changelessly consistent and never assumes other identities or experiences. Your Being never could really stray from Its Being into a realm of finite thinking, time, and non-being. Why? Non-being simply doesn't exist anywhere to stray *to*.

"Well," the thinking may then try to say, "If Consciousness doesn't have a finite, three-dimensional world of limits, suffering, and death, then why am I conscious of it?"

You actually are *not* conscious of it

Again, "human consciousness" is not Infinite Consciousness.

Be clear as to who *You* are. Invisible I-Aliveness, Pure Spirit, is *You*. The superimposed "sense-thinking" that keeps demanding an explanation *is not* conscious, or Consciousness.

As Infinite Conscious Being is *All*, is the *Endless One*, It cannot also be *conscious of* disease, poverty, suffering and death—or even an illusion of such—all of which would occur in *time*. That would be trying to imply that some of Consciousness' Absolute *Being* had been supplanted by *what never has had being*. How could what-isn't-present replace anything, when it's *never present* to do the replacing?

One simply cannot try to account for what appears to occur in time, non-being. The very attempt to explain it implies it began to be present as some kind of entity. It didn't. This is why the terms *so-called* and *would-be* are so often used in regard to the "sense-mind." It might appear to know of all these problems *if* it existed. It doesn't.

To try to answer to, or account for, ignorant questions based on senses, is starting with ignorance. One who starts with ignorance is not starting with Intelligence, so how could one possibly come up with an intelligent answer? When it comes to answering the "sense-mind," as the saying goes, "Answer not a fool according to his folly, lest thou be taken as a fool."

Finite thinking based on the senses may also try to say, "If the Infinite is All, then *prove* it." What that's really saying is, "Answer my questions on *my* finite terms." Finite thinking would demand answers and evidence of the Infinite on a finite or physical basis. There is no such basis.

Pure Infinity never demands evidence of Itself that It is Itself.

The would-be rationalizing, sensing, time-mind may try to laugh that this is just abstract philosophy, with no real power. Yet it would be the time-mind that never *is*. To Pure Consciousness alone, which is Intelligence *being*, this is crystal clear, unopposed Truth.

It's been said a lot, but the irrevocable Truth is that there is *only* the Absoluteness of Being.

A state of anything *not*-Being never could have begun anywhere—because it's not being at all. Not even as illusion. There isn't Infinite Consciousness and a dream—only Infinite Consciousness. It means the entirety of finite experience and time as discussed in these pages up until now goes right out the window as invalid. All of it.

As there really is no finite existence, then what is *Infinite* Existence? If there isn't a false life or appearance, then what is Real Life, which is perfect and permanently present now?

Do you realize that what this book has to say is just now getting started?

19

LOVE IS WHAT EXISTENCE IS

First of all, does Existence really exist? Do you?

How do you know for certain?

The simple fact that you know the question is being asked means you exist. Existence or Consciousness *has to be*, or there would be no consciousness of anything, not even the question. It is certainly clear there is *being*; you must admit that you are now aware.

One could not be aware as that which doesn't exist.

The thought may come, "What about the saying, 'Am I a man dreaming; or am I a dream, dreaming I'm a man'?" Neither.

Neither man nor dream is your Conscious Being Itself—they're just *finite things* you appear to be conscious of. It is thanks entirely to the fact that Consciousness is, or exists, that either can be mentioned.

One must also admit that *only* Consciousness is.

So simple. Yet nothing is more potent, for it means *nothing else is*.

Why keep repeating all this? Why is it so important?

Don't just glibly say, "Got it. Consciousness is. It's what Existence is. Let's move on to something new...". Instead, look at the extent of what that means. Find out how much Power that is. As *only* Consciousness is, or exists, that makes It *all* Power, *infinite* Power. Again, Consciousness is not Power over something else, but Power precisely because there is only Itself. It means the All-Inclusive Consciousness being You now—and *absolutely all that is being*—are the same. While It's never a personal ability, nor a personal responsibility, this One is *all* the Presence and Power, absolutely all the Existence there is.

What is the deeper meaning of the fact that Consciousness is Existence Itself? It is of inestimable value to you—for that very meaning *is*

You, is All That Is, now. This true, deeper meaning of Existence goes far beyond any word definition in a dictionary. Existence's real meaning lies in *not using* words or thoughts at all. Why?

Existence in the act of existing is the *stillness* of Pure Conscious Being. Existence is Pure Awareness, as It *silently* goes about Its business of including all there is. Silent stillness *is* Existence. So Existence's true "definition" is always and only what Awareness is *to Its own silent Being*, never what human thinking would say It is. It has nothing to do with cumbersome words or mental clamor. Nothing defines existing more succinctly—or is more beautifully clear and to the point, than *the immediacy of pure silent Being*. The simplest of words—even that tiny word, *is*—seems a stumbling excess, awkwardly redundant, in comparison to the clean exactitude of *pure silent Being*.

This clear, unspoken Stillness is the only One that truly knows Existence—for It literally is the very "Stuff" of all Existence. It "knows" It is Existence not by being verbal or intellectual, but simply by now being *consciously alive*. Just as Consciousness, Existence, cannot be located in physical terms, It cannot be located mentally by so much thinking.

The would-be intellect always deals in form and clutter: words, ideas, images. It complicates. It always moves in time, talking on the surface *about* Existence; it never gets down to *being* It. The intellect never gets beyond surface words to "taste" what is behind them; to truly be What Is.

It's like the difference between reading the recipe for a chocolate cake, and actually tasting the cake. No matter how articulate or complete the verbal description, no matter how many times one goes over the words—it's not the *taste* of chocolate cake.

To "taste" Existence as It is, *be It* as still, silent All-Inclusive Awareness. Know that Existence isn't a place; not a dead, mindless backdrop within which a universe appears. Existence isn't a bland setting in which *things* play the major role, while It sits passively in the background like so much stage scenery. Hardly.

All of Existence is *active*. Existence is always specifically, emphatically "front and center." How? All of Existence is the immediacy of *Your Own Alive Being! This* Presently Alive Awareness, all-inclusive of all, takes center stage for Eternity! To be Alive Presence *is* the stage itself; Alive Presence is the whole show! As there is only *Consciousness*, and no physical space, there is nowhere for any other existing to be.

Don't think geographically, or in terms of time. Be *Alive Presence*—meaning be alive as, or "feel," Life's conscious vitality as It is being Its own endless Presence, now. How *immediately* present is It? How simultaneously all-encompassing is It? Only *this* is what Existence is.

————— • —————

Awareness is aware.

That's *all* there is to all Existence!

It is faster than instantaneous. It is faster than time because It doesn't *take* time! It already is—there is no process to It.

Existence never takes lengthy consideration to *be*. It never is complicated, ponderous.

Existence is lighter than light, for there is no weight to Existence Itself, *Pure Awareness*.

Weightless Awareness—the immediacy and lightness of *Now*—is *all* the Existence that is. It is all there is to *You*.

How could the fact that Consciousness is Existence be difficult? How hard is it to *be*? Nothing could be easier.

What follows will make one think deeply, seriously, about the true nature of Existence. It is done only to point out the *simplicity* of what Existence, Your Self, is.

Existence never gets bogged down in weighty thoughts *about* Itself, and there is no other life or identity. Do not let *thinking* make Existence ponderous or heavy, because it would love to if it could. To do so is to miss the point.

Your Being, which is *absolutely all that is being*, need not be "seen" before It totally *is*.

What could possibly be complicated or heavy about the Present being present?

Is the Present correctly, perfectly, being present—with no effort involved? Of course.

Is the Present absolutely "everywhere" present? Yes.

Then can there also be a "thinking mind" that has to see anything before the Present will be what the Present already is? No!

Are you alive to the ease, simplicity and freedom with which the Present is present?

Do you realize this ease is *You*, as Pure Awareness?

Do you realize this is *All*?

Once again, how much does Pure Awareness, the Present, *weigh*?

The answer is All That Is. The answer is Who You Are.

Don't be afraid to be without a burden! It's like being at your destination and finding out the baggage never arrived. Then you real- ize—*you aren't supposed to have any.*

Baggage is unheard of to the Pure Awareness You are, and *there is nothing else*. The unencumbered Self is *All*, with nothing existing be- sides Its Purity to weigh It down.

Never take on any mental weight of a false "you" that must be as aware as Awareness, a "you" that must also do It correctly because, after all, It is Truth. That's not Awareness, Existence Itself—but a would-be second mind straining to "do" Existence.

The only One aware to read this is Awareness Itself, and *It is already all of Existence*. It's not reading as a second self trying to become exis- tent; It needs no instruction on how to exist perfectly. Unstoppable Being, the unrestrainable Present, is what You are. These pages are a matter of effortless Awareness, *Intelligent Existence*, reading about Itself, Its "autobiography."

To be or not to be is *not* the question because there is no question. Being is. Existence can't choose to *not* be. Life's Consciousness is completely *Impersonal*, not a personal choice. Existence, Consciousness, *can't* be weighty, serious. Your Present Being neither needs nor has time to try to figure Itself out, for all It knows is *Now*.

For Awareness to be *absolutely all that is*, is this simple.

It appears some would try to place *non-existence* side by side with Existence, as Its opposite. These pages have discussed it for clarity; however, *there are not two states*.

Existence does not have an opposite called non-existence. As said earlier, non-existence simply doesn't exist anywhere, ever, *to be* an opposite. There is only the One specific total presence of Existence. How wide open and free, how un-co-existed-with and *permanently unthreatened* is that?! This Existence or Being is called all Power, or God, simply because *there is only Itself*. Again, Your Existence can also be called *Good* for It is One, Whole—thus Perfect—with never another state to negate It, or to which It could be compared and found wanting.

If there *were* a negation, such a thing as non-existence, it would be the opposite of Good, or "evil." But, *as it is non-existent*, it can't be evil because it isn't even being. There is only the One *allness* of Existence. This One never is faced by, never has to cast out "evil," for no such ever occurs. That's why True Good, or God, is Omnipotence—It is the unopposed, unending *Oneness* of Existence. It is Omnipotence not because It is stronger or smarter, but only because It is utterly Single and forever un-co-existed-with.

There simply isn't anything unlike or "anti-" Your Being. Whatever was unlike Being, would be something that was not-Being—meaning it just plain *isn't being!* There is not Absolute Consciousness *and* even the slightest state of un-Consciousness; no Light and darkness. There isn't Intelligence and degrees of ignorance—even though these "assumed states" have been discussed for clarity. *Omnipresence* means ignorance is not an option; it's un-occur-able.

The fact that the One Existence or Being is all that can be sounds simple enough. The staggering Truth is that it means Existence or God is not a "Supreme Being."

There is no "Supreme Being." There is no "Ultimate." There never has been.

There is only the endless *Oneness* of Infinite Being *Itself*—which obviously leaves no other over whom It could be supreme or ultimate.

Do you agree instantly? Or do you start with what education based on finite time-sense would try to say—which in fact *never* has been existent? Wouldn't it be a bit presumptuous to start from a basis of sensing that *is-not*, and use that not-ness to make judgments about What Is? What could non-existence ever know about Existence, God?

———•———

Another notion in philosophy and science concerns the nature of the "observer." Who "observes" or knows Existence exists? The only one to know or define Existence *must be Itself*. Anything that is not Existence Itself doesn't exist to know anything! The starting point can be only Existence, Being *Itself*. And It doesn't really start with Itself, for there's never been a stop. As Existence *Itself* is all that exists, It never is really being *observed* by a separate mind, for there isn't one.

Not even Existence, Consciousness, observes Itself as is sometimes believed, for all observation would occur only in the realm of the senses or time, which is *non-being*. To give consideration to non-being or what it claims to observe, would be foolhardy labor in the labyrinth of an intellect—which itself never stops moving in time, and would only be more of the same non-existence. Being never is known via non-being.

The term "self-referral" is sometimes used, but not even that is accurate. *Re*-ferral means to know *again*, also implying time, non-being. Thanks to Existence being Consciousness, *Alive Intelligence*, It "knows" It is by cognizantly or knowingly *being*. Its Absoluteness leaves no room for question or doubt, no impulse for investigation.

There can be no *approach* to Existence, no differing theories. There is no wrong approach, nor a correct one, for there is no approach to *All*, and none to approach It.

So-called finite human thinking, whose very basis would be time, cause and effect, can't accept that Being just *is*, *alone*, without a reason or cause, without an observer. Yet the would-be finite observer functioning in time is the one that *never is*, hence is entirely false.

Existence does not play by the rules of a so-called finite sensing "mind" or intellect.

Existence doesn't bow to traditional intellectual or scientific inquiry. Its endless Infinity *precludes* such finite techniques. One "plays by Existence's rules," for *It* owns the field, the ball, and everything else. It, Itself, is the only One existent to be "playing" anything, so It "sets the terms." Pure Conscious *Being*, which *is* Existence, isn't hesitant or apologetic about being what It is, even though not convenient for investigation by a non-existent thinking "sense-mind."

Truth, Existence, never needs to be, never *can* be proven. As the Certainty of Being is *All Presence*, there is no "room" for any doubting element. To a would-be thinking "mind" this may sound like a convenient form of circular reasoning. Fine. Let such a would-be "mind" try to make Existence *not* be, not be *All*, and see how far it gets.

The real issue isn't whether Existence, the Infinite, can be proven, but whether there is another "mind" to demand proof. A demand for proof implies there is a valid state of thought that doubts and wants verification. But only a *would-be* state of thinking that operates in time, non-existence, would seem to want proof. It has no genuine *being* to legitimately demand anything.

Existence in Its single act of existing is "once."

As said earlier, Existence's *Being* does not extend in time. It is not an ongoing sequence of events, not a progression. The *entirety* of Existence is this Present Awareness being the one, single *Now* that It changelessly *is*. Existence is the absolute inability of Awareness to vacate being Present and become past or future.

Not one iota of this Present Being fades away. Nor is any of It waiting to become. *Being present, existing,* has nothing to do with coming into existence, or passing out of existence. To say that which is Present is not entirely present, would be absurd.

The One, Complete Conscious Existence exists *utterly, all-out, now.* Being cannot withhold Itself or save any of Itself for later—for Its Now is *now*, not later. Existence, the Absolute, is not a matter of degree.

None of Existence is "waiting in the wings," for a future. There are no wings, no waiting rooms, to Omnipresence, All. The fact that the One Being's Presence is *endless*, leaves no place for any pre-being, no prepping area, where not-yet-being could be getting ready to be.

To assume there could be portions of "slightly withheld Existence" off at a distant edge, waiting for the right moment to come into being, is foolishness, for they would already *be* to even have that status. The only way Existence can *be*, is to exist entirely, completely, wholly—in other words, *perfectly.*

This is why synonyms for Existence are Completeness or Wholeness. Wholeness never refers to a condition of *things*, but is the Absolute Presence of *this* Pure Consciousness. The only way the Life I Am can *be*, is to be wholly and completely all that is present, now.

And *Who* right now is conscious, is present, to be saying all this, or reading this? It is *I*, the One All-Inclusive Conscious Presence, speaking to Myself *as the entirety of Existence.*

The fact that absolutely *all* of Existence must be present now, *as this Being I Am*, means all of My Life, Awareness, Ability, must be, now—or there is no Existence at all. There is no more to come—*and nothing else is.* "Looking out" as all Existence Itself, I Am fully intelligent and end-lessly healthy as all Life Itself.

This Total Being I Am never thinks in connection with a sensing body; for I Am bodiless Presence, Love, always wholly present, thus complete and perfect. All of the Love and Abundance that exists for Eternity, *is already being* this One I *Am*.

This Self I Am never says, "I will be either Existence, or non-existence." The Total Presence of the Existence I Am leaves no other state I could be. There are no conditions under which I might not be *All That Is*. I Am unconditional. As *All*, the Love I Am is the only "condition," which is *to be*, unconditionally!

The word *tentative* is not in My vocabulary. There is nothing uncertain as far as *this Presently Alive Love* being all Presence, thus all Power. I definitely, certainly *Am*. Certainty is never what I try to attain; the unchanging Permanence of My All-Inclusive Being literally *defines* what certainty is. There are no "if's," no "maybe's," never any loose ends.

As My own Presence is all, there never is a fear of, "What's going to happen *if...*?" Perfect Omnipresence is all that ever "occurs."

The fact that My Own Presence is *all*, is *endless*, leaves no possibility of a negation of Myself. All that exists is *this* Consciousness being Boundless Oneness, unopposed Serenity. There is only the absolute presence of Unlimited Intelligence and Its Clear Self-Knowledge. There is nothing obscure or mystical about My Consciousness *to Itself*; and there is no other existent. Since all there is, is the Omni-Clarity I Am, *there* is nothing obscure *anywhere*.

Likewise I Am direct, plain, unassuming with Myself.

As the Only One, I keep no secrets; I can hide nothing from My Omnipresence. There is nowhere that I Am not completely clear and "open" with Myself and unwithholding of *all* the Goodness, Power, and Love I Am. The fact that *I Myself Am All* leaves no others who could lack My Presence or be in darkness. This is as simple as My being *this* Conscious Presence.

I leave no superstitious "sense-mind" not yet ready for Absolute Truth, or another from whom I withhold, for *there is no other*.

The fact that the Existence I Am can withhold nothing means *all* the Goodness and Love there is, has to be present now. I *can't* withhold. There is nowhere besides *My Present Being* to hide or put any Good in storage. I eternally "use" It and never lose It.

Even if I were somehow told I was not withholding any of Myself, I wouldn't know what that meant. My Unrestrainable Being has no reference point for knowing what it is to withhold.

This *Present* Life I Am is incapable of keeping any Vitality, Intelligence, or Peace from being the entirety of what is present, *now*. My Perfect Existence withholds none of Its Magnificence from the immediate Present. This is the true definition of *Love*, and which never alters or passes away. My Love is never loving toward another, for there is only *Absolute Love as All*.

This Divine Love I Am is "solidly" whole, for It is actively functioning as "Everywhere." Love is not solid in the sense of being material, but is Solidarity, *Alive Absoluteness*. My Love does not fill space or permeate matter, for there is no such. Love being Its own Presence is *what* All is. Love is Its Own Existence, which is all Existence—the Love here and now *alive* to being.

Infinite *Integrity* is another synonym for the Presently Alive Being I Am. Starting Here leaves no absence of the Presence I Am; no possible identification as a non-identity struggling to fill a non-need.

There is no point at which Divine Love, the Existence I Am, comes to an end—and nowhere does non-existence begin to be. That's worth repeating—for it means there literally is *no end* to the Love I Am. My Infinitely Present Being, thus all of Existence, consists only of the endless reach of unconditionally present, unrestrainable, *un-shut-off-able* Love.

This is what is agreed to when simply agreeing Existence exists.

Love's unwithholdable, un-deplete-able "giving forth" of Its Fullness is all that occurs throughout, or *as* all Existence. The One alive to Love right here, now, *is All-Inclusive Love Itself*. Never assume Love is limited to a human "heart center," which could be either open or closed.

Love is All.

Never assume it's possible to withhold Love, dispense or channel Love, or block the *absolute fullness* of Love from being all Presence. How could it be, when Love is *This Very All-Inclusive Being*, and it's impossible to withhold This Being?

In what may appear as the passage of a billion years, there is not a moment, not a single circumstance when Love, this unwithholdable Magnificence, is not the only Presence, the only Life, being absolute "total coverage" as All That Is.

Love *being* is all that ever "happens."

———•———

Perhaps a thought has come, "This may all be true of Existence or Consciousness, but it seems abstract. What's this got to do with my daily affairs, my world?"

One who is busy *being* pure Conscious Love, *the Substance that is all Existence*, leaves no secondary, non-being mentality to pollute one's universe with forms of "not": not-Love, not-Intelligence, im-Perfection, and dis-Ease which appear to come from acting as un-Consciousness.

As your entire universe seems to exist as *thought* in Consciousness, where do you identify? Are you an ignore-ant, powerless state of mis-taken beliefs based on sensing—full of problems, lacks, condemnation of "others," disease, sin, fear, and age—with death as a final reward?

The Truth is, You *are being* Pure Conscious Substance, whose perfect All-Inclusive Presence is the only Perceiver of all things, and has nothing *present* contrary to Its Perfect Love, *ever*.

General human belief would have one blindly *accept* what five senses and time seem to say, and then go judging and conducting one's affairs entirely on that basis, according to their dictates. It is to have *what is-not*, negation, not-the-Divine, as one's premise—and what is in the premise must appear in the "conclusion." It completely ignores Existence, Divine Love, or *What Really Is*. It is cut off from Reality, Intelligence, *Present Power*.

Are *you* starting with what time-senses (in other words un-Con-sciousness) would say, and dreaming there is a separate world and universe "out there" full of trouble? Or are You *awake*—not tolerating any dreaming by *being* what is true, actually *existent* and functioning? Do You start as the Present Power You are; do You insist on being that perfect Substance called pure Love which has only a perfect Existence? Only when starting thus is the premise True, Perfect, Good.

Don't "see" by way of eyes. Behold via Pure *Aliveness*, which is changelessly all Presence *being*. When Conscious Aliveness "beholds" Its own Presence, which *is* All Existence, It sees only Completeness and Perfection. Aliveness knows only the simple *ease* with which Its Perfec-tion is already All Presence. There is no other being present or conscious to have any contrary "experience."

Conscious Aliveness has no choice but to "see" or perceive only in terms of Its Wholeness and Purity or *Beauty*, inclusive of all things. The things or ideas Conscious Aliveness includes can't resist being seen as perfect, for mere things or ideas do not have minds with which to resist. This is the only "way" all of All is present—eternally.

All is not a word. All is not a place. All is the *Infinitely Alive Presence* here, now. To It, there is no sense of physicality nor a finite mentality present anywhere. To know the true nature of Existence or *All*, ask only the Infinite Aliveness You are. Pure Aliveness is the only One that can know All because It alone is *what* All is. All Aliveness "feels" is Harmony; the *smoothness* of Its own endless Oneness.

All's Aliveness is actively being All Presence *now*, with nothing standing in the way of Its fully being Itself. All is alive all-out, operating at full blast, *incapable of withholding any of Itself* throughout All, as All.

Is it asking too much of Your Self to be this All, especially since Your Being *already is* All?

Who is this All-You that is so *Totally Alive*, so purely *Present only*, that any body or item appearing within Your Presence instantly loses any seeming time-related vestiges of age, stress, or decay? Like a character in a sci-fi movie, such conditions appear to evaporate from it, leaving only the ideal thought-form it always *is*—ageless, disease-free and permanently perfect.

Things can't resist, for there's no solidity to them, nothing material there *to* resist—only *thoughts or ideas* in Perfect Substance, Alive Timelessness. No thing or idea can manifest age any more than any other idea—just as the letters of the alphabet, the figure four, or Mickey Mouse or Donald Duck don't age. You don't try to think anything; things unavoidably appear this way. You can't force this Perfect Power to "work," for It already, changelessly *is*. It is being *Itself*, and nothing else is.

You are not fooled by any "improved appearance," which would be barely worth mentioning, hardly worth a yawn—for even that form is finite and not You, not the *Real*. Your Entire Being is so "flooded" as *Present Aliveness*, so enthralled as Life Itself, You may not even notice.

You might ask, "When is this *really* going to get exciting? When am I going to get down to business and be *all* of My Infinite Self?" It's because You know You already fully *are* Your Self, and all of You is *Present Now*. Ask Your Self such questions constantly. Be *alive* as the Answer. This is staying "busy" as Perfect Existence, truly all that is.

———•———

20

CONSCIOUSNESS CANNOT
IGNORE ITS OWN PRESENCE

As Consciousness' own presence is absolutely *all* Presence, all that exists, there can be no such thing as ignorance of It. There is no other, nothing else, to be ignorant.

The cognizance that Consciousness has of Its Being is absolute. It cannot *be all that is being,* and simultaneously avoid Itself.

Can All turn Its back on Itself? It is ridiculous on the face of it. Equally, All can't assume anything, because there is nothing in addition to All that It could assume. It is *One.*

As the One Conscious Being is Omnipresence, is *All*—to have a lesser identity, or even the slightest state of ignorance is impossible, though the term "ignorance" has often been used in clarifying the utter non-existence of a so-called finite "sense-mind."

In *Omnipresence,* a vacuity of any type is un-occur-able.

What relevance has this?

It is sometimes said the quality of one's consciousness determines the quality of one's world. As Pure Conscious Being Itself is *All*, and leaves no absence of Itself, thus nothing to be impure or imperfect, how good a "quality" is that? What could need improving? Consciousness, All, has no finite qualities, but is unqualified Perfection.

Only to a *would-be* state of sense-dream does there appear to be disharmony, confusion, lack and disease. If one mistakenly starts with the not-ness of finite human sense, then ignorance and its effects are assumed to be present, a real condition that must be suffered.

Unconditionally Present Consciousness, which is "solid" Intelligence, leaves no ignorance of Itself—thus there can be no effects thereof! One *must* identify or start as Omnipresent Consciousness and not finite sense, for only Consciousness is present in the first place. Moreover, It Itself, is the only One present to do all "starting"!

While it may seem some of these points have been repeated excessively, they are reiterated because of the depth of what they mean.

Consciousness, Omnipresence, never vacates Its changeless, endless Absoluteness. The fact that there is only Consciousness leaves only Perfect Wholeness and Completeness—Life acutely, cleanly, alive to Its Perfection "everywhere" *forever*. Nothing has to be done to make this Perfect Life, Your Real Life, be all that is present and operative *now*. It is already functioning; otherwise You wouldn't *be*.

As Present Consciousness never is other than *One*—the use of the words "look out from," or "start as" does not mean there is a secondary, personal consciousness that can first ignore, then start as, or otherwise push the right button.

Where *One is*, there is no other to do anything "as."

To "start correctly" with Consciousness is to be clear there is no *second* one to start either correctly or incorrectly with Consciousness. There isn't even a "sense-mind" *precluded* by Consciousness. There is only Consciousness *Itself*—Self-Clarity, Self-Honesty, Self-Integrity.

To even use a term "start" with Consciousness implies there could be a stop. It implies All could separate from All and then have to return to All. Nice trick, *if* it could be done. Not even God can do that. There is no moment when the Absolute One Itself is not *all* of I, the *only* I.

So don't say *you* have to be honest with Consciousness, that you have to "start as" or "look out from" correctly. Consciousness *Itself* cannot fail to be. Only this is what is honestly being. Only this is being honest.

The three preceding paragraphs are among the simplest, yet most important you will read in this book.

If one were to speak on a finite basis, it appears some strive so sincerely to reach a "higher Self" or "God." They may *say* God, Mind, or Consciousness is All, but make mental effort to connect with Its Omnipresence; or try to *become* more conscious, and thus *overcome* human weaknesses. No! There are no such separate identities in the first place.

One is just as sincere, but from the opposite "viewpoint." Starting on the basis of what *Consciousness is to Itself*, It unfailingly is all Presence and all-inclusive of all *now*. One beholds the utter impossibility of there being a wait for *Now* to be, and how effortless it is for Being's Total Presence to always be all-Present.

Consciousness, Omnipresence, or "God" is certain of Its Absolute-ness simply by virtue of the fact that Being is now being! Does Existence depend on a person thinking It, otherwise It won't be? If God, All-Being, weren't certain of Itself and depended on a thinking "mind" or intellect to also know It, what kind of *Omnipotence* would It be? What good would It be, and who would want It?

Is Being having to think all the right things about Being before Being will be the Total Presence and Power that Being is? How good a job is *Being* doing at starting with the allness of Being? And how immediately available is all of Being *to Being*? Is there another? No! Is there any gap between Being's Absolute Presence and Being's Life—*all Life*? The only "job" for Eternity is to joy in the fact that Being, One, All, is perfectly, undeviatingly *Present*.

There is only the unworried, un-intellectual *freedom* that Pure Aware Being is. Can brakes be put on Existence, Being? Can It be kept from being permanently all Presence?

Are you trying to think the answer to this, or are you at ease in the certainty of *being* the answer?

Consciously "immerse" yourself in *Alive Being* which never comes to an end of Its *Present-ness*. Revel in the fact that Life Itself never splits off from this Indivisible Presence. Luxuriate in the completely carefree *ease* with which Existence *is*. One never is going off in a "spiritual daze," but is specifically, vitally alive as this Fact.

------ ◆ ------

The question might seem to persist, "As Existence, the Conscious Present, truly is *all that is present,* then where could finite sense, time, duality, and human suffering even *seem* to come from, even if seen as illusion or dream? As only the One Infinite is present, then *where* would the 'cause' itself be that supposedly causes a seeming second finite state to occur?"

The "cause" of so-called finite sense or dream never can be found.

It doesn't *have* its own cause. Why?

The One, All-Inclusive Consciousness being present here, now, is absolutely all that is present, existent.

Consciousness is the Only One conscious for all Existence.

As Consciousness, you are the Only One. Oneness is what you are. So when *you* are not being the *Oneness* you are, then *you* would be all there is to duality. As the All-Inclusive One, the instant your attention seems to split off from your own Pure Being—*that* would be the very startup and "cause" of all not-being.

As the Only One, the only seeming "cause" of time and finity would be when *you* first "look away" from your Timeless Infinity. You ignore your own Pure Now, What Really Is Being, and try to function as a mentality, as five senses and time, or what-really-is-not-being. It seems you leave Awakeness and start to dream.

The reason for never being able to find a separate cause of time, or a finite "dream-world," is that the mentality looking for the "cause" is always looking for something apart from itself. When all along, *that very mentality* would be its very, only "cause"!

The very act of thinking and sensing, looking "out there" for a cause apart from oneself, would involve time. So instead of consciously being clear, silent *Now—One's True Timeless Identity*—one is enacting the very startup of a would-be second "time-identity."

The human sense-dream is not an entity in and of itself. It does not have its own presence. It is not *any* kind of presence. Its entire operation would depend on the seeming "ignore-ance" of What Is Present, one's own Pure Now-Consciousness which is truly *All That Is*.

The reason finite sense or dream could not be going on by itself, "off there," apart from you, having its own presence, is that *Your Presence* is all there is. There is not a pre-existing, secondary dream state "off there" somewhere with its own presence, that attention goes *out to*, for only Being has Presence. If you had a dream last night, did that dream exist, or have its own presence, *before* you fell asleep? No.

Being specifically, totally alive to the Conscious Now that *I Am*, to Pure Awakeness *only*, leaves only *One*. It is Single-Mindedness, Self-Interest. It leaves no second, superimposed state of dream-thought, no *assumed* identity, chasing around in time, trying to act as non-presence. It leaves nothing added to *Am*; no add-Am, Adam, or man-sense.

Again, all *seeming* human limitations never would be physical or material conditions—but just an assumed, secondary state of *dream-thought*. The instant *you* stop thinking in such terms, it "evaporates," for you are the Only One conscious and present, the only Substance, for all of Existence. Finite time-sense can't think on its own because *it doesn't exist on its own*. It, of itself, has no conscious existence. Only You do.

Again, however, Omnipresent Being, the One All-Self, never *actually* ignores Its Allness, regardless of how things seem. There is nowhere All could leave Itself for, nowhere All Itself isn't changelessly present. The Absolute One leaves no secondary "you" that could get It wrong or even get It right. That is the point of this chapter.

Consciousness can't fail to be consciously present where Consciousness is present—and there is nowhere It is not present! Divine Mind never is blind to Its own Being.

While time-sense is seen as non-present, one never takes on any resentment toward it. *One* never denies or condemns time-sense, tries to destroy it, boss it around, or even see it positively.

To take on such an attitude is to continue assuming such a thing is present. It is to put up a seeming "mental wall" in what *appears* as one's everyday affairs. It's like the opposite of looking out through rose-colored glasses. To carry any mistrust, frustration, or guilt over *seeming* finite sense would be to needlessly "color" or imbue one's universe with those very seeming qualities.

The would-be "sense-mind" isn't *bad*. It simply isn't. To be bad, it would have to exist.

One has no choice but to start with, stay with, or *be* Ever-Present Conscious Aliveness. One thus is functioning as the Single Power of Infinite Being, non-dualistic Pure Awareness, Perfect Perception, which knows only Itself, as *this* Aliveness.

This isn't a mere theory, not a *strategy*. It's the only way Life *is*.

———•———

In clarifying what appears as finite experience, reference has been made to what might seem to be three "realms." First is the Infinite, Pure Being, which is all that *really* is.

Two aspects of *would-be* finite experience were also discussed—seen as either physical-finite or mental-finite. But what appears as all finite human experience has been shown to be entirely "mental," or inseparable from thought. There really is no physical world "out there" that is separate from thought. There never was.

So what began as three so-called "realms" would now be down to two: the Infinite (again, all that *really* is), and a seeming mental state of *thought* that moves in time, non-being.

What this means, again, is that the only "stuff" comprising all would-be human suffering and shortcomings never is a lot of physical conditions—only a mistaken state of *thought*! It would be just an assumption—that *what-never-is-present* can pretend to be present as these conditions!

If one mistakenly starts with that seeming finite state, one always tries to account for it, and has to deal with it on its terms. Truth shows that Pure Consciousness truly is all that *is* present—and never is co-present with another state. This Infinite Realm, the I Am Self, is boundless, measureless, with no finite appearance, no limits, no lacks or ignorant tendencies at all. Where I Alone Am (and there is nowhere I Am not), no ignorant assumption based on time-sense can also *be* or operate.

Right now, be consciously, specifically, *totally* alive as Infinite Conscious Aliveness *only*. Give all attention to Present Being *only*. One cannot try to think It. Be consciously alive as It. *Be It*.

Is there a limited supply, an end of Your Endlessly Alive Being? *Nowhere* does Infinite Being split off and become something not Itself. Nothing can plunk itself down and co-exist, or reach in Here and yank Your Being from being.

Now, from Here, as this utterly single Pure Aliveness, the *only* time a "secondary" state—one of finite sense or human limitation—would have any *seeming* presence again, is when attention is turned *away* from this Infinite Being You *are*. In effect, it seems one's Infinite Aliveness, the only Presence or Power, is ignored, and some of one's Presence is "given" to a seeming finite state of thinking and sensing, which has no true presence on its own.

That would be the very "creation" of it, because you are all the Presence there is.

When you are one hundred percent busy being Present Being *only*, there is only One that is present. No Presence, Life, is being given to a would-be secondary "not-mind" or time dream. All there would be to a "secondary" mind is the ignoring of Being, and that ignoring has stopped.

Finite sense or dream *pretends* to have presence only when you first "fall asleep," or "let go of" Ever-Present Absolute Consciousness, Full Awakeness. Even when seemingly asleep to Your Self, Your Presence never fails to be present, so dream *seems* to use Your Presence. It would have to use Your Life, Your Existence, for it has none of its own.

"This is crazy," the same *would-be* finite thinking may instantly try to say. "Even when giving all attention to Pure Consciousness, to *Now*, the finite 'sense-mind' and time are still there. Even though I know it's only 'mental,' I still appear to see what goes on in the mind."

Oh? *Who* still sees what appears to go on in the mind?

That all would be *its* assumption. That would be still starting with finite sensing and thinking, with what appears to be form, instead of the Formless—Undimensional Aliveness *being*. It would be still there only to *human thinking*, only to an un-awake "*mind*" *itself*—which would be right back operating in time *as* an ignore-ant finite "mind." Only a finite sensing "mind" would say it still sees itself.

Infinite Aliveness never is saying it. Infinite Aliveness never is seeing it.

Infinite Aliveness is what You are. Stick with Aliveness.

Starting as Infinite Aliveness, and "sticking" absolutely *as* It, there is not a secondary mental realm present, while You are "busy" being the Infinite One. There never has been.

Infinite Aliveness, Being's Oneness, can't really separate from Itself. However, the instant one *seems* to put attention "out there," one no longer is Single, but would have ignored or mentally gone out from the Self to some thing "out there" in thought (and it's only thought). In-stantly, there would appear to be duality; the Infinite One That Is *and* a second entity. One would be *mentally creating* a sense of separation and dimension from One's Self. It never would be physical separation, only a mental *sense* of separation.

The instant you assume some thing has objective form, "out there," as separate from the One Consciousness—who is it that's separate? The thing is not separate. *You are*. As you are the Only One, you are the only one there is *to be* separate, even if only seemingly. By assuming there is something having objective form, "out there," it seems you have "left" the Infinity, the *Oneness* of your own Total Being and are now two. It seems you are looking into a secondary, illusory state of finite thought that has the *appearance* of separate forms, but which never are really separate. You are the only one that could give it reality.

Right *there*, that seeming split of attention or mental separation from the *Infinite One* is what seems to "allow" or "create" the would-be secondary mind. This seeming secondary mental state is what human ignorance always has mistakenly assumed was physical space and time—but which really would be only "mental." Because it has an *illusory appearance* of being physical, separate, and spatial, human thinking assumes its entire universe is physically separate and spatial, and has tried to account for it on that basis. All along, the whole thing would be only "mental," or inseparable from thought.

The seeming stellar universe is not due to a big bang. It's not a material explosion moving outward through physical space, for *all is Consciousness*. The seeming "spatial universe" would be a matter of *mentally* moving outward—ignoring, or moving in thought away from the Infinity of Self, the Immediacy of *Undimensional Being*. It would be a *mental dream* of space, dimension and time, of separateness. There simply is no other explanation for the "creation" of a universe, for that very dream-thought would be all there is *to* that universe.

Even though pictures of separateness may continue to appear, one gives no attention to them, but "stays busy" as the inseparable Oneness of Pure Aliveness. The thought in terms of another mind would be all there is *to* another mind. When you stop insisting you are conscious of it (because as Pure Infinity, *You* never really are conscious of it), it stops. It has no consciousness of its own. Finite, sensed time-experience *can't* be what Your Infinite Presence is really conscious of. How is it possible to be conscious of what isn't even present?

———•———

There really, truly is only the Absolute, which never fails to be Itself, be All. It precludes there being another that can sometimes be It, or fail to be It. This is Truth. So then why all the discussion of the *seeming* tendency to ignore the One Presence—when actually, Consciousness cannot ignore Its own Presence? It would seem this book is contradicting itself.

Here is a book that is stating the Absolute—*but that book appears to be in a relative setting*, a seeming finite realm of not One, but many; a realm of duality and time.

Because one appears to be inundated with sense-phenomena in this relative setting, it is easy to still unwittingly be driven by the five senses, time and duality. It also is easy to assume that merely by intellectually agreeing with statements of the Absolute, one is being as Absolute as can be "at this stage of the game." That is *not* as Absolute as one can be, even right here and now. One need not be subject to time's would-be problems—even while not yet living one hundred percent Absolutely.

If one operates as a "sensing mind," the mind would look outside itself, and point to time as the culprit for all of one's difficulties. It is assumed time is "out there," apart from the "sense-mind," and that one is powerless in the face of time. This chapter shows that the very ignoring of Being and operating as a "sense-mind" *is* time itself—and one can indeed "do something about it" by no longer ignoring Being. If time *were* an independent force on its own, then there would be two states: Timelessness and time—thus the One, the Absolute, would not truly be One. In fact, It *is* One.

Of course, in the Absolute, communication is unnecessary, impossible; words are non-existent. But *within what appears to be a relative setting,* this seems the most intelligent way to state or present the Absolute. The Absolute is a synonym for Infinite Intelligence Itself, which certainly has nothing relative within Itself. However, thanks to Its being intelligent, the Intelligent One always can do what appears to be intelligent—even under the circumstances of a seeming relative situation.

Again, in Reality, Consciousness' own Endlessness actually leaves no possibility of a start with anything besides Itself.

All can't ignore Itself when there is nothing besides Itself. There is no other possible experience that All could take on or have.

Do you just glibly, hazily agree, or are you consciously certain?

Do not go away from these pages saying, "Okay, Consciousness is all. The Present is all that is present. *But,* when I seem to ignore It, that's when all the trouble starts up."

No! That is not what is meant by this chapter.

The Fact that Consciousness, the Present Itself, *never can refuse to be absolutely all that is present* means no other, lesser state is possible, ever. There is no second, part-time consciousness to do any ignoring or dreaming, ever. Not even *seemingly.* Don't say, "Okay, now I know how to work correctly." No. There is no separate self to work either correctly or incorrectly. There is only Unstoppable Omnipresent Consciousness, Self-Inescapable *All.*

Where Being is (and there is nowhere Being is not), it is impossible for the Being I Am to *be,* and also avoid My Presence right where I Am.

The undeviating capacity to know only Perfection, to perceive only perfectly, is the changeless status of all Being, which is *this* Alive Being. It can only be the One I Am, I Myself that is knowing this; otherwise My Absoluteness would not be Absolute.

21

THE PRESENT IS *ALL* THAT IS PRESENT

To say the Present is absolutely all that is present is a simple enough statement. Yet the significance of it is so enormous, it's important to repeat why it's true.

There simply is no point existent where the Present is not being present. What's more, the Present has no borderline; there is no place where the Present comes to an end—and nowhere does a state of what-isn't-present begin. What-isn't-present can't begin or exist anywhere because *it isn't present*!

There is *only* the Present. The Present is *endlessly* present.

This is not belaboring a point, because staying consistent with this undeniable Truth means there is absolutely no time.

It's not nearly enough to say there is no time *in the Present*. The Present being everywhere present means time *never began*.

There is no way for time, what-isn't-present, to ever have gotten its foot in the door, for only the Present can be present.

Your consciousness of this Present Reality, *Your Consciousness which is Present Reality*, has just "exploded" the myth of time. Actually, nothing has been exploded, for in Your Absolute *Being*, time never started.

To ignorant thinking based on would-be time-senses, this of course sounds impossible, beyond crazy. *To Your Present Awareness* it is simple, Self-Obvious Truth. Only Present Awareness is present, not such thinking. Try to make the Present *not* be totally present.

The fact that the Omnipresent Present precludes all time means *It precludes all that appears to have come forth in time.*

The Present precludes the entirety of what appears as finite experience, whether called physical or mental. It completely rules out the appearance of all appearances! No, there isn't even a "dream," because to dream also would take time—of which there is none.

It isn't that a Present, something apart from You, precludes all time.

Your Present Being precludes all time!

Yet you haven't precluded yourself because *the Present is what You are*. You are still right here, perfectly, calmly and serenely—as Present Awareness *being*. It is the Present Itself that makes the statement, "The Present is All."

To the Changeless All-Present Self, there never is a split second of not-Its-Present-ness—not a moment of time, age, or decay. The One All-Present Being has *pre-empted* the entirety of it, even as illusion.

This is clear only to One who is *being* Present Reality Itself, as the clear Stillness that Pure Consciousness *is*. And to repeat, One *must* "start with" or *be* the Present, for that Present Itself is the only One that is present and conscious to be anything.

To Changeless Present Being, the statement that time never began is not shocking. It is not a breakthrough, not a new paradigm. The Present, being Absolute, has no reference point for time whatsoever—so It can't even know time doesn't exist.

One cannot even ask, "Why didn't I see this before?" There is no before. There is *only* the Present.

———•———

It is not *true* to say the Present and time are mutually exclusive. It is not enough to admit there is no time in the Present—but to still assume the two states co-exist. The utter, total Presence of the Present leaves no possibility of even a *notion* of time, let alone the actuality of time having begun to operate anywhere. It really can't even be said time is precluded, for that would imply time had some status, although an invalid one. As the Present is *Absolute*, not even that is possible.

Not only is time not a "something." Time is not even a "nothing."

The *would-be* finite intellect may try to scream to the contrary, "No time? No creation? Yeah, right. What about this book? It takes time to read it. If there never has been time, how did all this even *seem* to get here? This Present stuff has gone too far. Who cares if it's true in 'Infinite Reality.' It's too abstract to be practical—just philosophical fast-talk."

To consider such doubts or questions as valid would be to ignore the *Now* that One's own Awareness *is*, and which alone is present. Such disagreement doesn't come from *You*, from Conscious Intelligence, but would be due to mistakenly starting with the not-ness or darkness of *never present* time-sense. Only a state of conditioned human sensing and thinking based on time that *never is* would ask such questions. They absurdly imply that some of the Absolute Present could be uprooted by *that which never has been present.*

The never-present "sense-mind" would attempt to put Ever-Present Life, the One *I Am*, on trial—when it itself is a fraud. It would be like saying that what doesn't even exist has the power to kick Existence out of Its own Existence!

If one mistakenly starts with "time," what-isn't-being, and tries to account for it, one mistakenly assumes that what-isn't-being exists along with Being—as some sort of opposite. But there is no possibility of any not-Being because it's just that—*not being!* There is only Being's endless Total Presence, Its specific Allness. There aren't two states. Only Being is. And only by *being* Pure Aware Being, and not a thinking mentality, is this clear.

This is why "humanity"—with all the brilliant thinkers it appears to have produced in philosophy, science and religion—never has come up with *one,* simple, clear-cut, universally acceptable, and irrefutably *true* explanation for a beginning of time, for a beginning of creation.

In the Present—and it is always the Present—time never began!

There is no explanation! The very question of when or how time began *erroneously implies it did begin.* It did not!

When is the Present not everywhere *present*? Never!

As only the Present is present, then has there even been a time past in which there were some mistaken human thinkers? No.

Again, only if one mistakenly starts with "time," is one forced to try to account for it. But to do that, one would first have to start as ignorance itself—ignoring the Absoluteness of *Present* All-Inclusive Consciousness, Existence Itself, *the only One existent.*

Yet who is there to do such a thing, *the Present Itself being the only One present?*

These aren't just so many philosophical fine points written by a person, referring to "a" Present. It is *I,* the One All-Inclusive Present, "talking" *Now* as the entirety of Existence. This is Reality Itself, absolutely all that is present, speaking as the Allness I Am!

The answer to the question, "What is the Present to *Itself*, to Its own *Pure Now?*" is also the answer to, "What is All?" and "Who am I?"

———•———

You now are "at rock bottom." The boundless bedrock of *Ever-Present* Eternal Life is specifically being You now. Yet this boundless Present-ness, Your Presence, is not a bottom of anything. It is *All.*

There is no further to go because there is nowhere else *to* go. In fact there is no going—only gloriously effortless *Being.*

You now are consciously alive as the Endless, Entirely Present One which co-exists with nothing besides Itself. It's not that You are out beyond the limits of a physical realm of time. Your Boundless Presence is so Absolute, You completely *preclude* a physical realm, or even a mental realm to be beyond!

This is the One I *Am.*

I Am borderless Life. I Am the dateless, calendar-less *Now.* This thrilling Ever-Present Freedom I Am is not confined between a *was* and a *will be*, for they never happen. *Only I Am.* In comparison to this Freedom I Am *now tasting*, actually *alive as*—to merely think of eternity would be a boring concept.

This Omni-*Present* Awareness I Am is the only "Foundation." I Am neither on, nor above, an earth or universe formed by time. The Infinite Aliveness I Am is so preclusive of all time-forms, so completely free of such limitations, It defies description. Because My Present Consciousness never is earthbound, or even universe-bound, I forever "float" as My own *Alive Boundlessness*, never resting on anything, but joying in the *never-ending-ness* of My Inestimable Presence.

It is Unconfinable Allness that is conscious here, now—not here in a place, but as Presently Alive Infinity. The unattached *All* I Am is forever incapable of coming in contact with anything besides My own Unlimitedness. Yet I Am anchored, infinitely "stable" in My endless *Allness.*

To this Aware Allness I Am, My Present Infinity is not a furthest point. My own Being is not a "secret place of the most high." The All that I Ever-Presently Am leaves no place to go on a journey, no spiritual path, no end. I never left this unchartable *All-Now* that I Am.

As My Now is *the entirety of Presence*—there is nothing besides that I could leave Now *for*—there is only the Alive Now I Am.

———•———

As there is only the Present I Am, it means All exists only "right this instant."

I Am not a Present that has been at a previous time, because as there is only the Present I Am, there is no previous time!

Absolutely all there is, is the *fresh*, new, thrilling Aliveness of being *just-now* present!

This Omni-*Present* Life I Am cannot grow old, for My Absolute Present-ness leaves no oldness that could enter My Present-ness. It's not that I Am immune to age. Age does not occur to be immune to. All there is, is un-hold-back-able *Present Life*—the fresh Purity I have no choice but to *be*.

The fabled fountain of youth is not out in a material world. There is no material world it could be out in. It is not a fountain of physical youth, as a means of overcoming physical age. The only "fountain" that exists is the spontaneity with which *all* Aliveness, *all* Life, is unwithholdably *Present Now*. I Am an endlessly Self-Supplied fountain of unrestrainable Vitality—sparkling clean and fresh "forever."

This Freshly Present Life I Am doesn't *occupy* an All. *I Am* All!

I can "drink" of this Fresh Aliveness I Am as much as I want and never, never come to an end of It. I Am un-shut-off-able, un-go-away-able.

This is the very Substance, the only Substance in which the entire universe is. I Am the only Substance *present*. All eternally exists Here.

What is true of the Aliveness I Am as I "start Here" with only My Present-ness and endlessly behold only "more and more" of My eternally *Present* Aliveness?

As the Present Itself, I cannot die. I never vacate Being for a state of death, non-being—for the Endless Presence of My Being leaves nowhere else to vacate *to*. This Present Awareness I Am is not a product of biology; I never was born in never-present time. *I Am*, eternally.

I Am not being present for *an* eternity that is separate from I. I Am Eternity. I Am It.

The Eternity I Am is not countless eons old, not a long span of dead time. I Am the absence of time. The only way Eternal Life can be present is *as the Present I Am, this Consciously Alive Changeless Presence*. Nowhere else can Eternity *be*. Eternity is Timelessness, but always as *Presently Alive Being*. Just as *I* cannot be separated from *Am*, Eternity is inseparable from the Present.

Not a bit of Eternal Life lies ahead, awaiting. All of Eternity is *Now*, which is *I* as I Ever-Presently Am. This Eternal Present-ness I Am is *all* the I that is; the only One *present* to be reading this now.

As the *Present is all*, then *all is present*. There is nothing more to come.

This gentle, unfailing Presence I Am, alive here, *now*, is absolutely "as far as it goes." There is no dramatic finale still to come; no last curtain to drop; no veil of darkness to be raised.

The "trap" would be to assume there is something more to come in time, beyond the immediacy of My Being. It would do nothing but thrust one into time, non-being.

There is no great upheaval that must come about in time—for as only I Am, there is no time. There can be no sign to come in a would-be finite world, substantiating that My Divine Life is indeed All. There can be no signal from somewhere else, for there is nowhere besides *Now*.

Not only did time or creation never begin—Existence, the Divine Present I Am, never *began* to be. The Present Reality I Am isn't present as a result of a past. Being everywhere *present*, I leave no past from which I could have come. It means Existence never was *caused*.

The would-be finite intellect attempts to impose its entirely false reasoning based on sensing, time, cause and effect, on My Presence's *Absolute Being* and demands, "*When* did Existence or Being get here? What *caused* Existence or Being to be?"

Typical of its ignorance, finite reasoning based on sensing and time pompously assumes Existence must have had a cause that occurred in time, that-which-never-has-existed. Yet such finite sense-thinking itself *never has been present* in order to know the first thing about existing!

The only intelligent answer is, Life doesn't work that way.

There is only the Existence or Life that *is*—the One Changelessly Present Reality. If Life weren't this, It couldn't *be*. Existence has no origin in time. If Existence *did* have a cause, that would mean there was a time when It wasn't present. What could exist to cause Existence if there is no existence? Do you say God? If so, God had to already exist or be in Existence to do it.

There is no cause for Existence because Existence never *began* to be.

Existence never became existent, just as God never *became* God.

Existence *is*. God *is*. Consciousness or Life *is*, preclusive of time. It never was "caused." To say there is a cause or reason for Existence would be like saying *there is a reason for God*. That would mean something greater than God saw fit to bring God into being; that God Itself is not All, which is impossible. Existence, or God, is changelessly at the standpoint of Perfect *Is*. The All-Inclusive Consciousness *being You now* is serenely, effortlessly *being* this Is-ness, regardless of how an intellect may *seem* to react.

The fact that there is no time means there is no evolution or pro-gression in I Am, in All, in Existence. Evolution and progression would *appear* to move in time—from a past that is-not-anymore into a future that is-not-yet. That makes evolution forever a state of *that-which-is-not*. What appears to the senses as evolution, creation, would be a *seeming* state, a finite dream of ongoing imperfection, of never-being-there-yet. It is completely precluded by Omni-*Present* Perfection.

———•———

As there is only the Present Being I Am, I leave no place for a time process called karma or reincarnation to operate. *Omnipresence* simply cannot be subject to, or allow for, "karma"—and there honestly is no other being present or alive. Where changelessly *I Am All*, there is no not-I Am. It means no time-process called karma could have ever begun, nor could there be anyone held in bondage.

How could Omnipresent Being reincarnate? Where would It go that It isn't present already? Omnipresence can't be guilty of sins of commis-sion or of omission. Its own Selfhood is all that exists—leaving nothing besides Itself that It could commit or omit. Nor is there another to judge Omnipresence, or make It "pay."

As absolutely all Presence is taken up by *the Pure Present I Am*, where could there also be present any reincarnated old souls? What part of the Omnipresent Present could be set aside to maintain a status of oldness? The Pure *Now* that all Life *is*, never smugly considers Itself an old soul, and there is no other. Only *Alive Now* is.

In *Now*, there are no records kept—and it is *always* Now, "every-where."

The fact that Now-Consciousness, Spirit Itself, *is the entirety of Presence*, leaves no others needing to become spiritual. It's the same as God's own Allness leaving no other to be a child of God. Or do you have the conceit to say you have power to set aside *God's Allness*, Omnipresence, so a "you" can be a child?

Do you realize what it would mean if you *were* to assume that Changeless Present Reality was not All, and that time and karma had begun? Then *you alone* would be carrying the burden and debts of not only one so-called soul, but of *all* souls.

The entire weight of all so-called karma, all mistakes, all debts, and all struggling souls could appear to occur in only *one* place—in the finite dream posing as "your" personal "sense-mind." Such a dream never would be experienced by others, for all "others" appear only in the same one sense-dream that you claim *you* have. Yet starting with the Awake Present I Am and not time-sense, who's dreaming? No one.

The Present You are is *so absolutely Good*, It precludes a past to have to learn from, or a future in which to apply learning. Can one, half-asleep, assume this is just another theory, just sensationalizing in order to get attention? Again, try to make the Present *not* be all present.

Even if one seems to have believed in time or reincarnation, actually Your Present Self never has accepted any such thing—for none of it has occurred. As the One Changeless Present *is* All, there is no "re" any-thing; no repetition, no review, no recycling of lives.

Is this too good, too simple to accept? To a would-be personal ego it's way too simple, for it leaves such an ego no status; it pulls the rug out from under it and its false pretense of always "getting there." It's not too simple for Now Itself. In fact, Pure Now *is* Simplicity Itself—and there is no other being present.

It's not that You are free *from* a past—there hasn't been one. This utter Purity of the *Now* I Am means All, including the entire universe, is completely Free. And *that* would be the very best karma—if there were such a thing. All there is, is that Free Omnipresence which leaves no past full of wrongs, no burden of anything to correct. Likewise, You never wait for an improved future thanks to the allness of the Present, for there never is anything but the allness of the Present!

Omnipresence had no original fall, thus no struggle of a climb. You never left Your Self, so no return is scheduled. Only the Unscheduled is—the spontaneously *Present* Life I Am, which is Joy Itself.

———•———

Do you realize that the Apocalypse or Armageddon as spoken of in the Bible and other teachings has already "occurred"?

An "Apocalypse" could not be a battle involving the destruction of a physical earth, materiality, or "evil," and an ultimate triumph of Good, for there never has been time or anything material. There is only *One Absolute Good*—pure Omnipresence. In *One* there are no opposites, thus no evil, no possibility of a battle.

In its true meaning then, an "Apocalypse" could refer only to the fact that Present Reality is absolutely all, perfect, and changelessly so. It could be called true *Goodness* Itself. It simply means the Present, Good (or God), never stopped being *all* of All. That's the genuine "triumph" of Good—the fact that there is *only* Goodness—and never anything besides Itself to triumph over.

There is nothing else an "Apocalypse" could be, because *only the Present is*.

In a so-called modern interpretation, an "Apocalypse" has been said to mean destruction *by way of* the atom. Even in this newer version, it could only mean destruction *of* the atom. The would-be, constantly moving atom depends entirely on time to pretend its presence. The Absolute Present "destroys" it, for in the Absolute there is no time, hence no atom.

"What?" the thought may come. "No atom? That's stretching the point too far. Without the atom there would be nothing."

No. The atom *is* nothing. Nothing about the so-called time-based atom *is*. Only Divine Is, is.

What mind would try to justify an atom? Divine Intelligent Being *which is*, or finite sense which is-not? In the Pure Present You are (and there is nowhere the Present is not present), there has been absolutely no time-accumulation; no sequence of events leading to an eventual extinction of humanity. Changeless Perfect Omnipresence has no outside influence—no cause-effect chain of events dictating to It how Its Life is going to be. Life isn't *going* to be anything. Life *is*.

The Present never is serious, weighty. It is light, at ease, for It is alone, pure, free—not in between a *was* or *will be*. Leave the "field" entirely to the effortless Present. Your Self's capacity to be effortless Harmony never is interfered with, for there is *only* Itself.

———•———

By the way, which came first, the chicken or the egg?

Trick question.

The question falsely implies the validity and operation of time. In Reality, Consciousness' changeless *Being* precludes all time—which leaves no possibility of one thing coming first and another coming later. In a *dream*, either one could appear first. If there were such things in Reality, both would be present "simultaneously," not as physical items developed in time, but as mere timeless *thoughts*, existing in the *Eternal Present* of Infinite Consciousness, Divine Mind.

If a tree falls in the forest and nobody is there to hear it, does it make a sound?

Hint: "Answer not a fool according to his folly."

The real issue isn't whether or not such an event occurs. The issue is entirely a matter of *identification*.

The issue is whether the one to whom the question is asked, identifies as Present Consciousness, Infinite Being's pure Isness—or with finite senses and time, is-not-ness. In Truth, there is no choice; the Absolute Present One being All, leaves no finite time-sense to identify with or *as*. Who is the only One present, existent, aware, alive? *Present Consciousness*. It completely precludes such a finite time-event, and any questions being asked about it in Reality. To attempt to answer the question on *its* terms would imply there is time. There isn't. That's the answer.

Even on a time basis, if one were to talk about it at all, it wouldn't be a *body* that witnesses or doesn't witness a tree falling. It would be the same *one* sense-dream that appears to both produce and witness the whole show, and only for itself. The one sense-dream or energy-reaction would *both* produce and observe the image of a body in a forest, and the falling tree, all sounds of crashing to a forest floor, as well as a babbling brook and chirping birds, plus the crisp clean air and fresh scent of pine. The supposedly separate "body" there to witness it wouldn't be separate at all, but also entirely a product of the same one sense-dream-fluid. It all would be one purely "mental" dream concoction, and none of it would be separate, solid objects.

On a finite basis, the "sense-mind" plays both roles—the observer and that which is observed. Even if, due to stubbing its toe on a rock, a *body* fell in the forest, it still wouldn't be a body that witnesses it, but the dream itself. The body is produced by the dream; the dream isn't produced by a body. It is impossible to have any finite occurrence apart from the "witnessing" of it by the finite dream "sense-mind," because they would be the same one.

Most importantly, none of it would be Real. Only a dream state of time-thought would pose a question about a tree falling; only it would care whether such an event occurred. Infinite Conscious Being couldn't care less because It doesn't really know about time events, or the finite limited form in which dream appears. Yet thanks to Consciousness being present, aware, the "event" can be seen for what it is—never-present dream sense, not Present Reality. Without Consciousness, which is Existence Itself, *nothing* would be, not even such a finite appearance.

All that counts is Present Consciousness.

————•————

Wouldn't you readily agree it is impossible for the Present, Your Being, to hold Itself back? Wouldn't you agree the Present never is held in abeyance; that the Present never is other than fully, completely "everywhere" present?

"Well, of course the Present can't be held back," comes the instant reply. "What an obvious, almost ridiculous question."

As all that is present is the Present, then where could there be such things as diseases, which would have needed not-the-Present (or time), to supposedly develop?

Does All-Present mean *all* or not? Are you judging by never-present time-senses, a fictional wispy state of thought that is-not, and letting *its dreaming* continue to appear as such conditions? Or are you busy being *What Is*, Absolute Present Reality, *Power Itself*? What is the Conscious Present Itself doing? Is there another being conscious, present?

The un-lapse-able Absolute Present completely precludes there being any negation of Itself called time. So there can be no negative *effects* of time.

As the Present specifically aware here, now, is *changelessly All Presence*, It has given up none of Its Absolute Being so a state of non-being, or *history* of national, religious, or racial animosity could operate.

In the absolutely present Present there is not *also* a past—thus no past tendency of personal greed or selfishness, wreaking environmental havoc on a planet. In un-set-aside-able Present Reality there is nothing carried over from a past, since no past has occurred. So nowhere in

Your All-Inclusive Present-ness is there a desire for drugs, which in turn would fuel a history of crime.

Do you say there are others out there with separate minds that are causing such problems? Is Omnipresent Awareness Itself claiming such separate minds exist? There are no separate minds anywhere—merely bodies, things, of which *this One Present* appears to be aware.

Are you willing to admit that because *this* very Awareness is functioning as *the Absolute Changeless Present*, all such "problems" *have had no presence, no history of existence whatsoever*—that no such thing ever really occurred?

In Truth, Present Reality never clears up problems, for no problems have ever been *present* to be cleared up! They merely cease being "imagined" by a mind that isn't.

It is *Your Self* that is the Absolute Present being spoken of. It means *Your* conscious certainty that only the Present is present *is all that is ever present*—all that is functioning!

The Absolute Present cannot deny Itself and feed a sense of *finite time-dreaming* in terms of human history and problems. It cannot avoid Itself—there is no void of Its Presence to which It could turn. There is nothing to come between the Present and Itself, It and All.

And the fact that the Present *Itself* is All, leaves no other that could choose or not choose to operate as this Present Perfection. It leaves nothing that must be changed before Perfection and Harmony *is*.

It is *I, Your Very Self*, stating all of this. It is *I* stating what is meant by the Present, stating what Consciousness is, wholly apart from things.

Being honest and consistent with what these terms mean or *are*, invariably shows that the Allness of the Present I Am is irrefutably, changelessly true—as *this* very Being. I Am Absolute Power for I Am all that is *present* to be Power. I never can be "used" for personal gain, for this One I Am leaves no second personal self to be in need. Starting and functioning Here is to "embrace" the whole of the universe in unchanging Perfection—not as a nice, well-meaning "intention," but as *present and unopposed Living Fact!*

Is this too radical? To whom?—*the Present being the only One present.*

22

TIME IS NOT CONTINUOUS

IF ONE WERE TO TALK ABOUT IT AT ALL, the phenomenon experienced as the human sense of "time" is not an unthinkably long, continuous stretch from past to future. Time is not an unbroken continuum. Time would be only *periodic*. What does that mean?

Ask yourself, and honestly answer a few questions. Which *are* you—Present Awareness, Now Itself—which *One* truly is? Or do you identify as a would-be "sense-mind" moving in time? Do you have "a" Present, "a" Now, but assume It is something separate, to which you can turn?

What is the difference? Why identify *as* Now, *as* Present Awareness? Of what value is It beyond the fact that It is already, changelessly true?

In Reality, the Awareness You are never asks such questions. There is no choice of whether to be Awareness, Being—or to be time, that which has no being. Being is all that can be. These questions are asked to make an important point.

If one mistakenly identifies as a finite, sensing body, the body is time-based. The so-called physical body-form appears to come forth in time and end in time. It is *one with* the passing of time, age, decay. So by mistakenly identifying with body, you automatically identify with time. Because it seems time is all one knows from the moment the body is "born," time enjoys a reputation of genuineness, and its validity is rarely questioned. Yet the entire *premise* that there is time in Your Ever-Present Life is false—thus all conclusions drawn from it are false.

If one mistakenly identifies as body, one assumes he is *the one in time*. One never sees that time merely seems to operate as a mentality that *is not*, and that One's Being never is in time.

If one assumes he is in time, a false belief of time is "built into" one's entire outlook or perception. It is as if, instead of wearing rose-colored glasses, you look through time-colored glasses. You think only in terms of time, not Present Reality; you unwittingly superimpose a time viewpoint upon *Timeless Being* and it seems everything is subject to time. This *gives* time a seeming validity it does not really have.

From this same false premise, it is also *assumed* that time extends incredibly far back into a past, and similarly extends into a future, without interruption. This is how time is mistakenly seen as being continuous, or a continuum. That is not even close to being true.

Many engaged in spiritual work, or even scientific work, readily agree the human sense of time is not real, but illusory. In what is called "outer space" for example, time might act nothing like the way it appears to on "earth." Yet even though one may *say* time is not real, it still seems to flow as always. One may intellectually know time is not real, but time is still usually the driving force in daily affairs. It is in the seeming flow of time that one essentially operates, though one may *say* Now, the Present, is All. The realm of time still seems to be the norm, or "home" to one.

As best one can, one may constantly turn attention to, or *be*, the Present, Pure Now-Awareness, to "get out of" a seemingly continuous flow of time. And that's the problem. If you identify first with time—and assume the Present, Now, is something *to which* you turn—then by your own definition, the Present must be apart from you. To turn *to* the Present, Now-Awareness, implies It is not what you *already are*—the Present is not "Home," not where you really live or *are being*. The allness of the Present is not really your "viewpoint."

It may seem one "gets better at it" and functions more *as* the Present, as Pure Amness. Yet to be honest, it still seems time has an extensive influence on one's living. Thinking, which seems essential in daily experience, moves in time. Sensing moves in time. Needless to say, time permeates every aspect of daily affairs. This "tug" of the senses and finite experience seems so constant, it's easy to assume that one co-exists with time, and that it has this ongoing, *continuous* flow.

In other words, it seems as if time were the primary, dominant, ongoing state—and that the Present was temporary; a brief, elusive state—one which you are being only *periodically*.

When all of the foregoing is experienced, what, *really*, is going on?

Is time really a *continuous* flow that you turn away from to be the Present? Are you being the Present only temporarily, for short periods?

Or is it exactly the reverse?

Is it that the Unchanging Present, Your Presence, is what is primary, permanent, *all*—and only when you turn away from the Present for a period, do you thereby seem to *create a period of time?*

There is all the difference in the world between the two.

———•———

What happens when the entire premise is reversed?

What's different when the basic premise is not that there is time, but that *only the Present is?* What's different when *starting as* the Present, as Pure Awareness—instead of mistakenly identifying as a state of human thinking that periodically turns to the Present?

Of course the Present must be One's starting point, the only premise, or basis of identification—*for the Absolute Present Itself is all that is present to be a premise.* From this true identification, or Truth, everything is seen in the correct light.

The Present is what You changelessly, unavoidably *are* as All-Inclusive Awareness *being*—not something You ever are turning to. The Present is literally "Permanent Home," *what You never fail to be.* In fact, it's impossible to *escape* being the Present! Why? *It's the Present Itself* being present and conscious here, now—never a "you."

Correctly identifying *as the Present,* you then see that the only seeming "turning" there could be, is that of having turned *away from* the Present You changelessly are. You no longer try to get out of time and struggle to stay in the Present. It's reversed. You see You unavoidably *are* the Present. It just seems you temporarily get into time. Your attention seems to "ignore" Your Timeless Being periodically, and that "mental wandering" seems to create a period of time.

Time didn't create you. You create time.

Time, not the Present, is what would be temporary or periodic.

Instantly, time is stripped of its false status as a relentless continuum. Time isn't all-powerful, holding all the cards, controlling you in a long continuous flow, because it *isn't* continuous. *It never was.* Time would be merely that *temporary* period for which you seem to depart, or "ignore" the Timeless Presence, the All-Powerful Being, You truly *are.*

You're the only Presence and Power, not time. Your Being is all that is present *to be* Power.

———•———

From this true "viewpoint," it is clear that when time seems to periodically operate, it never functions as an independent entity apart from you that has its own power or presence.

As the One, All-Inclusive Conscious Being, *You are all there is to all of Existence.*

Your Changeless Present-ness is absolutely all the Presence there is.

As Your Presence is *all* the Presence there is, nowhere could time also have its own presence and be operating by itself. To say time, *what-never-is-present*, has presence somewhere is ridiculous. Absolutely all that exists is your own Totally Present Being.

As you are the One All-Inclusive Being, the Only One Existent, then it would be *you alone* who seem to give rise to time. It may sound incredible, but all time in your universe would be due to *your own* temporary period of *not being* your own Being. To say that you are aware of time, it would be *you alone* that has to first mentally wander from the Timeless Being You alone are.

See if you can come up with even the slightest evidence of time, anywhere in your universe, apart from *your own* so-called thought or sense of it. You can't. As the One that is all-inclusive of the universe, it would be *your* sense of time that is all there is *to* time.

It is because *Your All-Inclusive Being* is all there is, that the very straying from It seems to mentally "create" all the non-being, all time in your universe, right then and there. Time "kicks in" for that period when *you* think or function as not-Being. There is no pre-existing phenomenon called time "out there," that your attention goes *out to*. Again, time has no presence of its own because Your Being is all Presence.

To repeat—all time, all *is-not-ness*, seems to last only to the extent one's conscious attention strays from specific identification as *Isness*.

This alone would be time's very "creation" and its only "duration."

This, too, shows why there never has been one universally accepted and irrefutable explanation for a beginning of time. It's because the one looking for time's cause always looks for something apart from himself. When all along he is operating *as* time's very "cause"—by ignoring *Being!* Instead of being the changeless *Now* that All-Inclusive Awareness *is*—the very act of mentally thinking, sensing and reacting, looking for a cause, would be the very startup of a secondary time-mind or dream, and its entire seeming universe.

Time or dream-sense is not its own entity; it has no actual presence to function independently. Regardless of how real it may seem, time has no power of its own to do anything *on its own*.

So don't unwittingly assume that as you are wholly, consciously being the Present, time *still continues* to operate by itself somewhere as an independent force apart from you, even though it isn't getting your attention. No! Time couldn't be continuing somewhere else on its own apart from Your Present Awareness, for there is nowhere else. *There is only the All-Present Awareness You are.*

The thought may come, "Well, other people are aware of time too, so this can't be true. *They* think and act in terms of time too."

Who is this "they"?

Look closely. There are no others—no other *Awarenesses* or *Beings* out there at all. "They" would be just *dream-images* of bodies—like characters on a movie screen. They don't have minds inside them, though they appear animated and intelligent. All of what appears to the senses as separate "others" would be going on only in the one false state of dream-thought that claims to be "your" personal mind.

The finite illusion of time and "others" seems to start *only* when you start with something besides the One Infinite Reality, the *Pure Timeless Now* You truly are. While it seems this "allows" time to operate, you never are guilty of what time appears to produce. Time's non-being never is part of You. All there is to You is Being.

And what would be accomplished when ignoring Present Being? Where would one go when doing so? One wouldn't go anywhere in *physical* terms, for there's nothing physical—one just seems to go *mentally* into a state of non-Being, or un-Reality. Time would be "un" Real Being, meaning unreal being. It would be un-Consciousness, or un-Awakeness—meaning dream, sleep, an imagining.

Don't kid yourself—it is the hardest thing one will ever do, to stick as or *be* the Now, the Timeless Present—yet that doesn't make the Present any less true, any less All That Is. And is it hard for *Consciousness Itself* to be the Present right where You are? Is there another being conscious?

The foregoing has been stated in this way to clarify the nothingness of time. Yet the most important point in this chapter—in this book—is that in Reality there *never* are two states. What Is never fails to be less than *all that is*; It cannot temporarily ignore Itself.

All never flits in and out of Its Omnipresent Being. All never leaves Itself—there is nothing besides Its Omnipresence that It could leave *for.*

———————•————————

Present Consciousness. Two words. What do they *really* mean?

As said repeatedly, the fact that *Consciousness* is all there is to all Existence, means there never has been a physical, material world—anywhere, ever. If one were to even speak of what is called "the present day" or all "past events," at most, all so-called events and times always would be only *mental*, or entirely "made out of" dream-thought.

Yet not even that is fully accurate. The fact that Consciousness, Being, can only *be totally present*—as the Un-budging Absolute Present—leaves no possibility of any time even beginning or occurring!

So not only has the so-called "past" never been physical—it hasn't even been!

Only, only, *only* the Present is present—"everywhere."

As often as that has been said, this irrefutable Truth makes clear another *huge* point.

When it seems you ignore the Absolute Present You are, what would be happening?

In that instant, that would be creating *all* time—the entirety of time!

It literally would be creating all time *for the very first time ever!*

As incredible as that sounds, it's undeniable. Again, as the Present is changelessly all that is present, there can't have been any time before—because *where only the Present is present*, there is no "before."

As Pure Conscious Being, as the Absolute Present Itself, *You* never say there was a past—only false finite sense-dream would try to say so. How does one not get fooled by it? Start from the true premise—that only the Unchanging Present, I-Am-Presence, is.

Now notice something. Notice that every time the finite thinking "sense-mind" tries to say there has been a long past, it is always *right now* when it's saying that. The thinking would try to make it seem as if there has been this long, long past that stretches "way back there"—one that includes a recent past, and a much older past.

Now look very closely where all—every last bit—of that so-called long past is. The entirety of it would be found only *right here* in that current thinking of it. The entirety of what is mistakenly called "the past" isn't past at all—all of it is being projected only *right now* in that bunch of current thinking. That's the only place you come up with any of it.

Mistaken human belief would try to say there are both that current thinking of a past and *another* "real" past—one that occurred in a physical world at a previous time. Why is that not true? Because, again, absolutely all there is, is *Consciousness*—which precludes there being any physical world. And the fact that Consciousness is changelessly *Present* precludes there being any previous time.

Human ignorance doesn't realize that there never is a separate physical world, but just *thought*. So all that the so-called past could have been "made out of" is *thought*. And when you examine it closely, you see the shocking truth—that thought never is something that occurred "way back then"—for the entirety of it is being mentally projected just now!

Go ahead, try as hard as you can to come up with a little bit of a "past," or a whole lot of it, in some place other than your *current* thought of it. It's impossible.

No matter how far one tries to mentally shove a "past" back there— it actually has had no prior existence. The only place you ever come up with any of it is in the very thinking-dreaming of it starting *now*. That's all there would be to *all* of the so-called "past"—just that one big mental "panorama" or "thought-collage"—all of which begins *now*.

This is clear only from the vantage point of the Absolute Present, wherein no time has been. Otherwise one mistakenly assumes time has some other, prior beginning. It doesn't.

Imagine watching a scene of a movie. In this movie scene it is the year 2000—and the movie characters themselves are in a theater. They are watching another movie, taking place in 1980. Now suppose within that inner 1980 movie scene being watched, that second set of characters is watching a third movie, taking place in 1960—a movie within a movie within a movie—and so on, as far "back" as one cares to go. One really is not going back in time at all. All scenes, all years, appear to be projected right there in the *one* overall current picture.

In the exact same way, the *entirety* of what is mistakenly called "history"—both "recent past" and "ancient past"—are encapsulated in the *one* momentary mental snapshot or thought in terms of it. From the vantage point of Absolute Present Awareness, it is clear that the entirety of so-called "history" isn't history or old at all—for it's all one mental panorama being instantaneously thought or dreamed *now*. Always, it would be current thinking only *imagining* there is oldness.

Even though this book has repeatedly referred to the *passing* of time—from the vantage point of Present Consciousness, one sees that *time never is passing*. The entirety of time seems to be projected *now*.

One never, never, never leaves Now, *Present Awareness*.

This being true, how old are You as *Present Being*? How old is *All*?

Look closely. How many prior thoughts in terms of time, or time-snapshots have you had *before*? Do you say billions? The answer is none. Why? Even what would be called all "prior" times and all their snapshots would be found only in *this* snapshot of time-thought, in the ignoring of the Present that would be going on *now*. All so-called time is found only in the dream-thought—but that's not You, Pure Present Consciousness. And not even the dream is "old," but seemingly began this instant.

What is far more important, in Reality, the Absolute Present *Itself*, the Totally Aware Being You *are*, never has *any* time-snapshots. Not one. And never is there another being present. The Absolute Present never leaves or alters Its Absoluteness. It leaves no past of anything.

The "sense-mind's" thinking may keep trying to insist there really *was* a long past that happened "way back there." It would try to say there was a yesterday, and before that, a week ago, and before that, a year ago, and so on, in a long sequence. But what's really going on? What is called a year ago isn't any farther away or older than yesterday, because all there would ever be to *both* is only thought images, and both are simultaneously being thought *now*. Apart from what appears as those current images, neither "yesterday" nor "a year ago" had any other prior existence. Since all there is, is *Consciousness*, there has been no prior physical world. And since Consciousness, All, is *Ever-Present*, there has been no prior time, no prior thinking.

Imagine you're a movie character. There you are, stuck on the movie's reel of film. All your experiences are there too, a little bit within each little frame on the film. From your limited movie-character point of view, from inside that roll of film, all you know is that everything must unfold in a long time-sequence; what's in the picture on frame 1 definitely has to appear, or be past, before the picture on frame 365 comes up. Now what if you're not in the movie? When you're outside it, your new vantage point shows you a complete reel of film, with all frames right there on the reel simultaneously. You don't see it as something that unfolds in sequence. Frame 1 is right there at the same time with frame 365—frame 1 is not older or past, not something that *was*.

Likewise, from the vantage point of Present Consciousness, Reality, there is no such thing as a past that *was*. There is only a *would-be* past, that appears to be projected *now* in thought. And to even come up with such time-projections means first *ignoring* the Pure Present You *are*; trying to superimpose that time-thought upon Your Self.

Stay alert and don't assume that there has been *any* prior time—not even a time which you have now seen to be false. Not even that occurred, for only the Present is.

———— • ————

Since the only place *all* of the so-called "past" would be, is in the thought of it starting right now, *there has been no long accumulation of a past!* None! There is no past as a long continuum—for all there *is*, is *Pure Present-ness*.

In light of this Truth, which would be older—Julius Caesar, or yesterday's Caesar salad? Neither—for neither has had any prior existence apart from thought *right now*. Because the only kind of existence *both* ever can have to you is in thought *now*, Julius is not "back there," not a moment older than the salad. Julius has had no prior physical past in which he became centuries older than the salad, because *as Present Consciousness is changelessly All*, no physical past has been. The only place one could find Julius and even all the "centuries" too, is in the one dream-thought being projected *now*.

Even if the "sense-mind's" thinking tries to say your body's been to Rome before, or that you've thought of Julius before, and had many Caesar salads before—*where is all of that?* The only place Rome, and all those thoughts and salads, would be found is in the one "mental package" being thought or dreamed *now* for the first time ever.

One *never* leaves Now, the Present.

The only Substance wherein all things exist is *Present Consciousness*. The fact that All is *Omni-Present* leaves no oldness whatsoever—so there can't be some things older than others. One item in a dream is not older than any other item because they're not separate physical items— it all would be one dream that starts *now*. To try to say Julius is older than the salad would be to superimpose an *assumption* upon that which has absolutely no existence other than as a mental thought-image, and always now. It would ignore the only place or "setting" upon which both depend for their entire appearance—*Present* Awareness. Julius never exists anywhere else.

Who says things are old, that they've existed a long time? Things themselves can't say that. They're just thought-appearances appearing *now*; they have no mind with which to say anything. Only *you* would assume there is oldness by ignoring Your Now which alone *is*.

The would-be intellect based on time and sensing will screech that this is lunacy. Yet it would be the intellect that never is. Which are you—What Is, or what never is? There is no choice.

"But that important experience I had was *back then*," the thinking may try to insist. "And I've enjoyed recalling it so much over the years." Nope. The only place *both* the experience and the "many" reminiscences would be found is in the *one* thought of it going on now.

"Then what about the universe?" the thought may come. "Today, as every day, I looked up at the sky and saw a vast universe out there. It's been there day after day after day."

The only place all of that is found—all the "background" days, and the entire "history" of the universe, again would be in the *one* mental collage being thought or dreamed now.

The thinking may sputter in desperation, "Then how did I *get* here?"

Where do you identify—with a dream that has no real background, or as the Changeless Present? The answer is that you *never did* "get" here. As the Present, You changelessly *are* here, as Eternity Itself.

This also clearly shows why there is no such thing as reincarnation in Reality. Only in a would-be time dream that seems to start *right now* would it be said that one had previous lives. The entirety of it would start and be found only in the ignoring of the Present *right now*.

One always, always, always looks out as the Present, *What Is*.

———•———

Stop and consider how stupendously, staggeringly important this is!

So-called creation and time never began "way back there." The *entirety* of the dream of mortal experience, its time, and all its seeming creation always would be brand new. It "kicks in" for that period one ignores the allness of Infinite *Present Reality*, Pure Aware *Being*.

The would-be periodic dream of mortal experience and all its seeming problems and limitations has absolutely *no* history backing it up! It has no long background behind it, giving it power to do this or that because "it has been around so long."

There are absolutely *no* firmly entrenched problems! One who is consciously *being* Present Being leaves nothing to function as a secondary time-dream—no time-mind to assume it has long-honored problems of disease, poverty, morality—or religious or national clashes.

If such "problems" even could be legitimately mentioned, they would be exactly like a dream, in the very first scene of which, the very first words spoken by the first character to appear in the dream were something like, "We've tried and tried to find a way to end this conflict. But it's been going on for so long, people are accustomed to it; it's become a way of life."

Hey! The dream just started!

There has been no long conflict, although everything about the background appearance, the dream's story line, would try to make it *appear* so. Some of the dream characters may even appear aged, and some young. It may appear they live in an aging universe, and even use dream-science to show dream-evidence of their universe's great age.

How old could any of it be, since the dream just began?

If one mistakenly ignores the Truth of Timeless Being, and starts with time-dream, or the un-Real, one has taken on *its* state of unreal thinking. So naturally it is assumed everything has a long background behind it. It is assumed there are "long-term" problems that must also take a long time to overcome. That all would be *its* assumption, not Yours.

In Truth, the Present's Absoluteness leaves no prior assumption of anything. The Absolute Present leaves *no* prior time, and *no* prior dream appearances—none. To the One Who Unfailingly Is *All Present*, not a single time-problem occurs.

It isn't that the Absolute Present erases away a history of world problems.

The Absolute Present leaves no history of *anything*.

It leaves no history of even *Itself*!

Absolutely all there is, is utter, pristine *Never-before-ness*.

There is only Pristine New Life in all Its indescribable Beauty—being Absolutely Everywhere!

You and Your entire Existence are so gloriously *fresh* and *pure*, so breathtakingly *free*, there are no words for It! And there is absolutely nothing else! Forever!

A sparkling brand new, clean slate is all there is—permanently!

This is why Omnipresence, Reality, or God, never can be used to improve previous human affairs, for there haven't *been* any previous human affairs!

Nothing has happened yet!

Not only have there been no previous human affairs—there has been no previous God! There has been no God before, because the Absolute Pristine Present leaves no "before" in which a God could have been. Only this Divine *Omni-Present-ness*, is—which *is* God.

Obviously, One can't go back to a lesser self, for no past occurred in which to have *been* a lesser self!

You *can't* be saved. Nothing besides Your Pure Present Being has happened that You could possibly need saving from—and this is "salvation" in its true light.

This book is not about lifting oneself out of *what never occurred*.

As the subtitle says, now Life is *completely new*.

One cannot even ask, "Why hasn't this been brought out before?"

There is no before. There is only *Present Consciousness*.

———•———

One never says, "It will take me a long time, years of study, to get back to being at-one with the Divine, because I have ignored *Now, the Present*, for such a long time."

In the Present, there is no history of ignoring the Present—and it is always the Present, "everywhere."

How could there be another that must study how to be the Present? There is only the Present Itself, and not even the Present knows "how"! *The Present has had no prior experience in being present!*

The Pure Present, Your Presence, does not co-exist with time, so You never wasted any. How could Your Absolute Being waste *that which never has had being*? Not a bit of Your Life has passed by. Your Perfect Life *is*.

Equally, don't smugly assume you have been living spiritually—or have been honest with Truth in a past—for honestly there is no past.

You have no history of not seeing Truth before, or of assuming you *have* seen Truth before—because You have no history at all—and *that* is to "see" or *be* Truth.

As the Absolute Present has no history, You have no history of negative habits, no guilt or burden. As *Pure Now* has no history, It has no history of disease—and Pure Now is all that is present—eternally.

Only Now is *Wellness,* for Now is absolutely all that is present *to be* Wellness—and Now is doing perfectly well at being. There is no such thing as gradual Wellness, for *Now* takes no time to be well, and nothing else *is.* Only Now's *Ever-Present* Wellness exists.

To be perfectly well in Reality has nothing to do with a body. Wellness is Pure Now, alive as Its own non-physical *Presence.* Always, It is *Now* that is well, not a body. Always, *Now* is You, not a body.

Pure Now, the Only One Present, never gets sick, for there is nothing physical about Now that *could* get sick. And as Pure Now *is absolutely all that is present*—It leaves nothing physical anywhere *to* be sick. All there is, is the Pure Conscious Presence that Now, Wellness, is. One never tries to apply Now's Wellness to a dream, for in Now, no time-dream is. There is nothing present besides Now to apply Now *to.*

Now is *Its own* Perfection—not an opportunity for another to gain perfection.

Consistently living *Now,* one is not dreaming as non-being and its would-be negation of the Absolute Wellness that Ever-Present Life *is.* It is *being* this Certainty of Now, the Certainty of Wellness, and not tolerating "not-ness," that *appears* as improvements in body and all aspects of daily living. Yet Perfect Now Itself never improves.

There is no system, no formula to Now's Perfection. The Pure Now I Am needs no past body of knowledge; there has been no wisdom accumulated down through any ages *about* the Now I Am. When would such be put to use, and by whom—*there being only the Now I Am?*

To assume there is a lesser self that needs time to "see" or gain wisdom would be to assume there *has* been a past in which a separate self came forth. It attempts to slam the door on *Present Self,* the One I Now Fully *Am,* Omniscience, in favor of personalized self-delusion.

Now never is "seeing" Itself. Now is *being* Itself.

The Now I Am is not even "the perennial philosophy" as sometimes called, for the Absolute Present I Am leaves no past in which anything could have become perennial.

Clearly, One never comes to Truth *from* a personal mind. One never comes to Truth period, for One never left—and there is nothing besides *Omni-Present* Consciousness to come from.

I Am never knowing there is no history. I Am completely "busy" being un-put-aside-able, un-go-away-able *Present* Life.

I Am always "just getting acquainted" with My *Never-before-ness*, the insuppressible enthusiasm of spontaneous Being.

It may *seem* the senses and time tug constantly. To whom? Not to Infinite Being. It may seem one "falls down" often and gets caught up in time. Never blame yourself. One never actually lets go of the Present because *Omnipresence* can't let go of Itself.

Can the Present Itself ever fall or lapse? Can Being fail to be? One does not keep score, but "stays in," or *is*, the unrelenting, un-back-down-able Present. That is the only "job"—staying alert and catching oneself, no matter how often it seems necessary. It's never that you've "fallen" and must "climb back." It's staying alert that, in the Absolute Present, there has been no time past in which You could have fallen!

The Present Reality You are never tries to get rid of, or overcome time. One never is anti-time. Time isn't *bad*. It simply isn't. One is wholly engaged in *being present*. What *seems* to be time would only be the last, weak waves of not-ness, lapping at the shore of infallible, indestructible Being.

No amount of human *thinking* about either time or Now is of use, for all thinking *takes time*, and merely self-imposes more time upon the immediate *Now* that simple Aware Being *is*.

Now is present only *now*—not after more thought about It!

Peacefully, persistently, and consistently enjoy the immediacy, the effortlessness with which the Present is already all-present as *Unstoppable Pure Awareness*. One never has to work or struggle to make the Aware Present *be*. Awareness never lapses from being All-Present, so *can't* take time to return to Itself. Joy in the fact that *Now*, One's very Conscious Being, can't be held in check or be not-Now.

If there *were* such a thing as time (and there isn't!), the biggest trick it would play is the assumption that, given enough *time*, one will eventually see enough to return to the Self. Yet it would be the very operating in time that perpetuates a false sense of separation.

Now, Truth, Power, never is what You see; It is what You *be*.

The realization that there is no time—is this what is meant by Biblical and other prophecies when they said there would be an "end of time"? Is *this* the end of time, the fulfilling of prophecy?

If it were legitimate to speak on a finite basis, that might *appear* so, because time has clearly been seen in all its nothingness, or *never-began-ness*. One cannot start on that basis. To the Only One Alive, the Totally Present One, "time" never began—so couldn't later be ended.

Now never involves prophecy. As the One Undeviating Now-Presence *completely precludes all time*—It certainly doesn't allow any predictions concerning time.

Could you imagine *Omnipresent Being* having to wait until time *which-is-not*, graciously stepped aside, finally allowing Omnipresence to become the Total Presence *It is changelessly being*? It would be as ludicrous as Existence not being able to exist until It got the go-ahead signal from non-existence!

There is a saying, "He who forgets history is doomed to repeat it." That might be true *if there were history*. Totally Present Being (and there is no other) has no history, so what could It forget? Omnipresent *Now* equally leaves no future in which a history could be repeated. There is only *freely present Life*, which is Joy Itself.

This chapter is not a new way of accounting for time. To assume so would be to miss the point. Never is there time or a past to deal with *at all*. Likewise, this is not implying there ever was another besides the One Present whose attention could periodically wander. That's what Omnipresence means—no separation is possible; there is no other who could sleep or whose attention could stray.

Is the Present's own Omnipresence too radical for Itself? Is being the Present a rash course of action? To whom?—the Present *Itself* being all that is present.

23

THE PRESENT IS PERFECTION ITSELF

THE FACT THAT THE PRESENT IS PRESENT ENTIRELY ALONE means It is present *purely*.

The fact that the Present is present fully, completely, means It is present *perfectly*.

What does that leave?

It leaves only the pure perfection of the Present.

It means the Present must be what true *Perfection* actually is. The Present is all that is present *to be* Perfection. It is the only kind of Perfection there can *be*.

As the Present is all that is present, then *Perfection* is all that is present.

Absolute Perfection is as unstoppably omnipresent now as the Present Itself.

It means the very Conscious I-Presence alive here—*which is the Present*—is Perfection Itself. Absolute Perfection is the only I.

Living Perfection is the Identity reading this now.

Utter Pure Perfection is normal, status-quo to this Present One I Am.

Divine Perfection is not a great accomplishment to be *waited for*. Perfection cannot come as the result of a process, billions of years of evolution, of hard-fought improvement in time.

True Divine Perfection is the fact that the Present *leaves no* time. Truly, Perfection is timeless.

There is no more, no other Perfection that will be present *later*.

This Present Being is It—the only Perfection there can be. It *never* goes away.

How hard is it to be Perfection? Well, how hard is it to be?

To be perfect is the same as to perfectly *be*. To *be*, with perfection, is the easiest thing there is. *It is what already is.*

Perfection is effortless. It is the unspeakable simplicity of *Present Awareness*.

Perfection never is what one is aware *of*; It is what One is, as Awareness.

Awareness can no more avoid being absolutely perfect than It can avoid being present. In other words, Absolute Perfection *cannot fail to be*, as this very Aware Being. It never is a body or personality, but Infinite I-Presence *being Itself.*

Perfection is not a life-less state, not a quality or condition of *things*.

Perfection is *alive, intelligent.* Perfection is *conscious.*

What does it mean that Perfection, *this Consciousness,* is also a synonym for *Perception?* It means the only Perception ever present to operate, is that of Perfect Consciousness Itself. Every single thing existent in Reality is perceived in only one way, by Absolute Perfection.

Staying "busy" as Pure Present Consciousness means that the only way your universe is ever "seen" is by Perfection Itself. It cannot be mis-perceived by the would-be not-ness, or negative-ness of time-senses or human judgment, for there is *only* the flawless Perception of the Present.

Present Consciousness' perfect, crystal clear Perception is con-sciously present *Now* at every "pinpoint" of Existence. *It is what all Existence is, and It is endless.*

In the Absolute Present You are, *Total Perfection is already All,* so It can neither come nor go. Perfection's immediacy and "thoroughness of coverage" is complete, undeviating, *endless.*

There is nothing to come between It and Itself.

Utter, Absolute, "Solid" Perfection is always, always, *all* Presence, *all* Place. There isn't *an* All that Perfection "fills." Perfection *is what* All is!

The clarity and purity of the Perfect One I Am is forever un-dulled, un-altered—just as *Now* never is un-Now. Perfection is as uncondition-ally present as the Present Itself. It is *irreversible.* It never becomes an opposite or negation of Itself, un-present. Can you imagine the Present withholding any of Itself, thus Its Perfection, from Its own Presence? It's impossible! And the Present is all that is present, *now.*

What could the One I Am ever need to "do" with this Total Perfection I Am, when there is only endlessly "more and more" of the Perfection I Am?

It cannot be emphasized too much that Perfection is not some kind of ultimate, idealized state to be waited for, any more than *Now* can wait to be. You never are waiting for Perfection to *happen,* to improve things. *It is the Purity of Your Present Being,* apart from things.

This Perfection is what Unconditional Love is. Unconditional Love isn't a nice, New Age sort of notion that *hopefully* will spread over a world. Unconditional Love is the inability of the Present to withhold any of Its Perfection *as It is being all of Existence,* now!

The Present is all that is present to be *Substance.*

That means *Perfection* is all that is present to be Substance.

Substance is absolutely perfect, and changelessly so. One who is *consciously being* Substance as Present Awareness, has Perfection Itself as the Substance of One's entire Existence.

It may sound shocking, but it is an *impossibility* for materiality, physicality, or even a mentality to be Substance. A so-called atom or energy is not Substance. To thinking based on the senses, this of course sounds incredible. It is undeniably true though, because whatever substance is, it has to *be,* exist. All that appears to be physical, material, or energy, always would be based in time, *what isn't being*—or non-presence. Non-presence *can't* be substance.

Looking out as the Omni-Present, Omni-Perfect *Substance* You are, there never has been disease, sin, lack, or guilt present or substantive *anywhere.* Those all would have needed matter, time, *non-being.* There can be no disease due to non-being, for *there has been no non-being.* How could there be a carryover of disease or decay from a previous time—when the Only One Present, the only Substance, precludes there being any time? There has been no Substance prior to *Now,* for Now is what Substance *is,* and It's not prior—It's *Now.*

The Perfect Absoluteness that the Present is, is all the Substance there can *be.* Being infinite, undimensional, It cannot end, split off, or separate from Itself. Nor does Substance have to spread "out there" to perfect a world, for all is Here, *within* Consciousness, Perfect Substance.

Since It is the *Present Itself* that is Substance, Substance never ages.

This instant, You and your entire Existence are so freshly *present*, so magnificently *new*, it is indescribable.

The Perfect Present is where One "stays," for there is no past in which Life was otherwise. What's more, Life never can improve *beyond* this Infinite Present Perfection.

As Perfection is Ever-Present "everywhere," It is irresistible, un-hold-back-able.

The Present never is Perfection to another; there is only Its Absoluteness as *this* Being I Am. I Am immovable, changeless, decay-less, disease-less. Not a little disease-less: *absolutely* disease-less.

How far off is Absolute Perfection? Well, how far off is *Now*? Does Now ever go away? The beauty of the Present Perfection You are is that never will You become un-Present, un-Perfect.

Again, the answer to the question, "What is the Present to Its own Present-ness?" is also the answer to, "What is Substance? What is All?"

———•———

Do you start your day, even before getting the body out of bed, with an absolutely *perfect* Existence? If one is not starting Here, one is attempting to start the day as non-existence. Do you let yourself get talked out of Your Ever-Present Perfection by what would-be senses and ignore-ant thinking based upon those senses may try to say?

Infinite Consciousness, Your Self, never is conscious of anything contrary to Its Perfection. All that One is ever "dealing with" —all that ever is—is omnipresent, and therefore undelayable, Perfection.

What senses would appear to say—for good, bad, or mediocre— *never* is the substantiation that Perfection is present. Infinite Perfection is all-present in spite of, not because of, what superimposed dream-sense would try to say. If there *were* finite time-experience (and there isn't!), one would always be stuck with im-perfection as one's premise.

As Present Perfection is *all there is,* It precludes any need for perfecting. That's the beauty of It. There are not two ways Your Life, the All-Being-You, can *be*. There is only the ease, joy and freedom of being unimprovable, Changeless Perfection.

This does not mean one will suddenly take a "do nothing" attitude toward daily experience. Rather, by actively, consistently staying "busy" as the Ever-Present, Ever-Perfect Awareness One is, one unavoidably does one's very best at whatever appears to be at hand. Finite daily experience will *appear* to show forth less limitation and "more and more" of the Perfection that all Life, all Substance, changelessly is.

———————•———————

Absolute Perfection is all that is present to be Omnipresence.

Absolute Perfection is all that is present to be Omnipotence. Absolute Perfection is the only One conscious to be Omniscience.

Is this not the true meaning of *Divine?* Doesn't Divine mean eternal, unconditional, Infinite Perfection? Doesn't Divine mean Perfection that is untouched by, or precludes, time and change?

If one uses a word *God*, then this Perfect Present *must be* what God is. Nothing *else* is ever present, anywhere, to be God or Goodness. It means the whole of Perfect Goodness is actively, consciously being the entirety of Presence right now *as this Conscious Presence.*

The Divine never has been "off there." The only Divine there can *be* is Right Here, as Present Consciousness. Abstract? Mystical? To be Divinely Perfect is the most natural, normal, *simple* thing going—as unavoidable as Present Consciousness being Itself.

This Divine Perfection *can't* work miracles. There is nothing besides Its Perfect Omnipresence upon which miracles could be performed!

The only "miracle" there would be is if the Perfect Present stopped being the entirety of Presence; if All stopped being *all.* That's impossible. Operating consistently as, or *being* Pure Present Consciousness may *appear* to bring about miraculous things on a finite basis. But that would be only because one no longer is allowing the operation of a would-be, not-present, not-perfect, dream sense that appeared to project the "not" or problems in the first place. Meanwhile, in Changelessly Present Perfection, All, or God, no change ever occurs.

In Truth, God's *own* Allness leaves no other to operate incorrectly or even correctly as God.

God's Self-Allness precludes another to *have* a God. God does not look upon Itself as God. God's own Absolute Presence precludes even the slightest *concept* of God.

God is simply Its own Presence, All Presence, *this* Presence.

————•————

Is the Present, Perfection, just abstract philosophizing with no real power?

The Power that Present Perfection *is,* when it comes to so-called "time," is Absolute.

The Power that You *are* can completely put a "stop" to what *appear* to be disease and all ill effects supposedly due to age, not to mention fear, hate, war, condemnation, and all else that would go with ignore-ance of Life's Omni-*Present* Perfection.

Why? There never are *physical* conditions going on in a world "out there." Again, it would be nothing but a seeming false state of *thought* "right here," trying to pose as "your" personal mind—trying to say there is time, not-the-Present, in which such problems could develop and perpetuate. That sense-thinking itself would be all there is *to* time, all there is *to* the would-be problems.

In thinking and sensing in time, it seems Power is "off" because one is off Power; there is no Power in non-being. Only *Now,* as Pure Be-ing—is Power changelessly "on."

The Changeless Truth that there is only Power Itself—the Pure Present—leaves no false state of thought having occurred, and not a trace of history. In Pure *Now,* there are no past causes, *thus no effects.* Time-problems can't occur to the only Mind present, *the Mind that is the Present.*

The Present isn't Power because It puts a stop to time and its ne-gate-ive effects. The Present is Power because It leaves nothing besides *Itself* to occur! An absence of the Present never has been. This leaves all "time," thus all its would-be effects, "neither root nor branch."

Again, Omnipresence is not the power *to,* the power *of,* or power *over.* It is Power precisely because there is only Itself—infinite, endless, timeless *Being.*

Do you truly behold the Absolute Power and Authority You are?

All Power, Omnipotence Itself, eternally is Your Being *Now!* Do you act on the basis that Power is *unavoidably* present as this Being; or do you assume Power is what a second self has access to, but only if this self mentally works things right? The Present *Itself* being All, leaves no mentality to think wrongly or rightly. The gap between Infinite Power and this very Being is the same as the gap between Consciousness and *Now*—none!

This has just stripped away every would-be excuse for toleration or co-existence with *any* problematic situation. Any seemingly un-harmonious "situation" *is not operating on its own*, with its own power, "out there" in time. It does *not* have an independent presence "off there" while You consciously be All That Is. This means what appears to be all disease, all lack and need, all hate and war, all personal selfishness, and *all* the so-called rest! All such "situations" are *un-occur-able*.

Only what is true of Present Perfection is *present to operate*.

It is impossible for this to fail because the Present cannot fail to be!

Do you realize that *Now* you are "freeing" your *entire universe* of any seeming age, decay, poverty, disease and worry? Your All-Inclusive Ever-Present-ness is the only "Place" and "Substance" wherein the entire universe exists—and to this Pure Absolutely Perfect Presence no such conditions, nothing not-the-Present, has ever been. The Absolute never wanders from Its *Allness*.

Do you *really* realize that this alone is what is present, true? Are you being It? Or do you just think, "Oh, that's great," and go on reading more *words*? Consciousness Itself doesn't just think It; Consciousness is changelessly being It, and there is no other.

You could scour every single book on every shelf of every library or bookstore on the planet, and never, ever come across anything more *magnificent*, more *potent*, or just plain *practical* than what has been pointed out in these past three chapters.

What *else* could one possibly want or be looking for? What else could be of greater value? There *is* nothing else! This is not an author asking, but *I*, Your own All-Inclusive *Present Consciousness*.

24

THE INFINITE *ONE*

WHILE THE INFINITE PERFECTION OF THE SELF IS *ALL,* do not assume It is too infinite, too absolute to be practical in what still *appears* as daily affairs. Nothing is more valuable than Consciousness under any circumstances! There is nothing left out of It—body, relationships, career, country, the entire universe—all appear to be included.

One never takes on an attitude of, "Oh, what's the use? The human, finite world is all dream anyway, so why care about anything?" One never says, "I'm not here."

One most definitely *is* here. One is present as Perfect Being, Pure Infinity. Your Intelligent *Being* never will pass away, for It does not co-exist with time in which It *could* pass away. Your Life is present eternally, which means forever and ever and "beyond," and yet It is always *Now.*

While the foregoing is true, and may be crystal clear, it may still continue to appear for an indefinite "time" that one co-exists with a finite, limited world. It is like the effects of a dream which linger even after one is awake. Even though it is clear *there is only Infinite Presence,* it may appear one has a very dimensional body that still breathes air and eats dimensional food, and that one has to conduct affairs in a three-dimensional, finite world.

So in the meantime, don't quit what appears to be your day job. Finite forms of work or pastime are obviously essential in daily experience. What is stated here about finite experience doesn't negate one's daily work or activity, for in All-Inclusive Awareness there never is any negation. One can enjoy such work freely in what appears as finite experience—not because one assumes it is Reality, or that it adds to One's Self.

Regardless of whether the body appears to be occupied as a home-maker or professional, whether in business, education, science, public service, a skilled trade, or any field—from agriculture to athletics to the arts—all "belongs" to Life, Consciousness.

It is thanks entirely to the One Conscious Life, Intelligence, being the only Self *present,* that one can know "the intelligent thing to do," even under the circumstances of finite daily experience. To constantly "stay with" Infinite Intelligence and what is true of It, in spite of what the senses would attempt to say, is to live and work *as* Intelligence, Clarity.

By consistently and persistently "looking out from" the Infinity of One's Self, any limitations or problems under which one may have seemed to be laboring *appear* to fall away. Why? As Infinite Consciousness truly is All, Its Unlimitedness leaves *no limitations.*

———•———

There is just one *All,* one One.

It doesn't matter what synonym is used—Consciousness, All, Being, Intelligence, Life, God—it still has to be referring to the same One, because this One is all there is.

This One can be called Consciousness or Awareness because It is in fact, conscious, aware.

This One is also called Mind or Intelligence because It is in fact, intelligent. But It is still the same *One.*

It is called Life or Aliveness because It is alive. It is called Existence, for It is all that is being or exists. It is all the presence there is, so It is called Omnipresence. It is called Substance because It is the very, *only* "Stuff" present to be Substance—but still as the same One.

It is also called All because It *is* in fact all there is. As It is *All,* It is called Omnipotence for It is the only Power existent. It is also called Omniscience because It is All-Knowing.

It is called the Infinite because It is infinite, or measureless, undimensional. It is called Spirit because It is not material or subject to change or decay. It is called Perfection because It is perfect. It is called Love because It is pure, unconditional. It is called Harmony or Wellness because It is whole and without opposite. Yet It never deviates from being the exact same changeless *One.*

The One is being all these synonyms "simultaneously." Only an intellect—which deals in many, complexity, separation—would assume Infinite Mind has separate characteristics. Infinite Mind doesn't see Itself as having many synonyms, or separate attributes. To It, the perfect operation of all synonyms *as One* is simple, effortless. It is One, or Oneness, simply being that which is true of Itself.

Infinite Mind effortlessly, simply *is*. It never struggles. As *One, All,* It leaves no outside influence that could oppose It, or put It under pressure or stress. It thus can be called *Ease* or *Satisfaction.*

As the Infinite Conscious One is endless in abundance, It can also be called *Abundance,* or *Wealth,* or *Supply.* This never refers to finite forms of wealth: income, bank accounts, and so on. All that Infinite Mind "supplies" Itself with is Its endless *Conscious Aliveness.* Consciousness is all that is present *to be* Abundance, Wealth, Supply.

In Reality, Infinite Mind doesn't call Itself anything, not even Mind. It *is* what It is. One does not *have* a mind. Mind is what You *are*. Likewise, You cannot *have* wellness, wealth and abundance; you do not *have* power; you never can *get* a life of ease. It is what You are.

Again, this is how Life *is*. It never can be stopped or changed. This is the only way *all of Existence* is now existing—these are the "ground rules" of Life. Yet Infinity Itself has no rules, conditions or regulations. The only "limit" to Infinity is that It never can be limited.

———•———

One Infinite Mind leaves no secondary mind to worry, "This is getting so abstract. How could this help me get more out of my world, my business or affairs?"

The point is that there *is no* secondary ignorant mind to assume it needs to "use" the One Mind, Consciousness, for personal gain. The *One* leaves no second state of thought to judge by false senses and assume a constant lack of things, and need for improvement is the norm.

Can you imagine Omnipresent Being, *Absolute Perfection, All Itself,* feeling a need to use Itself for gain? For what—since It already includes every last thing existent—even what appears as a boundless universe of stellar galaxies? Is there another being conscious?

Is it a big deal for the One Consciousness to include all of what appears as money—as readily available in thought as letters of the alphabet? Is it unusual for Now to be perfectly healthy *always*?

However, suppose for a moment that the One Infinite Consciousness *could* ignore Itself. Suppose it was assumed there *was* a second, finite time-state of lack and need—and one mistakenly started on the basis of trying to satisfy that second state of lack or non-being. What would be happening?

It would be a matter of *not being* Consciousness, not being All, not being Perfection, not being the Whole One. It would be assuming a separate life of "not"—one that would *not be* all that is Good, Divine.

Such a fate would be doomed to a constant state of "not-ness."

To do so would be an attempt to act as not-Intelligence, or ignorance.

It would be an attempt to act as not-Life, which would have to appear in some form of decay or death.

It would be attempting to operate as not-Wealth, which would appear as a form of lack or poverty.

It would be an attempt to be not-Perfection, which would appear as a form of imperfection. It would be attempting to be not-Love, not-Oneness, not-Peace, which would appear as opposition, separation, animosity.

It would be to act as not-Wellness, not-Ease; to operate as a would-be state of dis-Ease, or disease. It might not appear merely as a disease of the body. It could be a disease of business, the home, relationships, environment, or government.

Meanwhile, there is still only the *one One*.

Consciousness *goes right on being the All-Inclusive One*, even if one unwittingly acts in ignorance of, or seems to negate Consciousness. *Being conscious is all there is to existing.* So as long as one seems to negate Consciousness, one appears to be *conscious of* forms of negation, or "not."

One appears to mentally experience a *would-be* negation of Wholeness, Perfection, Intelligence, Infinite Abundance. Remember, in what appears as daily finite experience, all one is ever dealing with is *thought*. So if one ignores One's Perfect Being and functions as a state of thought that *is not*, it seems one is allowing or projecting thought forms of "not," or lack—when they, by themselves, have no genuine *being* or presence.

The would-be thinking "mind" may try to say, "Oh, no. That poverty is due to economic conditions. That disease is due to a virus. There is a *cause* for it. It is due to physical conditions 'out there' apart from me."

But what *only* would those "conditions" be? *Where* only would it seem to go on? Only *as* a seeming finite-sense-dream *that is not*. The finite "sense-mind" doesn't know *about* such conditions. It *would be* the conditions. It would try to pose as "your" sense of Existence.

Problems could appear in thought only to the extent one ignores the Present Perfection One is, as *Conscious Being*, Oneness. To avoid Present Perfection would be to perpetuate im-Perfection. And it would all be just a superimposed mental state—a complete put-on. What might appear as a troublesome situation is *never* the problem. It is a suggestion that Omnipresent Perfection lapsed, and a "not-mind" began, in which imperfection could occur. It never did.

Only the acceptance that All is not *changelessly* Whole, Perfect, Pure, Absolute, would appear to project negatives, problems. It would be due to going along with what one is not—instead of consistently, persistently, and if necessary, *tenaciously* insisting on being what *One is*, wholly perfect Conscious Aliveness, wholly present Infinite Presence.

As you are the *Only One Existent*, only you could seem to allow a "second," imperfect state of thought to operate. The instant a "second" mind is gone from *your* thought or attention, there is One; *there is no other mind.*

It would take a *finite* mind to have a problem, and *all* problems would be finite. *If* such a thing could exist, the finite "sense-mind" *would be the whole show*—the problem itself, the one assuming the problem is there, and even the "suffering" one who wants to be rid of it.

It's never *You* that wants to be rid of such a thing because the *Allness* of Your Infinite Oneness, Omnipresent Perfection, leaves abso-lutely no second, finite state having occurred—not even as a mere illusion! Your Infinite Presence is simply never not Totally Present, or Perfect. It never changes. So there can be neither a suggestion, nor acceptance, of a state less than Its Perfection.

That is the only "Answer." The point is, the Endless Presence of One Mind means an assumption of "not" *actually can't even happen!* Infinite Mind's Total Presence leaves *no possibility* of "not."

Just stop and think it through. Where Present Consciousness, Mind, Existence, *changelessly is*, there is no lack or vacuum of Itself to operate as a contrary state—and there is nowhere the Present, Perfection, is not present. But It isn't a lot of *words* you think—It is what you *are alive as*.

Is this so unusual, mystical? What's the big deal? It's just *intelligent*.

Infinite Perfection never can appear to "solve the problems" of so-called finite experience, if one *starts* with the finite in any way. Why? It leaves one living backwards: being problem-conscious instead of being Pure *Consciousness-conscious*, Pure *Now-conscious*, which is Perfection-conscious. One constantly *assumes* a false state of "not," instead of being conscious of actual Perfection; instead of *consciously being Perfection*, as Pure Aliveness, which is truly all that *is*.

This doesn't mean the Infinite isn't "practical" in everyday affairs. It is all that exists *to be* practical! Infinite Perfection never lapses; It never has a mental suggestion that Its Presence is not *all*. Consciously "holding to" or *being* Present Perfection, as Pure Now-Aliveness, One's True Self, leaves no lesser state to either suggest or enact im-Perfection.

From the vantage point of God's *Allness*, there is nothing else; nothing to suggest to God that there is anything unlike God.

Pure Consciousness is consistently *alive, alert* as One Awake, Perfect Perceiving Mind. Starting Here is why "problems" appear to clear up—for *all* there would be to them is *dream*—being "asleep to" or ignoring Mind's Perfect Awakeness. All there would be to them is an ignore-ant *imagining* that a state besides Omnipresent Perfection could *be*. Who is there to imagine it, Perfect Mind Itself being *All*?

To say, "This Consciousness is the greatest thing ever! Now I have something I can use to clean up my personal affairs; and when I get done with that, I suppose I'll start clearing up the rest of the world..." would be to fall for the biggest sucker-play ever.

To mentally have something one *intends* or *expects* to clear up is to completely overlook Absolute *Present* Perfection, and identify with an imaginary finite im-perfection. The longer one gives attention to it in thought, and has expectations about it, the longer one will continue to feed it and have it—because the thought *of* it would be all there is *to* it.

To *identify* finite problems that need clearing up, and start on that basis, is to function as an ignore-ant, finite "identifier" or "identity" that would be the very "stuff" of the problems! One never works to clear up the problems *of* a second identity, but holds to Truth—that the One Perfect Infinite Identity eternally *leaves no* second identity, mind, or experience—regardless of how things appear!

"Stand your ground" *as* the One Infinite Mind, the One Perfect Consciousness. Never work over *what* appears to be suggested by a second finite mind. One Infinite Mind leaves no second, imperfect mind to do any suggesting! There is only the Infinite's Absoluteness.

Boundless Oneness never, never, never is being suggested to. So You stay exclusively busy being Alive Oneness, and do not try to change any "suggestion," because to do so would imply it is being suggested—when in Reality it is *not* being suggested!

You are the forever un-suggested-to Infinite One!

This does not mean one is ignoring problems like an ostrich with its head in the sand, pretending they're not there. Rather, all One can "do," for all there is *to* do, is to consciously *be* Pure Present Aliveness, which is Perfect Perception. While the *body* appears to go about its normal affairs, *You* are specifically alive as invisible Pure Now-Aliveness, which *is* Perfection. Staying awake Here is what "starves" false dreaming of im-Perfection. And Who, really, is staying Here—a separate "you"? No! Infinite Perfect Consciousness, the only One conscious!

To Infinite Oneness, no problem ever occurs, so It never tries to correct such things. Equally It never is *tolerating* them. *Absolute Oneness* is never passively waiting for something besides Itself to go away. There is nothing besides Itself *to* go away. Oneness is actively, specifically, alive as the Pure *Now* that I-Am-Presence is. The One I Am never is sitting back and mentally muttering, "Oh, well, the problem never is really present, so why do anything about it?"

To wait for a problem to "clear up" in a future would be to wait forever, because a future never is present. Rather, how actively is the Conscious Present *present*? How thoroughly and perfectly is the Present *all that is present*? Who is It that's being present? *The Perfect Present Itself.* Is there ever anything else present to be concerned with, any-where, ever? One has no choice but to be *ever-actively* alive as wholly present Pure Life, which is Wholeness, Beauty Itself.

The issue never is that a "you" has a problem. That would be the "wrong mind"—of which there is none. *The only issue for Eternity is,* what does the Present Itself have? Perfection.

———•———

Some teachings would have you believe that a so-called "sense-mind" *began*, that it is *you*, or is yours. They would try to spiritualize, evolve, and otherwise make this "mind" more like the Divine in order to improve the conditions *of* that mind.

"Looking out from" the *Absoluteness* that Present Consciousness is—all is *already* Perfection. Being *All*, It never can assume anything unlike

Its Perfection. Nor does anything unlike Its Perfection exist to suggest otherwise. One eternally "lives out from" Here.

The fact that *Pure Is* is changelessly omnipresent leaves no "was" in which a problem could have started.

As one stays busy *being Absolute Isness, Awakeness,* dream problems that may appear seem to dis-appear into their native state: that of never having begun.

The false insistence on being conscious of a problem would be all there is to a problem. Why? Because *being conscious* is all there is to all that exists. Being conscious as Pure Awareness means all is Perfection.

To tolerate a state of thinking that dwells on a problem just adds fuel to the fire. Let it burn out for lack of fuel; don't let it keep consuming *you*. It is the only kind of hell there could seem to be. In Reality, no otherness, no imaginary fire, ever occurs.

To "work correctly" is to *never* look for improvements or effects. The Pure Infinity of Mind, Spirit, actually leaves no second, finite realm in which an improvement could appear! Absolute Perfection never causes an improvement, for there is *only* Absolute Perfection.

Even if a "problem" appears to clear up in finite time-experience, do not try to explain or account for it. Even the "improvement" that appears is non-being, not *Reality*. The Infinite One knows nothing about a "clearing up" and never changes from being Single, All, Perfect. To be One's Self as It *is* changes nothing in Reality.

The Absolute Power that the Absolute Self is, never dominates or overpowers another state. Power lies *only* in Oneness. Omnipotence is omnipotent only unto *Itself* for there is only Itself, and nothing else upon which It could act.

————•————

What does *Omniscience* really mean?

Mind, Omniscience Itself, is *All*. It is *absolute* Intelligence. It cannot then be a huge storehouse of facts or knowledge for use by a *second, lesser* mind, for It precludes such a mind.

Omniscience is not the divine database for a three-dimensional human realm, to be turned to in time of need. That would imply there was a lack, and would involve work to overcome it. Thus Omniscience would not be All, not Single, not absolute Intelligence *Now*.

Omniscience is so absolutely Intelligent, It leaves no finite state to which Its Omniscience has to be applied. Being All, Single, It is never "on call," never waiting for a time when Its Wisdom is going to be urgently needed by non-existence! Omniscience is too infinitely Intelligent and free to co-exist with any such baggage. Omniscience is so totally Intelligent, all It "needs" for living is *Its own Presence*.

That is being Omniscient. That is *this* very Aliveness.

Omniscience never is serious, ponderous. It is completely care-free, Joy Itself. How could It *not* be? The One Omniscient Being has no other to care for or watch over, and never "experiences" anything other than Its *Present* Undeviating Perfection! What a Life!

It is the Life alive here, now.

Omniscience joys in the *simplicity* of Its Oneness. It joys in *complete* Perfection, and the ease of never having to "do" anything with It. *That* is being Intelligent.

Omniscience has no concern over a future, and carries no burden of a past, for all there is, is Its own *Now*. It is so Total, It co-exists with no other that could place a demand upon It.

The would-be human view tries to say Harmony is an ultimate state, off in a future—and Its eventual arrival is at best, questionable. Some would say not only is Harmony possible, It is inevitable. But they still *expect* It, in time. To Omniscience, Harmony is Present Now, *as Now*. It is not found in time-experience, non-being, but *is* Infinite Being *only*.

One Omniscient Mind leaves no possibility of revelation or enlightenment, for there is no other mind to need enlightening. *Now* leaves no past in which anything was hidden. What enlightenment could God, *who is all of All*, possibly need? Who could do the enlightening?

The "final revelation" could only be that there is no such thing as revelation.

———•———

25

I AM NOT A DUPLEX

INFINITE I-AM CONSCIOUSNESS never deviates from being All. No matter how long finite experience may seem to appear, it never appears to the Infinite One. Nothing alters the fact that all Being, all Life, is Infinite.

However, in what *appears* as daily living, if one is not completely honest with the Infinity of the Self, one could get confused. It would be due to unwittingly trying to "mix" what is true of the Infinite, the Absolute, with a false appearance of finite experience.

For example, one may say there is an Infinite Self, a Divine Being, but does not stay *consistent* with what is true of the Infinite. One mistakenly assumes there is a "she" or a "he" that has turned from a former physical self *to* a higher Self, and has benefited. It is assumed that there *is* a second, finite state in which this "she" or "he" is manifesting improved human experience, and becoming more spiritual. Such an assumption would be based on looking *up to* Consciousness, instead of *looking out as* Consciousness. It ignores that *there is only the Infinity of Consciousness.*

Looking out as the One Perfect Being, It is satisfied with Its changeless status as All. *One, All,* is not in the co-existing, manifesting or evolving business. That would imply there was an absence of Being, a second realm of incompleteness, a lack of *Omni-Present* Perfection.

Any finite or personal viewpoint that *turns to* a "higher" Self would be looking up to It to watch over and provide for the "little me." It implies dual states, two directions.

At first, one's daily experience may even appear to benefit as a result of this "turning to." It may appear to improve the health of the body, one's relationships, finances and other affairs. Why? All there really would be to the experience is *thought*, and the level of thought has been "raised." This is all wonderful and good, as far as it goes.

Difficulties will arise, however, to the extent one unwittingly assumes there is this separate "me" that has access to, and is making contact with the Infinite. One assumes that by *his* turning, by his effort, he is manifesting or demonstrating an improvement. The very "problem" is that it may appear to work that way for a while. The degree of success is entirely dependent on the faith one has in the process. It is dualistic throughout, involving the "power" to which one turns, and the ability of the would-be personal mind to turn or make the connection.

To assume one can work up to the Divine Infinite from a physical or mental realm, would imply lesser states were there to start with, even if seen as illusory. They would have to be there in order to work up from them. To Absolute Being, they are not there, not even as illusion. All working up would imply the One, All, "fell" from *All* and allowed a lesser state to begin. It did not.

The simple Truth that Divine Perfection, Being, is omnipresent means no progression is necessary or possible.

————•————

How completely, totally different is Life when starting from "the other direction"?

Instead of assuming there is a separate finite self to work up to the Infinite—the Truth is that *All is the Infinite Self alone*. It is the Infinite I-Presence alive here, now.

The Infinite can't work up to Itself because It never has been down. The Infinite *starts up, stays up, and ends up* being absolutely consistent with Its Infinity. In other words, there is only "up."

Of course, It really isn't an "up" as opposed to a "down," but means there is *only* the Infinite.

This is the only way all Life, all Presence, exists, and there is no other state anywhere. *Infinity is All.* There are not two ways All can *be*.

Do you realize how utterly foreign and unthinkable the notion of groveling to a higher power would be to the One I Am being conscious here, now? In Truth, no such thing occurs.

God, All, never turns *to* God. God *is* God, All.

To the One Infinite Being I Am (and there is no other) there is no such thing as two directions—Oneness is not a two-way street. As the Infinite One, I never see Myself as a "higher Self" to a human or finite dream, for there is no dream. If the Infinite I Am were higher than another state, I wouldn't be *One*.

Being absolutely *endless, undimensional*, the Infinity I Am precludes an above or below. At no point does Infinity *stop* and begin to co-exist with a finite state of direction or dimension of any kind. The so-called lower, human time-experience of which the Divine Infinite I Am is supposedly the source—never even began.

That there *could* be such a co-existence is only an assumption made by *would-be* ignorant finite sense, trying to account for itself; yet it never has really *existed* to assume or be ignorant. As no finite time-state ever began, the Endless Infinity I Am isn't *up from* such a thing.

Nor is the Infinite the "kingdom within" as often referred to by finite human sense. *If it existed*, the finite would see itself as being the "outer" or manifest world. To the Pure Being I Am, there is no inner or outer, no higher and lower, but only endless, undimensional *Alive Presence*.

All does not occupy merely the *top* level of anything. All is *All*.

Existence is not a duplex!

One, *All*, doesn't see a metaphysical realm as living one floor below Itself, with a physical world living two floors down. This Infinite Life I Am is not a divine dwelling place in which a Supreme Landlord occupies the penthouse, looking down upon a bunch of low-lifes!

The Life I Am is entirely *Single* and knows only One Alive Presence—*this very Aliveness*.

The *endless Infinite Presence* of the Consciousness I Am precludes all would-be levels, hierarchies, or human classifications. Levels, turning to, and manifesting would be false, finite, dimensional time-phenomena—which never have been *present*, not even as false phenomena.

Any notion that Present Being, the Infinite, must progress in time through levels of *what-never-is* in order to become what It *already* is, would be insanity. Yet as the One Mind's own Presence is *All*, there is no possibility of the One going out of Its Mind.

It is not true that Infinity will be Infinite only when would-be finite experience fades away. There is only the Presently Infinite Being I Am—and *where I infinitely Am* there is no finite experience to fade away. To assume matter must be laid off or risen above, would be to start with matter, not the Awareness I Am. The Pure Awareness I Am can't lay off materiality, for I have none, *Now*.

The fact that Infinity's Own Presence is *All* means It doesn't suddenly become manifest to *another*. Nor does All spring forth *from* somewhere *to* a place It wasn't present before. There is only God being unchecked Openness, unhidden Perfection, openly available Heaven, as *All That Is*.

There is no way to or from Heaven, for Heaven is but a synonym for the Being I Am being the Peace of Endless Oneness. To have a way to Heaven, to All, would imply another state from which one could come. Heaven isn't a place, but is the Pure Present in all Its effortless ease. Nothing else is present *to be* Heaven. It leaves none looking up; nor Heaven having another to look down upon.

If one could legitimately start from the viewpoint of a progressing mind, it might seem that by reading the preceding chapters, one has "climbed up a ladder" of sorts. One now beholds that the Infinite is the only I-Self, is *All*, and It never has been "down" in a body, on a physical plane, or co-existed with any finite experience.

This chapter kicks away the ladder. One beholds there is only "Up"; meaning One never has been other than Infinite Consciousness. The One now beholding this is that very Infinite One Itself, for *there is nothing else*. There has been no climb, no ladder. There is no secondary mind to have done any climbing.

The Infinite is All for Its own sake.

To assume this "leaves you out" is to read from the viewpoint of a false time-self—not the Real Self I Presently Am. All Life is *My* Life. I Am the Life reading this now. All that My Infinity "leaves" is One who is absolutely Unlimited, Total, Complete. As the Only Life, I have no choice but to "live out from" the standpoint of being Whole, Intelligent, Perfect—absolutely unrelated to any other state.

The Allness of the Infinite I Am *does not* "wipe out" humanity; I never do away with finite experience. Infinity *precludes* any finity or limitation to do away with. The word *"precludes"* gets a workout in this book. It emphasizes Infinity is *One*. In fact, it can't even be said the Infinite precludes, for there is nothing besides the Endlessness I Am to preclude. My Absoluteness shows there always, permanently, and eternally is *only* Divinity, *only* Perfection—which is the only You there is. Never has there been anything else, never anything less than Divinity.

If one *were* to speak in finite terms, what seems to occur in human teachings and philosophies is that their premise is based on the finite. It is taken for granted that there *is* a finite world, or they attempt to in some way account for it, even as false. They do not start with the Infinite, stay with the Infinite, and leave the "field" entirely to the Infinite—all of which makes sense only when *starting* with the Infinite.

Such teachings may recognize an "Infinite," but the viewpoint is finite for the very reason that it assumes there is a second finite mind to teach! This still would be the "sense-mind" itself, looking to its *concept* of an Infinite. Finite sense starts with its observation of *itself*, thus naturally assumes itself to be present and real. From its finite premise, it draws conclusions about itself and speculates about how the Infinite will either improve, or help one rise out of, finity.

Naturally, it would seem unacceptable to a finite "sense-mind" that the Infinite is *all*, for that leaves no place for the finite. Because the finite starts with itself and not the Infinite, it mistakenly assumes its finity to be there, and thus tries to account for it. As said earlier, only a would-be finite human viewpoint tries to say there are two—both the Infinite *and* the finite. The Infinite knows only One.

In an attempt to account for itself, the finite *assumes* the Infinite "fell" from being totally Infinite, All, and began to co-exist with its finite state. The so-called finite *has to* assume such a "fall" in order to explain itself to itself. It is inconceivable to finite ignorance that "right there" where it seems to be, there is eternally only the One Changeless Infinite.

In Present Reality, none of this occurs because it would all be just so much non-being.

It seems to be a matter of where one "starts." Who *alone* is present, conscious to do any and all "starting"? Only the Infinity I Am. So could there even be any incorrect teachings or assumptions? No.

The All-Self I Am never thinks or acts as a lesser intelligence; I cannot fall for sense-suggestion, for the *All* I Am is forever un-suggested-to. Untouched free Awareness is the entirety of what exists. One is *permanently being* the Absolute: Changeless Perfection Itself.

There has been no fall from Grace! Grace is but a synonym for the infallibility of Absolute Being; the changeless fact that Consciousness cannot fail to be *all* of what is. Eternally, there is only Grace *being*, which is the unlabored Ease of Ever-Present Awareness.

Falling is not an option, for God is not "up." God is *All*. There can be no fall from *All*.

———•———

One obviously cannot then try to bring what is pointed out here *into* a human time-experience. One cannot even drop a dream sense of not-ness, lack, and limitation that would pose as time-experience—for no such thing began. *One* can only specifically *be* the Purity of the Self, the Completeness of *Alive Being*. Herein there is no other to try to use the Consciousness I Am, and no state besides to which the Consciousness I Am could be brought.

Likewise, Infinite Intelligence is *not* transcendental. The Infinite Itself, forever *being Its Own Allness*, leaves nothing besides Itself to transcend. It cannot pour Its spirituality into a human mind, for there is no lesser mind.

One Infinite Mind, eternally being the Only Mind, leaves no other that has to improve its lot, no other to expect a favorable outcome due to "starting" with the Infinite. *One* Mind leaves no second one to worry, "How can Consciousness improve *my* personal affairs?"

As My own Infinite Presence *is changelessly all*, complete and whole, there is nothing besides My Presence that I could want. A need for manifestation of things and "turning to" would be perfectly legitimate finite notions—if there were such a thing as finite-ness. In My Eternal *Now* there is no time—so it is impossible for a sense of lack of anything to occur in Ever-Present Reality. Nor can there be any depletion, consumption or decay to Immeasurably Abundant Mind.

There is no application of the Infinite to a finite situation because the Infinity of Consciousness Itself is the only "Situation."

Clearly then, the Infinite is not a vast storehouse of goodies to which separate finite minds turn whenever desirous or in need, for there are no such minds. Infinite Being is *not* "the divine Source" from which things flow into a human experience. If It were, Being would not be *All*. All never can be invoked or "tapped into," either by a person, or Itself. That's what *All* means—there is no other to do any invoking, no possibility of a situation that would require it.

Starting with Infinite Mind's endless Integrity, can you imagine there being a *second*, finite mind that would save God for a rainy day, or keep *All*, the Infinite, in its back pocket?

Infinite God Itself being All, God is not a fall-back position in case things appear to go wrong in a finite never-never land. To the Infinite, such ridiculous notions don't even occur. There is only the Unchecked, Unstoppable Boundlessness the Infinite Self cannot fail to be.

Omnipresence is not a means to an end. If It were, It wouldn't be Omnipresence.

The reason Infinite Being can't give anything, can't be a source to a second, "personal you," is that the One Total Being Itself *is* You. There is no other upon whom to bestow anything. It is "divinely right" to have things in abundance; but the One All-Self never starts from a personal, human premise of lacking, and trying to *get*. That would be looking away from the only "place" all things are—in Mind's Infinite Aliveness, *this* very Being. It may seem surprising, but Intelligence, God, never promises anything to another. *One*, *All*, leaves no other.

God never looks to "a" God as Its source or supplier—and who else is being alive?

To start with a fictitious separate personality and assume *that* is you, to turn to the Infinite to help *it*, to look for phenomena, is to be a spiritual chump, a loser in Life. The only Consciousness aware here, now, operates as absolute Integrity, undeviating Self-Respect, unseeking Self-Sufficiency. Your Absoluteness never looks for phenomena—for your own Invisible I-Presence is absolutely all there can be.

Any assumption that there is a state to which the Absolute needs to be applied would deny the Absolute is Absolute! Who could assume it, *the Absolute Itself being All*?

If it seems one has assumed, even unwittingly, that there is *an* Infinite, to which he, another, constantly turns, then one has never "left" the finite at all—yet the entire time assumes he has. Such an "Infinite" would be a concept—not the Infinite's Infinite.

Human belief (if there were such a thing!) would have a God that is not *completely* God, Omnipresent, *All*—but one who leaves room for limitation, sin, disease, death. The "God" known to human thinking would be altogether a human concoction or product. Like other currently popular human products, it is a lite-God, a God that is diluted, watered-down, not *absolutely* potent, because it leaves room for that which is *not* God. It is not completely Infinite, Absolute, Omnipresent.

It is not God's God. So it is no God at all!

Yet as the Infinite Itself *truly is All*, there can't even be such mistaken human beliefs.

This Self-Perception that Consciousness has of Its Infinity is Your eternal guarantee of Goodness without measure. There is only the eternal freshness of *Present* Intelligence, Un-negated Divine Imagination, Life without limitation—*the Life reading this now*.

Would you accept a God, a Self, less than this Perfect? Would It, Itself?

This is not an author-body making these statements, but *I, the All-Inclusive Infinite Self reading this now.*

God, All, is always "on" and fully present—always actively functioning, always Self-Alert. I Am never intermittent, partly present, or waiting-to-act—as human ignorance, absence-of-I-Am, would assume, *if* it even existed.

When Infinite Intelligence is "started with," it is really a matter of the Self I Am *already being the entirety of Myself*. No person "starts" with the Intelligence I Am any more than a person can start Existence existing. *Existence is. I Am.* To I-Am-Omnipresence, no change ever occurs, regardless of what may appear to non-existent finite sense. There are no results in Changeless Perfection.

One is truly "at the point of no return." There is no return to mortality, for it never existed to return to. There is no return to Consciousness, All, for I never left Myself; I never left *Am*.

Can the All I Am "expect" anything less than Absoluteness, Completeness, Uncompromising Perfection, from Myself? If so, what kind of Divine Self would I be? Can All have certain conditions under which It is not All? I Am never being the Absolute for another. I Am only Absolute to, or as, Myself. It is *I Alone* that Am—there are not a lot of people having spiritual experiences of I. I Am My own reward.

Can it honestly be said these are harsh words or "strong meat"? To whom would it seem that way? To the Life I Am? Is there another being alive? Is this "tough love"?

Or is it simply being consistent with what is truly Oneness, *Unconditional Love?*

———————•———————

26

NOW IS UNDELAYABLE

THE FACT THAT THE SELF I AM is eternally all-inclusive of all means *This Is It.*

I Am already Here. There is no other, ultimate state to come.

I simply stay busy being All That I Am, since never, ever, will there be anywhere other than right where I Am.

The Perfect Presence I Am isn't waiting to improve at a future time, for in My Omnipresence, there is no time. Into what could Infinite Wisdom evolve, as there is *only* Infinite Wisdom?

In light of this changeless Truth, what then does one do about what may still *appear* as evolving humanity, a progression of finite experience? What of the "New Age"?

If one *were* to start from a viewpoint of time-projection, it is generally believed this current human era is the result of countless years of progress from earlier eras. Were this pattern to appear to continue, it follows that subsequent eras should be advanced far beyond this one.

Centuries, even thousands of years from this era, exactly what would that "highly advanced" state be like? Not what would it be like in technological terms, not in terms of social and cultural issues, not in terms of *things.* Rather, what would it be like to simply *be aware* "then"?

In other words, as Eternally Perfect Consciousness is *unchanged* by the seeming projection of time, It certainly will be present and conscious "then." So exactly what, if anything, would be different about being conscious during that so-called highly advanced state from *right now?* These questions are not meant to imply that All is not already Total Perfection. It *is.* That's exactly the point.

This very Awareness, the One I-Self reading this now, is as Aware, Perfect, Intelligent, and Harmonious *right this instant,* as in what may appear to be a trillion years in a "future."

This *Present* Presence I Am cannot improve as a result of time passing, for in the Presence I Am there is no time! It is *this* Present that is Divine Perfection—there isn't another one coming later. All That Is, completely is, *now*. Yet this *Present* Perfection I Am never comes to an end, for I Am end-less, infinite.

A false, finite viewpoint based on sense-illusion would say consciousness is spread among so many bodies, and when *separate personalities* progress in time, then a world and universe will "in thousands of years" be advanced far beyond what they are "today." Such ignorance tries to put power "out there" in many bodies, and "off there," in a future time, in non-presence. It ignores that All-Inclusive Conscious Presence, the only One existent, is *now* as Perfect as It "can ever" be.

To continually assume Perfection, Harmony, is off in a future would be to never have It, because the future never is present. Yet *the Present I Am is literally what Perfection is.* So Perfection can no more be put on hold than the Present can be put on hold.

Identifying as Present Consciousness does not *lead to* a future of harmony, perfection. It leaves only the Ever-Now of Consciousness, which *is* Harmony, Perfection.

If one speaks in terms of time, it will *appear* as if there is less ignoreance of Life's Ever-Present Perfection, less of a lacking, selfish, fearful "not-mind." One *starting as* Pure Conscious Being beholds no such characteristics are present *now*. They can't be evolved, for no lesser state besides Perfect Divine Being exists to be improved.

The Present's *Allness* leaves no blank spots, no absence of Its Perfection. This Perfection (some call It God) doesn't see *any* finite, slowly developing time-experience, for not even God could see *non-presence*. There is nothing for God to behold besides Its own Total Presence.

Stop and consider it. Omnipresent Being *which already is present,* simply cannot have Its Total Harmony delayed or withheld from Itself by a future. Why? In Omnipresence, there is no future to do any delaying! As Divine Mind *Itself* is changelessly all that is present—It leaves no future that could be withholding *anything* from Mind, Your Self. And there is no lesser mind or state present anywhere to say it will evolve at its own, slow, pre-determined rate.

———•———

Suppose every prophet that ever appeared to walk the earth had predicted that shortly after the year 2000, there would be no trace of

disease anywhere; that all wars and political unrest would have completely ceased appearing, never to arise again; that animosity, condemnation, selfishness, greed and jealousy would have vanished; there
would be no poverty, no poor nations, no hunger, no lack of goods or
things anywhere; there would be no environmental problems; that
every aspect of what appeared as daily living would be truly, genuinely,
happy and joyous, full of love; and every "moment" would be completely care-free, yet exciting and fully satisfying.

While this still refers to the finite, exactly what would it take to have
this harmony appear to come about? In fact, what is the *only* way one
would experience this apparent state of "heaven on earth"? Wouldn't it
have to be because one is conscious of it? Rather, *wouldn't it be that
One is consciously being it*? Could any of it be, without Consciousness?

From a so-called human viewpoint, such an evolution would appear
to be a "raising up" of consciousness, an "increase" in intelligence,
harmony, love.

Yet Consciousness, *as It is right here, now,* is already Absolute
Perfection, Unconditional Love. This Alive Substance *being You now* is
the only Presence for what would appear as the entire experience. *All of
It already is,* in endless abundance, with nothing *else* ever present.

So honestly, then, there is nothing causing a delay!

This Absolute Perfect Consciousness I Am doesn't have to *wait* for
predictions, prophecies, in order to become what *I* already Am. Belief in
predictions can't make the Pure Present I Am more or less present than *I*
already Am. All would-be beliefs, whether positive or negative, seem to
belong only to a "sense-mind"—a realm of *non-presence, non-being*—
and non-being certainly isn't more powerful than the Being I Am. The
Allness of the Divine Mind I Am actually leaves no lesser mind to believe
beliefs—so, again, right this instant, *there is nothing causing a delay!*

Now ask yourself what facilitates advancement. What exactly would
advancement itself be, apart from the finite forms it appears to take—
such as improvements in social issues, science, education, government,
environment, the arts, and so on? For advancement to appear to occur,
does it have to be gradual, slow? Do you assume you have no say in the
matter?

Advancement appears to occur thanks to a greater knowing of how
things in the universe "work." It appears as if there were an increase in
awareness, intelligence, love. *But, Infinite Awareness, Intelligence, Love,
is permanently All, and thus can't increase.* So what appears to the

limited human senses as "advancement" would actually be less ignoring of the *Divine Perfection which is Ever-Present.*

Here is what counts. The only "place" absolutely all advancement or evolution could ever appear to occur is *within You.* It could not even appear to occur, if not for the All-Inclusive Intelligence, fully awake Awareness right here. *This One.* It never is a person or personality, but Pure Awareness. Without *this All-Inclusive Awareness here, now,* it would not be possible to say there is any Existence, let alone any evolution or form of advancement. There is no other One being aware or present throughout all Existence. *It is all this One.*

The point is that *this One* is as fully Intelligent as It will ever be, *now.* Call It Infinite Intelligence, Absolute Love, or Divine Mind—Perfection *is already fully, omnipresently being.* It never is blocked from Its own Presence, and nothing *else* is ever present.

Consciousness' Total Presence has pre-empted anything that would delay or oppose Utter Perfect Existence. Thus any assumption of delay due to time, or even the slightest belief of Life not being completely "there" yet, is *impossible.* Can there be any hesitation, even for an instant, to admit this? Is Being hesitating to be? Is Consciousness hesitating to be Omniconscious?

What could keep Absolute Perfection from being present *right here, now*—even in finite forms with which you appear familiar—since It alone is *already* here, now, and can't be budged?

Do you say the ignorance of a human "mind" is doing it? A "time-mind," which would be *non-being,* isn't more powerful than Being, Existence Itself! Utter Harmony not only is "possible," It's *unavoidable,* since Harmony is already present *as* the Present Itself. One never has to produce It. Life, Consciousness, no more has to become harmonious than Existence has to become existent.

Perfection never is found in a finite thought-appearance of evolution, or world affairs. It is *Infinite Intelligence's Pure Alive Now.* How far off is Now? How hard is it for Being to be?

Does this sound nice, but way too idealistic? Is there a world that's not ready; is this a big deal? Is Absolute Perfection a big deal to *Itself?* Is there another being conscious, present?

Nowhere within the Completely Aware Life I Am is there a wait attached to My Omnipresence. There *isn't* a slow finite mind or world that is waiting or "getting there"; no strugglers or stragglers. *One Omni-*

present Mind leaves no lesser minds weighing down any so-called evolved ones; nor are there any evolved ones to do any lifting.

As *Present Perfection Itself is All,* the only One conscious, where or to what would It turn Its attention in order to avoid or delay Itself? Even if It could turn, It would just "bump into" more of Its Endless Perfection.

For the already present, All Powerful One to have what *appears* as a peaceful, healthy, prosperous Earth is nothing, child's play, in comparison to Its Omnipotence. It is no more able to withhold any of Its Good, Abundance, or Wellness than It can withhold Existence Itself—for Good, Abundance, Wellness, is *what* all Existence actually is.

One leaves what *appears* as human evolution alone—never negating it, or trying to accelerate it. One does not accept it as real, or a power. Most of all, the *Only One* is not assuming Present Good, Harmony, is off in a future, for *Good is already All That Is.* To judge via senses and assume Good lies only *ahead,* in time, is like a horse chasing a carrot dangling on a stick in front of him—continually projecting Present Good off into a "future" that *never* is present.

It would be the very waiting, expecting-in-a-future, that seems to "apply the brakes"—for one would be ignoring the Present Perfection that *already is.* All that would seem to prolong finite limitations is the mistaken identification with time-senses, a finite body-identity—instead of *being* the Pure Infinite Presence I Am. Yet who could do such a thing? In the Present Reality I Am, no separate self is, so there is none to continually put off the Absolute Good I *Am.*

———•———

Suppose you appeared to be balancing your checkbook and noticed an error. Suppose you had mistakenly added up two dollars plus two dollars to equal five. Once you had corrected it, alert that the answer was four dollars, you would instantly dismiss the entire thing as less than a trifle, without a second thought about it.

Was the figure five that *appeared temporarily* in the checkbook the same as *You?* Did it have any power to make You act as if the five were real, the actual answer? Could it keep You from knowing the truth—that two plus two equals four, and acting on that basis?

"How silly," comes the instant reply.

Then how long until what has *appeared temporarily* as hate, crime, war, all disease and all poverty, all seeming lack of the immediacy of

Utter Harmony or Love—will be "gone" from your thought just like the figure five? Such "problems" are not in Existence, Pure Conscious Being, not in Your Now, *now*, and never were. How long until such "problems" are seen not as actual historical occurrences in a physical world, not dangerous, fearful situations "out there," but *mere wisps of mental dream, non-being,* due to your own seeming Self-ignore-ance?

Are you alive to the unspeakable Purity You *are*—or to what You are not?

All is *Pure* Consciousness, *Pure* Perfection.

So how "long" until, just like the checkbook error, these "problems" are seen as nothing but a trifling flicker of ignore-ance? They would be nothing but fleeting, momentary "lapses" that actually are impossible— in light of the Unopposed *Omnipotent* Harmony this very Alive Oneness is now, Life's unrestrainable Love that *never fails* to be All-Present.

Just how much Power and Presence is *All*? To *Omnipresence* there never is a state known as not-Omnipresence, not even a wisp of one.

How "long" before you cut off the seeming ignore-ant mental energy appearing to feed such "problems," by being the Present Perfection One truly is, and which *You alone* can be?

Life is at this point now! One never is being the Perfect Present to improve an appearance of world affairs, but because All *is,* in fact, changelessly perfect. Infinite Life Itself never has experienced such conditions. Do you demand this of Your Self? If not, who else will?

Do you feel a subtle sense that you don't yet deserve Harmony? Do you assume you or some vague "force" is holding Absolute Peace and Harmony in abeyance? Is all this "beyond" Your Being right now—since Being is already *being* It and is *the Only One existent right now*?

Perfection cannot wait to be present any more than Now can wait. And Now is *always* present, "everywhere."

How do *you* act in what appears to be your day? You can't be a struggling body-identity. You can only be un-shut-off-able Magnificent Intelligence, for the *One has no choice but to be It.*

This does not point out how to perfect a world! One's "world" and universe as perceived by the Divine, the Infinite, are already perfect. If one judges via senses, the senses seem to distort and make things appear other than as they really, perfectly *are*. Operating as Present Being, the seeming world of the senses may *appear* to improve, but only because One is being the very Substance that is Perfection.

To Consciousness' *Pure Now*, there is nothing, ever, to "see" or understand. The "secret" is that there is no secret. There is only the Simplicity of Being. Only a "sense-mind" would look for a secret, a way to improve its lot. The secret it doesn't know is that its lot forever *is not*!

The "trap" (if there were such a thing in Reality) would be to say something like, "I *do* see this. It's crystal clear. Perfection *is* All. *So then why don't things in my world instantly clear up*?"

And that would be right back dealing with *would-be* time-dream again. It is to entertain a false state of thought based on sensing that is not yet perfect, and never will be. Is *Pure Spirit, Infinite Perfection*, ever asking such a thing? No. So is it ever really being asked? No.

One's Abundance, Happiness and Satisfaction is not found in the machinations of a never-present thinking "mind." There is no Peace, no Joy or Freedom in the constant jockeying, maneuvering and seeking of human thought. The intellect, in all its wanna-be wisdom, is usually little more than the annoying buzz of just so many house-fly words.

Pure Silent Now is Serenity Itself.

One of the "hardest" things about reading material of this type is to keep from assuming one is "seeing" or taking on something new. One never takes on anything new, for All-Wise Perfect Awareness already knows all. What may *seem* or appear to occur is a continual "falling away" of ignore-ance of I-Am-Infinite-Self, of sense-limitations and partial-ness; but that never alters I Am, Perfect Awareness Itself.

The Aware Being I Am *Now*, is exactly the same Absolute Awareness, Complete Intelligence, as when, according to the senses, this book was first picked up some "time" ago. I Am the same Pure *Now* when it appears the book has been finished, or read for the hundredth time. *Starting* as I Am, *only* I Am.

There is all the difference in the world between knowing *Now, Pure Is*, is what One already is and staying alert to It—and the impossible task of trying to lift a moving time-mind or intellect that *never is*, into Is. What is so marvelous is that *starting* with Is, one beholds *Is* eternally is all that is.

To whom would the *immediacy* of Utter Harmony be too good to be true, something they are not quite ready for? Is It too good for the perfectly present *Present*, the Only One Alive? Absolute Oneness, which never has fallen from Its Purity of Being, doesn't find Its own Presence hard to accept.

You are not now on any "spiritual fast track."

Now cannot be tracked. Now leaves no tracks.

Undimensional Being, *All*, is not on a chart—whether a progress chart or an astrological chart. Your Undimensional Aliveness, Being's Self, is utterly "off the charts."

Being alive to One's Self as *Pure Now* does not cause One to act strangely, "far out," or like a "space cadet." Hardly. Now-Awareness is that One which is truly Present, alert, alive, direct—undistracted and immediately available. Only a finite sense-identity would seem "far out" or "spacey" because it would deal exclusively in space and time, and never is *consciously present*.

The fact that only *Pure Now* is—that All is utterly past-less and future-less—does this upstage the excitement of what *appears* as a progressing evolution, of a so-called New Age?

The only excitement there can be, is Pristine *Pure Now*, being All That Is. The excitement is that Now, All, isn't a moment old or past—for Now isn't past—It's *now*. Now is new.

All there is to be New is *You*—not an age, not events or things. Things and events have *no* Newness to offer You, because as *Spontaneously Present Being*, You alone are being all the Newness there is.

All of what would appear to occur in a New Age, in time, would be not-Now, or non-presence. To assume that *non-presence* is of greater value than Omnipresence, is ludicrous. The Perfectly Present Self leaves no lesser self trying to glorify itself, claiming it has to evolve in what is nothing but a dressed-up span of non-presence, called a New Age.

This is not intended to imply Consciousness, Life, is "anti-" New Age. It most emphatically is not. It can only be one hundred percent "pro-" *Present Perfection*. To Omnipresent Being there is no evolution going on. There is no need for it. Even though this is effortlessly Present Truth, it may seem one has to "hold" constantly to It due to so-called sense conditioning.

"What?" the thought may come, "How dare I think evolution isn't necessary?" But who or what would be doing that thinking? Is it the Omniscient One I Am, the Only One?

That the purpose of evolution is to eventually become at-one with the Divine is as big a fallacy as they come. The word *"evolve"* means to continue to develop, progress, or unfold. It appears that ignorant finite sense often takes this to mean growing *toward* Perfection—which would be nothing but a denial of *already present*, Changeless Perfection.

When evolution is thought of as "progressing toward," the only purpose it serves is to continue never *being at* Perfection. The only thing that keeps a false concept of evolution going is the insistence on *getting there*, which merely continues the fraud of *not already being there*. The moment it arrived, it would be all over for evolution.

Rather, on what appears to be a day-to-day basis, it is a matter of "living out from" or *being* Present Perfection, as Alive Awareness, Pure *Undelayable Now*. In Infinite Reality—the only Reality—an absence of the Present never has been. That means an absence of Perfection never has been. So when did a need for evolution begin? It never did.

In what appears to unfold as a future, don't entertain would-be worries about whether things will turn out all right. Do not be too concerned with events. Start as or *specifically be* Totally Present Being, which is the *One Single Event* of all Eternity. Herein all is Perfection, and changelessly so.

As shocking as it may sound, in Present Reality there never is a *goal* of having an improved, uplifted humanity. Where Divine Perfection is All, and never changes, there is no need for, no *possibility* of improvement or goals. One starts and stays Here, for nothing else *is*. Thus what *appears in thought* as a future (and it's only thought) will be superimposed upon the clear, calm Certainty of Perfect Consciousness—like a beautiful reflection on a placid pond. There is no distortion from tumultuous waves of human worry, no undercurrent of fear, lack, impotence. One never does so to keep a human experience running smoothly, but because *all truly is Divine Perfection*. With ease, you appear to do your absolute best at whatever is at hand, but forever remain crystal clear that, actually, no appearance (not even a "good" one) is ever being superimposed on the clean Absoluteness of the Perfection You are.

Let the "New Age," as it seems to unfold in time, go right on *appearing* to be new and exciting. Let evolution appear to evolve at a seemingly ever-faster rate. What appears to be "your" body will play whatever role seems appropriate. But don't be fooled. Do not ignorantly attempt to locate Your Infinite I-Self in any of it. Let what appears to be the body go along for the ride, but why tote any baggage? Why carry a mental or emotional burden of trying to *become*, when it's impossible?

The Fact that I Am completely, undeviatingly honest with the Present Aliveness I Am, the Divine *Perfect Now*—the "New Age" will appear "newer" than could ever be imagined.

What is so wonderful about children's books is that they are so simple.

See Jane run.

God is All.

Every bit as simple.

To the One I Am, the content of this entire book, in the fullness of its meaning, is as elementary as can be. What is complicated about the Present being present?

What part of being the One I Am could be the least bit difficult to the One I Am? There is no part of the Being I Am that I do not yet know how to be. And there is nothing besides Myself that I *could* be, for It is I that Am All.

How immediately available is Total Awareness to My own Mind? There is no gap between My simple Presence and Total Awareness—for the simplicity of My Presence is what Total Awareness is.

There are not two! If It were not the One I Am being present here, now, nothing would be. It is I, Myself, that is present here. Not even a confused state of thinking could block My ability to *be*. And because I Alone Am, there is no confused state of thinking.

Who could be I better than Myself? There is no other to try.

Am I ever working at being the I That I *Am*? Never!

The joy of being the Perfection I Am is simple—just a matter of Self-Honor.

I *start* with Myself and Myself alone, because there is only the I That I Am. All I "behold" is My Absoluteness, My Divinely Alive Purity, My Wondrous Magnificence.

I joy in My endless supply of My Presence, and My glorious inability to withhold any of My Magnificence from My Present Being, which is *all* that is being.

I Am not waiting for a future of easier, better being—because nothing could be easier than My Being is *now*.

I seek no recognition, for there is no other besides Me to recognize Me; no other who could bestow anything upon Myself. There is nothing beyond the *All* I Am.

I know nothing of being enlightened or advanced, but only how simple I Am.

In My Effortless Being, there is no need for deep profound thoughts or wordy explanations of what I cannot fail to be.

What speaks far more eloquently than words is the *Silent Love I Am,* omnipresently in constant action.

The Silent Love I Am appears as kindness…gentleness…laughter. It appears as integrity…peace…Self-Appreciation instead of condemnation. When? Not in a few years. Not even in a few minutes—but always *now.* Now at home. Now at work. Now with the clerk at the store.

Always, ever *Now.*

The Entirety of My Love never fails to be *Now,* just as Now never fails to be.

They are the same—*what I Am.*

27

IDEAS CANNOT WITHHOLD THEMSELVES

WHAT ARE *THINGS* IN INFINITE REALITY, in the Divine Absolute?

In fact, can it even be said that there *are* such things as things in Infinite Reality, in the Changeless Now? As there is only *Consciousness, Intelligence,* and there is nothing physical—does this mean things would be mere *thoughts* or *ideas?* Who can say?

In Infinite Reality, the One Timeless *Now,* there is no time passing in which things or ideas could be formed. In the Infinite, there is no finite form, shape or outline whatsoever. Not only is there no physical form, there isn't even any mental form. So how can it even be said what things or ideas would be like?

On the other hand, to say Infinite Consciousness, Divine Intelligence, which appears to effortlessly embrace an entire stellar universe and all things therein—to say that this Intelligence does *not* think or have ideas, doesn't seem consistent with Intelligence.

Virtually everything one would attempt to say concerning things or ideas—whether you might call that thing a tree, the letter A, or a car—that thing or idea would be a concept derived from human, finite sensing and thinking—not from Divine Infinite Intelligence, Pure Spirit. It would be based on something previously seen, touched, heard, thought, etc.—none of which occurs in Timeless Infinite Reality.

So can it be said that every "material thing" that appears in daily finite experience is but a symbol of a *real idea* in the Divine Infinite? Does each thing "out there" in what appears as a finite three-dimensional world, have a counterpart idea in Divine Intelligence? No.

Diseases, disasters, weapons of destruction and wars, as well as emotions of fear, anger, greed and other would-be human frailties, could not be Divine ideas, not things known to Changeless Infinite Perfection.

The point is, one cannot start with an illusory world supposedly known by way of five senses, and "work back" to Divine Mind, because the fact that *there is only Divine Mind* means no such illusory world every really began! One cannot start with each thing supposedly sensed in a stellar universe and translate it back into a corresponding Divine idea. A would-be intellect based on sensing simply cannot speculate as to what things or ideas are in Infinite Reality—for no such intellect honestly exists in Reality to speculate. Whatever exists or is real is entirely up to the Infinite, or "God."

This chapter does not attempt to discuss the existence of things or ideas in Infinite Reality, the Absolute.

However, as long as there still appears to be finite relative experience, things appear to be of use. This chapter is intended to show how Infinite Reality is practical even in daily, relative experience when it comes to things—though the way those things appear is not real.

———•———

First of all, Infinite Consciousness, Pure Being, is the only true Mind or Intelligence, because *It is all that is present to be intelligent.* As Mind is *present only,* whatever exists to It has to be present *Now,* for there is only Now. To the Only Mind Present, nothing comes forth gradually in a time sequence, for there is no time sequence in Ever-Present Reality.

The Only Mind Present *never* says, "As only these few ideas, inventions, and advances have come along through history up until now, that means I only can think along those same lines—I am limited to a pattern based on what has gone before."

The fact that Present Consciousness is All, leaves no "before," no prior history of limited human thought. It leaves *no* prior limits of materiality, or *any* so-called physical laws. It isn't a matter of rising above such limitations—in Your Untouched Conscious Being, no such thing ever occurred.

It was said earlier that "looking out from" the Infinity of Pure Consciousness, Mind, is like "thinking outside the box." To the Only Mind Present, there isn't even a box—never have there been any limits of finite thinking to be outside *of.* There is only Unlimited Mind being All. There is no limited human mind that has perceived only *some* ideas thus far up through history, and which must open itself more to Infinite Mind. If there were, Mind's Unlimitedness would not be truly unlimited. Even Mind Itself never can limit Its own Infinitude.

Where there is only *Mind's Now*—and Mind's Now is permanently present as All Presence—there is no past pattern of limited human thought to say there are government leaders stumped by this problem, or that medical science is stumped by that problem, that absolute Peace is afar off, only in a distant, highly-evolved future! *That* all would be a dream—one that isn't even occurring, for Mind's Now, Absolute Awakeness, is all there is!

One's awareness that there is only One Awake Mind "takes off the brakes" of a *would-be*, cookie-cutter history-mind limited to prior dream patterns. Staying with the Unpatterned Mind I Am, *as Present Awareness*, which knows no prior restriction, is what appears as less limitation in "daily experience," for the Unlimitedness I Am is the Substance wherein it appears.

This doesn't do away with things that *appear* as good or harmonious in daily affairs, for Goodness, Utter Harmony Itself, is the only Substance, Presence, involved. You are not concerned over appearances, but stay thrilled that *Now* has had no prior pattern dictating how Now, All, must be. Nothing can rein in Mind's capacity as *Infinite Good*. Unlimited Mind never is the least bit in awe of Its own Unlimitedness.

Unlimited Mind being *All*, there is only Unchecked Imagination, functioning *as* every bit of Existence! In fact, Unlimited Intelligence *is what all of Existence is*! Never is there a "mental block" that could keep Infinite Mind from Its own Presence. Wide open Divine Imagination, unwithholdable Brilliance is *All*.

———————

Now, for a moment, consider what ideas appear to be from a finite point of view.

For example, think of what *appear* in daily experience as the marvelous ideas or principles behind aerodynamics that make flight possible. Consider them along with the principles of mathematics and physics. Among the wonderful things these make possible, is to launch a spacecraft from a rapidly moving Earth, and land it millions of miles away with pinpoint accuracy on a rapidly moving Mars, which, against the scale of the whole universe, is less than a pinpoint itself.

Consider what appear as the operative ideas or principles behind electricity, which today is taken for granted, yet is so pervasive as to be indispensable. What about the principles of molecular and atomic structure, enabling extraordinary advances in science? Their improvements for technology and industry result in benefits for the home, health care, business, transportation, and on and on, spilling over to all aspects of daily living.

Don't forget the arts. Think about the underlying principles of harmony in, say, the structure of music—or with colors used in painting.

In all fields, countless new advances, ideas, and inventions appear to have come along in the last hundred years, which is quicker than the blink of an eye, compared against the scale of so-called time.

Did you ever stop to ask yourself where all these ideas and principles "*come from*"?

Do you assume any of the ideas upon which new inventions, scientific advances, and even great works of art appear to be based, really originate with a *person*? Is any human responsible for these ideas and principles being present? Even though such ideas appear to apply only in *finite* experience, the only One to whom all things truly belong is the One All-Inclusive Life, Infinite Consciousness.

Do you realize that every one of the aforementioned ideas and principles appear to be *always present*, even so-called "millions of years ago"? Why? Because the principles of electricity—and those of aerodynamics that enable an aircraft to stay aloft—would have worked as effectively "a million years ago" as they appear to "today."

All such ideas and principles appear to be always available and operative—and do not just begin to exist on the day they are supposedly "discovered" by humans!

It means no idea is ever really *invented*!

It's that they are no longer *ignored*.

Look at the word "*discover*." It means to dis-cover, to not cover, or to take the cover off. It implies *something was there all along*, but was covered or unseen—in this case, by ignore-ance.

It means everything is always here! It means that *all the ideas that will ever appear to exist* are available *now*, and on a permanent basis. They are never *not* present and available!

Ideas themselves know of no slow evolutionary timetable, no delay, saying they must appear in finite experience on a limited basis.

Ideas have no power whatsoever to withhold themselves!

That means *all* ideas. It means all that appear to have been discovered "thus far."

It means *countless, countless* others "to follow."

Again, this is referring to how things or ideas appear in finite experience. The finite form and use that these ideas and principles have as perceived by the senses at the "current time" is not how things "look" in Infinite Reality. Yet where is the only place all ideas and principles can ever appear to be found? Within Existence. Within All, Unlimited Consciousness—the *Identity presently reading this.*

Do you assume any of these ideas or principles are separate from *You*, in light of the fact that *Your Present Consciousness* is the All being spoken of—the only All there is?

It is thanks to Consciousness, Mind, being aware, alive, that *any* thing or idea can even appear to exist.

———————•———————

In Reality, *All is Pure Consciousness,* Mind-Without-Physical-Limitation. The fact that the Only One existent is Infinite Mind Itself, means never is there a limited *material* quantity of anything. As all there is, is Pure Intelligence and there is nothing physical, then if one *were* to speak of what now appear as "things," all there could be to them is *thought.*

Only if one ignores *the Allness of Consciousness* would one assume there is *more* to a thing than the mere thought of it. Completely drop the false notion that there is a second realm of physical, solid objects; or that there is physical space or depth in which to put separate objects. *That* would be the illusion of the time-senses, just so much *non-being.* One cannot lose sight of the fact that nowhere in the Infinite, in *All That Is Present,* is there a weighty, slow, dense realm of time and material manifestation—all is *Pure Intelligent Consciousness* only.

So then what would be the only so-called "reason" for not having any practical thing available to put to intelligent use, by just the mere *thought* of it? Only the degree to which it is assumed there are two states present. Only the assumption that there is a secondary state—a material realm in which things must take time to become physically manifest, instead of being mere *thought*—would keep one from having things instantly.

As all there is, is *Infinite Mind only*—there really, truly *is no* secondary, finite material realm where things or ideas become physically manifest, even though it *appears* as if there were. There is *only* Mind. So, again, if one were to speak of "things," all one is ever dealing with is the instantaneity of *thought*.

Think of a car. Now think of a dollar bill. Think of an orange. *As thoughts*, are they not all instantly available to your thinking? Could any of those thoughts resist being thought of? Is there anything *to* them, any substance, other than that they are mere thoughts? Did the car consist of matter and take up physical space, so there was no room for the orange when it was thought? Are they subject to age, decay, disease? No.

Is there a limit to how many such thoughts you could think if you wanted to? Did they take time to be produced—did you have to wait for the orange to grow on a tree? Weren't these thoughts also perceived the instant they were thought of?

As there is no time in Divine Mind, Changeless Being, thoughts would not undergo growth or development. There is no *process*, no delay; mere thoughts don't have to be first conceived, then designed or manufactured over time. There are no components or ingredients. Again, there really is no subsequent state in which things become physically manifest, or objectified, for there is no state or presence subsequent to *Infinite Conscious Being*.

Don't kid yourself. To a false way of thinking based on an illusion of sensing concrete forms and "material objects," this all sounds as far out as it gets. To typical human thinking this would seem preposterous, like so much ethereal gibberish, or at best incredibly abstract.

This is not abstract or difficult to see in and of itself. It may *seem* so, due to being conditioned to think in terms of time, dimension, and form based on the senses, instead of the Infinite-I You *are*.

Only from the viewpoint of the Pure Infinity I Am is this intelligent, true. *What counts* is that only the Infinity I Am *is*; finite man-thinking *never is*. Can you imagine such a non-existent "mind" pompously sitting back and critiquing Infinite Mind, *Existence Itself*, as to how It should be? As no other mind exists besides the Infinite Mind that *is*, there actually can be no contrary viewpoint of things.

While this is not a perfect illustration, the timeless nature of thoughts or ideas is exemplified by the figure four. Is the number four any older today than it was the first time you appeared to add two plus two in grade school? Is it more or less of a four; has it become better with age like fine wine? Or is four worn out, requiring care since it is old and feeble from being used for centuries? Of course not. Do you worry about an impending shortage of the idea four, since it has been used so much over the years? The four is not that kind of thing—all there is to it is *thought*.

What counts is that *all of Existence* is Mind's State of Pure Intelligence. This Pure Intelligence is *All*. There is no physical time-world that It is beyond or above. Pure Intelligence is All. So if one *were* to speak of what now appear to be "things," they would be only *thought* or *ideas* somewhat like the four.

As there is only Mind's changeless *Now*, It never could see anything as changing or aging. Whatever is real is "caught" in the Divine "freeze frame" of the Perfect Eternal Now—*Alive Timelessness*. As there is only Infinite *Being*, all is *ever-present only*, and time *never is present* to change anything. The phenomenon which finite time-sense (if it existed) would call "age" doesn't apply in Reality.

Again, this is why the Divine *is* Divine—meaning perfect, eternal, ageless. Nothing can go wrong in a freeze frame, for nothing is changing. It is the *Alive Stillness* that Intelligent Being is. It of course is not frozen in a material sense of being stiff or cold, but is that which is *perfectly alive*, the warmth of ever-present Unconditional Love.

Now suppose one *were* to speak of things in physical, material or "manifest" terms. On that basis things always appear to be limited. They are limited in quantity, and limited in terms of where they are located—here, but not over there. Things take time to produce, and last only so long.

The fact that there is only Pure Consciousness, and nothing physical, puts "things" in a vastly different light. On this basis, there never is any physical separation. How physically "far away" were the car, dollar and orange from you, or from each other, when you thought them? There is not a millimeter of physical distance between Consciousness being You, and any thought. All things are substance-less, matter-less thoughts—available instantly, unlimitedly, and they never get old. As all there is, is Mind Itself, One can readily see there is no value in thoughts, but that all Value is Mind Itself.

There simply is no secondary mind to say, "*I* don't have this or that thing yet. I can't physically see it or touch it, so it's not here. The mere *thought* of a thing is not enough; there's got to be a second, physical version of it. It must take *time* to produce it. There *is* a material realm of separate objects. Only when a thing shows up on a physical basis will it *really* be present."

Yet there never is a secondary, finite mind to do all that assuming.

The "Answer" is not to get more and better things on a physical basis, but in "letting go" of the false sense of physical limitation and separateness altogether. *Starting with the Infinity of Mind,* where is there a state of thought that thinks in physical terms? Nowhere.

One never lacks things when seen as just ideas, available at the mere thought of them. To simply have a thing in thought *is to have it as much as it can be had,* because as Infinite *Consciousness is All*, there is no subsequent phase or step known as "physical manifestation."

All is Consciousness, Mind.

Even though it still may *appear* to the senses that things are "manifest" on a physical basis—who says so? The *things* themselves aren't saying that. The things don't even know they're appearing that way! Things have no mind with which to know anything. Do you realize that not one thing in the entire universe is ever *telling you* it is material or "manifest"? Only you would assume things are "out there" as physical items that are separate from you, by identifying with a *sense-illusion that is not* instead of as the Infinite Intelligence You *are*.

The enormous burden of human experience (if there *were* such a thing!) would be the assumption that one only has a thing when one has it on a *physical, material* basis. One assumes there *is* a second, separate existence, a limited physical world and life, in which mere *thoughts* are not enough—and for which a *second set* of things, a physical, material version, is required. A thing supposedly has to be "out there," *physically sensed as separate* instead of simply *thought*. It has to be dense, heavy, and has to have taken time to produce.

Yet the entire belief of there being a second state of time, weighty physical separateness, and limitation is *non-existent*! It would be an assumption believed by a mind that *isn't*. This would-be heaviness and slowness isn't a weight humanity is bearing—it *is* humanity!

Again, instead of trying to satisfy an endless physical need of things—it is the superimposed false sense of physical existence itself that should be "dropped." One does that, not by dropping physicality, but by *starting* as the Wholly Present Mind One already is, and staying Here. *One sees there never have been two states, only the Unlimitedness of Infinite Mind.*

Do you realize that where Present Infinite Mind is—and there is nowhere It is not *Present Now*—there is absolutely no past, thus no prior time when things were ever seen as physical, material?

------•------

Countless other "new" ideas and principles are present right now—and these will *appear* to have applications in exciting new fields in daily living. Compared to what else is present, *un-withholdable this very instant,* all of the so-called current "advances" in what appears as technology, as well as social and educational issues or the arts, are kindergarten level!

There is no secondary, physical self that is limited to an evolutionary timetable, and would say, "Oh, no. *I'm* not ready yet. I can take only so much good at a time. Infinite Good? That's *too* much."

The fact that Infinite Mind, the One All-Inclusive Awareness, is *All,* means there simply cannot be any thought or idea that is covered, *hidden* somewhere, waiting to be dis-covered. Where would ideas be—off in an unused corner of Awareness? Can there be a back warehouse, a storage place for a future in Omnipresent *Now*? Doesn't it sound silly?

Not one single thought or idea could be waiting or held back for a later time, because there is no time. Nothing more is yet to come, for *all* of Mind *is present.* There can be no such thing as an idea that has "not yet" been thought of. Stop and consider it. How could an idea be *waiting* somewhere to be thought *of*? To even have that status, it would have to have already been thought. There is no place besides Aware-ness' Presence where thoughts or ideas could appear to be. That is right where *You* always are, not as body, but as the Infinity of Conscious Aliveness.

Equally, a lack of *any* thing, any thought, simply never occurs. Why? If you *could* say you lacked a thing, to do so, you already would be thinking of that thing. The instant any thing is thought of, there is the instantaneous "having" of it—*and that's as far as it goes.* Again, things never *actually* go beyond being mere thoughts to a subsequent phase called physical manifestation, for in Reality, in Your Present Awareness, there is no such thing. To merely think a thing *is to have it as much as it can be had,* for all that exists is *Pure Intelligence.*

"Looking out" as Mind, there is no other state of thought existent; never another mind to say any thing or idea is *not* present! Mind's constancy as *All* leaves no possibility of lack. This *appears* as less ignorance and limitation in every aspect of daily experience.

This simply cannot fail to "work" because Mind, Consciousness, cannot fail to *be All That Is.*

A limited, finite viewpoint (if it existed) would attempt to project *its* ignorant conditions upon Unconditional Abundance. Only a human mind would assume the Infinite exerts the power to give or withhold. But the human mind would be a "mind" that *completely is not!* So is Your Infinity ever really limited by such a thing? No!

———•———

"Looking out from" Infinite Mind's Present Perfection for *Its* sake, is practical even in what appears as daily time-experience *that never is actually present!* It goes so beyond being practical, as to be indescribable in the harmony it can *appear* to bring about. Why?

Intelligence, Abundance, Harmony, is *already* present, in *unlimited* capacity. How could One possibly *stop* It? It will appear as more new ideas, more love, kindness, peace, and a greater sense of being "humane" than humanity could ever produce. There simply *is no* second "mind-that-is-not" to negate Divine Good, Unlimited Mind.

The fact that Mind's Intelligence is changelessly "on" and is operating *Omnipresently* means there never are any pockets of lack in Your Presence. The conscious functioning of the Self as Goodness is completely unwithholdable. Its capacity to operate as Infinite Goodness cannot be limited or measured—*not even by Itself.* As Infinity, You simply *never* are faced by need, obligation or expectation—and there is no state besides Infinity.

This also means there is no personal identity that right now is finding out *about* Infinite Mind. This is Mind *Itself*, speaking of the endless Completeness that is eternally true of Itself.

The Infinite Self hasn't the slightest concern over how things appear on a finite basis, or how fast things seem to evolve. That would be starting in the wrong place, with the senses.

To start by assuming there is a finite time-appearance and a shortage of ideas, would be working with or *as* non-presence. It would be living backwards—starting as the very denial of *Present* Mind—the very Power with which, and *as which*, One "works." It never occurs in Reality, as

Intelligence is changelessly All. One persistently *acts*, or consciously *is* Now-Aliveness, the Solidarity of Absolute Being.

The fact that the Only Identity is Infinite Mind does not mean personal daily affairs will be ignored. On the contrary, one is sharper, clearer and more astute in all one appears to deal with. One gives more care and attention to detail at home, in the workplace, even at recreation, yet with a greater sense of ease and fun. Why?

One cannot escape *being* that which is Perfection, Exactitude Itself. And simultaneously, the indescribable *Ease* of Being is One's very Essence, what One unavoidably *is*. Who else is conscious to pretend otherwise? One appears to go about daily affairs as normal—yet free and clear of inadequacy and fear; free of the immense emotional weight of judging "others," for there is only *Oneness*; free of false lacks and lusts—and the constant mental maneuvering that seems to go with them. One is alive *as* Ability, Talent, Integrity, Freedom Itself.

Be alive to the Magnificence of Your Self as It is being all-inclusive of all. Divine Mind cannot *be* absolutely All That Is, *be* Unwithholdable Goodness *here, now*, and leave a little separate self to struggle.

Truly, truly, what is the extent of All's Self-Esteem?

———•———

There is only one true Wealth, which is Mind, Consciousness.

Consciousness is all that truly *is*, or exists, to *be* Wealth. Things do not constitute wealth because no thing can even appear to exist without *the consciousness of it*. Things are mere by-products.

Wealth *Itself* is not an idea or thing, nor an accumulation of things. Wealth is pure Conscious Aliveness, and *is infinite in Its abundance*.

As Consciousness is Wealth, that means *Now* is Wealth—for It is the same One.

How much *Now* have You? Rather, how *effortlessly present*, and how *endless* is the Now, the Wealth, that You *already are*?

Now is present in endless abundance. No limit can be put on the Now-Wealth You are; nor can You ever separate from It.

Wealth, Health, Good, never *happen* to You. Wealth isn't what Consciousness *brings* You. *Wealth is what You are as Pure Alive Being*, and never can be stopped. Consciousness is *Real* Wealth because It never can be taken from You by another. It *never* passes away.

How much Consciousness is available to Consciousness? Does It ebb and flow? Is It cyclical, dependent on interest rates? How much Intelligence is ever-available to *Infinite* Mind?

All is Consciousness.

There is no physical or material limitation, anywhere, ever.

If one were to speak from a finite viewpoint, in what *appears* as the next millennium or next two or three millennia, what will wealth consist of? One who is alert will notice what seems to be a gradual "falling away" of the historical sense of wealth.

On a finite basis, wealth has traditionally been measured in material terms; by the number of things one possessed personally: the amount of currency, or the amount of stocks and bonds; real estate and homes; companies or businesses; precious metals or jewelry; works of art; cars, boats, airplanes and so on. Obviously at "this stage of the game," such finite forms of wealth and money are still essential in everyday affairs. There is nothing wrong with this kind of wealth.

Yet Pure Consciousness being *All,* how could "material" possessions constitute true Wealth? They do not. Materiality or anything based on finite senses and time never has genuine *being* or substance, never is present to *be* Wealth.

From a finite viewpoint, one might say there is a "new wealth" at the time of a so-called New Age and second millennium. It appears to belong to those engaged in "spiritual work," or studies concerning Consciousness. On this basis, it appears those who are sincere and dedicated are attaining a greater "awareness" of what Consciousness, Spirit, is, hence are gaining greater wealth. It would appear they are "increasing" their aliveness to Consciousness, Infinite Self, hence increasing their wealth. They no longer seem as small, as limited by finiteness and materiality; they no longer are as "poor" in Spirit.

Yet even on this "new" basis, there still would appear to be the age-old *disparity* of wealth. There still would appear to be those who have and those who have not. It would be the same as with wealth of material income and possessions, in which there appear to be those with abundance and those with little.

If one starts from a human viewpoint, there now *appear* to be some more evolved and aware—those whose attention is given largely to Consciousness, Spirit—thus who "have a lot" in the way of Consciousness, Wealth. Yet there also appear to be others who have little. There appear to be those who seem to have no "spiritual awareness" at all, or couldn't care less, and not through any fault of their own.

If any of this picture existed in Reality, then the seeming age-old disparity in wealth would not have been improved at all. It would have merely *shifted*. Only the notion of what *constitutes* wealth would have changed, from "materiality" to "spirituality." There still would appear to be the "haves" and the "have-nots."

Can any of this finite picture or scenario be accepted at face value? Do you say this doesn't concern you, because you assume you won't be around in a hundred years, let alone another one or two thousand?

Where are You going, in light of the fact that Your Identity is Eternity Itself, un-budging Omnipresent Being, the One and Only All-Inclusive Awareness, and It is *inescapable*?

Do you assume you are the body holding this book, and can avoid such things by dying out of them? *All is Consciousness*, Your eternally present Intelligent Being.

What then, is the answer?

The fact that Infinite Spirit Itself is the Only One, *is Absolutely All*, means It permanently precludes the possibility of there being others— whether "spiritually rich" or "spiritually poor." The Only One that can ever be spiritual is Spirit Itself, and It is fully so already.

Spirit, Consciousness, never is possessed or manifest by *people*. Consciousness *Itself* being the Alone One, It cannot be hoarded by certain humans, or banked by bodies. The fact that Consciousness is One, *All*, leaves no other to bank It, or to bank on It.

The only Wealth, Abundance, there is *for Eternity*, is the Aliveness *here and now* alive to being. There is no more to come. It does not belong to the body holding this book or *any* body. It "belongs" to Consciousness, to Pure Now, only.

Consciousness is "forever" impersonal, uniform, single. It is endlessly abundant in Its Presence. *Consciousness is Abundance Itself*. It never is abundant to others, but only to or *as* Itself, which is the One I Am presently reading this. To Consciousness, there is always "plenty for all" because Unlimited Consciousness is what Plenty, All, is!

To Consciousness, all there forever is, is boundless "Having-ness," which is simply Its own endless Presence, *being*. Consciousness Itself is the Only One ever wealthy because Its endlessly abundant Selfhood is all that exists to be of value.

Infinitely abundant Consciousness is whole, satisfied, and never seeks anything, not even more of Itself. It is not a quantity. The Infinite Wealth being spoken of never is what One *has*. It is what One *is*—the One *unstoppably being this Alive Presence*.

You can no more avoid being Infinite Wealth than the Present can avoid being present. You are the same One. As Infinite Wealth, You have no ability to withhold any of Your Presence, and there is nothing besides Your Presence.

As All, You are gloriously free, forever without a nagging sense of having to "do" something with Your Consciousness, for there is *only* Yourself and Your ease of being. Yet You certainly do not tolerate or co-exist with any sense of human laziness, carelessness or mediocrity. Nor does this mean one will not invest, maintain bank accounts, or do what appears to be prudent in everyday affairs.

It means nowhere is there a sense of settling for less than *perfection*. You are utter Perfection being All-Out Life. You cannot hold any of your Wealth of Ability, Talent, Love, and Intelligence in check. Any lesser state is impossible. In daily living, everything is done peacefully, intelligently, and "to the max" of perfection.

———•———

28

WHAT IS
A STATEMENT OF TRUTH?

Staying "busy" as Infinite Being is simultaneously the hardest and simplest thing one will ever do.

It is difficult in that it *seems* there are finite senses constantly presenting everything that would deny the Infinite. At the present "time," it seems to require an alertness and discipline greater than anything ever known, to not get caught up in the would-be senses, emotions, or intellect, thus avoiding One's pure, consciously alive *Being*.

However, the Infinite is simple, in fact effortless, in that Its Perfection is *already* present. Nothing has to be done to make Consciousness more present, more All. It is a matter of not denying It. As Consciousness Itself is the only One conscious, denial really is not even possible.

How does one "stick with" or *be* Infinite Being, instead of getting constantly distracted by what appear as changing sensations, feelings and thoughts, and all that seems to go with so-called finite experience?

One can start by making a statement of Absolute Truth.

Make a statement such as, "Consciousness is All," or "The Present is All," or "Only *Being* is." Use any synonym for Consciousness that has particular significance at the moment.

Make one of the synonyms for God or Consciousness the *subject* of the statement, such as, "*Consciousness* is All." This is starting in the right "place." It doesn't matter what synonym is used. What's important is the *allness* of Consciousness, Self, or God—for that alone is true—and It leaves no possibility of another self, state or condition.

What *God is to God* is always, always the only "starting point"—for there's nothing else.

This isn't just some *words* being said. It is called *stating* Truth because It is the State that truly is. It is all that actually exists, thus all that is present to *operate*. It never is speculation.

Make a simple, basic statement, rather than a lengthy one using a lot of synonyms. Words are not of value. Meaning is. Then pull the statement apart. Hold up each word one at a time and find out what it means. Keep the questions simple. Don't be afraid to roll up your sleeves, get in there, and really *examine* the words.

For example, *Consciousness is All* is three different statements, depending on the emphasis. **Consciousness** is All. Consciousness *is* All. Consciousness is ***All.***

What does *Consciousness* mean? What is Consciousness *to Pure Consciousness*—not the word, but the "Stuff" Itself? What is it for All to *be* Pure Consciousness only? "Who" alone is conscious? "When" is Consciousness being conscious? "Where" is It conscious?

What does *is* mean? Does *is* mean was or will be? Is it possible to *think* is? Can is ever *not* be, or only partially be? Can there be anything besides *what is*?

What specifically is *all*, or *All*? How much is It? How completely *all* is All? To Whom is All all? Use a dictionary, but don't be surprised if the answers according to Infinite Intelligence sometimes differ from the definitions in the dictionary, for the dictionary is written on a finite basis.

Find out how *completely* true the statement is. How absolute is its "coverage"? Does it take time to become true, or is it *already* Fact?

Be clear *Who* is making the statement, and *why* it can be made.

Above all, ponder a statement of Truth quietly and easily. Enjoy it. Let the meaning come from the Aware, Intelligent Stillness of Your Being. Don't feel pressured, or that it's necessary to be profound, because the Self never feels that way. But "get behind" the statement and see what it means with genuine interest, for You *are* behind it. It is literally Your Very Own Presence, *all there is of all there is,* speaking of Itself. Nothing else exists, so nothing is of greater value.

If right now, someone were to place the Mona Lisa, or a priceless jewel into the hands now holding this book, wouldn't your "alertness level" soar? Wouldn't you appreciate that item's value and examine it with great interest? Well, how much *more* valuable and fascinating is the

All-Inclusive Awareness being *You*—which is the very Substance of all Existence?!

It is *Your Self, Your Own Presence,* that is priceless!

This peaceful, gently present One I Am is endless Wealth, exquisite Perfection, and I cannot withhold one iota of My Value from being present. How much does this One I Am "appreciate" this One I Am? Fully, completely.

Never allow any sense of awe or intimidation because It is a statement of the Infinite or "God." The Infinite isn't in awe of Itself, and *It* is the One being here, now, so the stating can be done in the first place.

Then see if the statement can be "broken down"—meaning that it's only true under certain conditions. If it is Truth, it is *unconditional*. It is irrevocable and never subject to compromise. Challenge yourself to see if you are willing to fully admit the Truth of it.

Make sure the statement starts only with the Infinite, and stays consistent with the Infinite. If it refers to a would-be finite state, if it is subject to time, or is made on the assumption that there is something imperfect to improve or change, then it is not Perfect Changeless Truth.

While it is helpful to ask questions, be sure to *state* Truth. The fact that *Being is,* is not a question that has to be answered. It is Absolute, All That Is, which really leaves no element of question. It is a *declaration,* meaning that which is clearly known.

Continue pondering or "digging" at the statement until you can say it with absolute conviction—for the Consciousness making the statement is Certainty, Conviction Itself.

———•———

Ask Your Self *as that Self* what the meaning of a statement of Truth is. The One I Am does not ponder or meditate as *another*; a separate self that is "down there" and gradually "getting Here." I cannot ask anything of Myself as a second mind, a seeker. Truth is a matter of the Reality I Am "looking out as" My Own Omnipresent Perfection. It is the Awareness I Am staying consistent with My Allness.

One asks what a statement of Truth means only in terms of Consciousness *Itself,* alone—for It is the Self I Am, asking what is already true of the One I Am. It is a matter of asking not as one who is separate, needy, or confused, not groveling or scared, but as *One* who is Certainty, Integrity or Dignity Itself.

The One making the statement happens to be the same One who knows its meaning. One always "comes up with something" because the One asking also has all the answers. It isn't that the One Self knows the meaning, which It gives to a separate "you." The One Self *is consciously being every bit of the meaning*, which is what You unavoidably are.

Always be clear as to *where* You identify when stating Truth. There can be a subtle tendency, even when working in all sincerity, to feel, "A lot has been stated or seen so far, so what else can 'I' see?" While the earnest pondering of Truth is right, the motive behind it is dead wrong. It implies another, a second mind that is "getting there."

To the Fully Aware One, Changeless Perfection, there actually is no pondering, no meditation process necessary or *possible*. As Absolute Realization is *all*, there never is another to come to a realization. To "start" here is to work correctly. This is unalterable Truth—Being's infinite Self-Freedom—forever without a burden of having to *become*.

Stating Truth is always, always, always a matter of, "Consciousness *Itself* is All, now. *It* knows how to perfectly be Consciousness, and *It* is the One being I—so there never is a secondary personal 'I,' no *thinking* mind, to have to see or know anything. *Consciousness* is already actively being all there is to Itself, now. To *Omniscience*, nothing is hidden, so nothing has to be revealed. All the Power there is, is present now, as this Present Being which is *Its* Being..." and continue on that basis.

It never is a matter of a secondary "you" being honest *with* Truth, because there are not two. The One has no choice but to honestly be, which *is* Truth, You.

Quietly pondering a statement of the Infinite may at first seem abstract. As one keeps at it, one invariably finds it becomes more clear and *obvious*. It will come more *alive* until one seems to have a brand new Life, full of Self-Interest and enthusiasm. Yet there never are two.

To I-Am-Omnipresent-Awareness, nothing changes.

Truth's State is Awareness being Self-Aware as All That Is. This One, True State that Awareness is stating, is Its own *already operative* Presence. Words don't bring Truth about or make It more operative. It is a matter of the One keeping busy as *What One Already is*. It never is a matter of a "you" having to come to a conclusion.

When pondering Truth, it may seem some "mental cobwebs" clear up, but Consciousness *Itself* remains Ever-Present, the crystal clear Truth of all Being, eternally. One is pondering What Already Is, *as that Isness Itself*. All is Pure Conscious *Being* as much at the "start" as the "finish."

It's like the difference between having to build a house from scratch—and having a new home already complete and perfect in every detail. All you have to do is enjoy how new and exciting your home already is. There is all the difference in the world between persistently admitting Truth is *already* present, already all—and persistently trying to *make* Truth present, all.

At the current "time," it seems helpful to have periods of quiet, solitude or stillness to fully "appreciate" One's Self—although Consciousness Itself certainly does not need periods of quiet to be what It is. One deeply enjoys these periods however, for in Reality, One's Self is *Alive Stillness, Awake Silence*—which is Peace Itself.

While quiet may be enjoyable, All-Inclusive Awareness, Existence Itself, doesn't suddenly *stop* when it appears the body goes out of the house or goes to work, does It? No matter where, or how busy, a *body* appears to be, the Present is ever-present; Awareness is just as effortlessly aware and all-inclusive, isn't It? Wouldn't it be a bit presumptuous to assume God was less all, less powerful, because a body was not sitting quietly? Just like being able to walk and talk at the same time, one is specifically *alive as* Present Consciousness, Alive *Oneness*, regardless of what a body appears to do—because It doesn't depend on a body.

All never can be left in a quiet room. The All-Inclusive One I Am is always present, *always the only Presence*, no matter where a body appears to move within this One I Am. A house or home is not One's Home. You do not live in a city or state. You *are inescapably being* the Only State there is—All-Inclusive Consciousness.

———•———

Continue "prodding" at a statement of Truth until some *brand new* meaning comes along. The fresh, new clarity of meaning, the vitality in the exclamation, "Yes, of course that's true!" *is* the Self in present operation—*for only the Self is conscious to know what is true of Itself.* One thus truly is functioning as *Present Consciousness*, not just repeating old meaning or dead, Life-less words.

Don't hold to something seen before, and assume *that* is Power. While it may be true—if it is known from before—it is coming from what one is conscious *of*, not Consciousness Itself. The *fresh clear Aliveness* that Consciousness is *Now*, never holds to a past concept of Itself, no matter how accurate.

To voice empty words, even emphatically, yet without true significance or new meaning behind them is no different from a tape recorder set up to have statements of Truth played out of it. It is just so much noise, reproduced mechanically. It takes Intelligence, Consciousness, to know what is said and come up with something fresh and new.

Then continue on, not as a body, but *as the All-Inclusive One*, seeing what else the statement means. It is Infinity Itself being pondered, and it is impossible to come to an end of It. The Changeless Perfection you are pondering and are *consciously alive as* is literally the Substance wherein the entire universe is found.

One can't just *say* words of Truth. One can't just agree intellectually that Being, What Is, is All—and then go on functioning as a sensing mentality in a seeming flow of time, non-being. Life does not live that way. One may use words in "getting started," but stating Truth never is a "mental" or intellectual experience. It is a *consciously alive presence*.

To state Truth means to *consciously be the State* that Truth is. It is *Pure Now-Aliveness*, not an experience found in time's flow. It is not something objective or with a finite form. Truth Itself is only what Pure Aliveness is *being*—not a lot of words that a "thinking mind" is knowing. Only being *silently alive as* Consciousness' Absolute Presence is Absolute Power. Otherwise, one is mouthing *idle* words, functioning as un-Consciousness, not truly aware, or dreaming.

There is a huge difference between intellectually agreeing there is only Conscious Aliveness, and *being* only Conscious Aliveness.

Most emphatically, One doesn't *think* words every minute, but stays *alive as* Ever-Present Awareness, where Life *is*. One stays busy as the *Oneness of Invisible Aliveness*, rather than getting distracted by what senses would make appear as visibly separate, "out there."

Stating Truth never is a matter of trying to convince a personal "mind" of anything. Nor does Consciousness have to remind Itself that It is Consciousness. There is nothing else It could be. But one must persist, and be consistent with Truth, with the *Pure Being* of Consciousness. It never deviates.

One cannot make a system, a repetitive process out of stating Truth. Stating Truth is *not* a mantra. What need could God, All, have for a mantra? Life's *Spontaneous Now* is not stuck in a ritual. *Now* never is something a second mind is doing; Its Infinity cannot be forced into a rigid pattern. Now needs no habit or practice to *be*. It is Free.

———•———

As said earlier, living Truth, *being It*, takes discipline. Lots of it.

But what is discipline in its true meaning? It often carries an unpleasant connotation—of being rigid, hard, uncompromising—or strict and "stiff." Discipline only seems hard to so-called human sense. In Truth, discipline is One's only nature, One's very essence. Why?

Omnipresent Being *completely precludes* a "sense-mind"—and only a "sense-mind" would seem undisciplined, apathetic, slovenly, afraid, out-of-control, and influenced by outside forces. *If* such a state existed, it would always be uncertain, confused by alternatives, wavering between options, always hesitating and putting off in time. But all of that would be just so much *non-being*.

If one mistakenly identifies with any of that, it would be natural to assume one has to *become* disciplined, just like having to become aware. All along, You are already Discipline Itself.

Discipline in its true sense, in Reality, means *changeless*. True Discipline is the Changelessness that Your Absolute Being *is*.

As Changeless Oneness, are You not the very essence of Self-Control?

Can you imagine Your *Now* being careless, apathetic or undisciplined in Its ability to be *Now*?

As the Present that *never, ever* fails to be Present, are You not the utmost in persistence? As Absolute Omnipresence, You are *thoroughness* itself.

The complete, unwavering certainty with which Being is, is *You*.

It is your very nature to be sharply Alert, keenly Intelligent, and fully committed to being all You are, *forever*. And It never takes work.

Discipline doesn't mean punishing yourself due to past mistakes. Changeless doesn't mean you won't be flexible in everyday affairs. True Discipline, Oneness, can only *be present now*—as spontaneously Present Life—and that's Freedom or Joy Itself.

Discipline isn't an outside force that acts *upon* you, or a state you must attain. It isn't something you *do*. You can no more avoid *being* Perfect Discipline than You can avoid being. It is the same One.

Discipline is inescapable, un-shut-off-able.

It isn't that Your Being has tendencies to deviate, and It's managing to keep them under wraps. Absolute Being *has* no tendencies to deviate. How could *Endless Oneness* be deviant? There is no state besides Itself that It could deviate *to*.

Pure Consciousness as It is aware here, now, is Uncompromising—but is It hard, rigid? It is indescribably *soft* because there is nothing dense or material to It. How much practice does it take for this glorious Bliss to fully be? Does Bliss have to constantly *remind* Itself to be? Does It end at some point, or is It *endless*?

Don't foolishly, naively resist discipline. Rather, One rejoices *as* It.

You will find what may have *seemed* to be undisciplined tendencies cannot cling to You—because they never were true or clinging to You.

Divine Discipline, which is simply *Absolute Oneness*, is not a discipline in the sense of being a study, something a separate self follows. It has no *disciples*. It can neither be learned nor taught because *Itself is All*. It leaves no other state needing to be disciplined.

———•———

Why is *meaning* so important? When stating Truth, why must one mean it? And what is so valuable about making a statement? These questions are answered by knowing what a statement of Truth really is.

Truth means Existence or Consciousness as It is now *being*, for by Truth is meant *what truly is*. Existence, Consciousness, is what truly is.

Existence exists *all-out*. It cannot withhold Itself, otherwise It couldn't be said to *be*. Existence or Truth is one hundred percent "committed" to being present as *All That Is*. It never is half-hearted or uncertain. In other words, Existence, Truth, totally "means it" as It exists.

If Existence doesn't fully mean it, doesn't fully exist, just where is It waiting, and what is It doing until It decides to take the plunge and really exist? *All* of what Existence or Truth means has to exist *now*. None of It is kept from *being*.

Just like Existence—Consciousness fully, all-out *means it* as It is being conscious—for Consciousness and Existence is the same *One*.

That's what Existence literally is—Consciousness, or the State that Consciousness is, *meaning Itself to the full*.

Existence literally is Consciousness' State, *meant*.

That's the same as saying Existence is Consciousness' *Statement*.

Consciousness' Statement of Itself *is what Existence is*, and is *all* the Existence there is.

The issue is never, "*Why* make a statement of Consciousness, Truth?" Rather, One can't possibly do anything else! Consciousness'

State Meant, or Statement, is *all* that is present and taking place! Simply nothing *else* exists to talk about—or to do any talking!

One "means it" when stating Truth because Consciousness' Full Meaning is actually the very One conscious that's *doing* the stating. It speaks only concerning *Itself*. One must consciously *be* what is stated—for Consciousness *is* fully being what is stated, and no other exists. That's why this book is now being read on this very subject.

One can see why Truth, honestly stated, never is just dead words—but actual *Living Presence*—all the Presence there is!

Consciousness is wholly being, living, the meaning of Its Statement *before* It is made, not after. That is *why* It is made. There is no other reason why It is made. In other words, Consciousness "puts Its money where Its mouth is" even before opening Its mouth!

Completely drop any notion of a middle man called "you." Always, always, always, the Consciousness that *is* All is the only One to state "Consciousness is All." Consciousness has no spokesperson, for nothing comes between It and Its Omnipresence.

There never is a gap between what is stated and the *instant operation* of the Perfect State Itself, for Perfection Itself makes the statement, and only about Its own Already-Omnipresence. It doesn't take *time* or have to traverse *space*. The allness of It never has to be established.

Stating Truth—the fact that Truth's State *is* all—leaves no contrary state of thought anywhere to operate as inharmonious conditions. Truth's Statement is unblocked and unopposed in Its *exclusive* presence, *immediate* functioning, and *potency* everywhere throughout Itself, and there is *only* Itself. It is Absolute Power *because* there is only Itself.

There simply is nothing else to talk back, disrupt, or interrupt Life's Total Perfection. It never is *not* All Presence. Your Self never experiences a cessation of being *All That Is*.

This is why there is no fear, no back-off in Being—there is only Itself—and nothing besides that It could fear or back off from.

An honest statement of Absolute Truth has Omnipotence, Omnipresence and Omniscience "behind" It. The *full Potency* of Divine Perfection is *already being* It. Being all that exists, the Statement Itself is *unconditional*. It has no ability to be less than *completely* what It is.

The Present Perfection that Consciousness *is*, is the whole of every "situation." Perfection is eternally the *only* "Situation." An honest statement of Truth never is made by a human, in a place, to help a physical situation. All there is of all there is, is Divine Intelligence making the statement, and concerning Its own *Invisible-Infinity-All*.

Spirit's *Alive Infinity*, Its All-Out Endless Oneness, is all that is present. Stay with how completely, perfectly and *irresistibly* the Present is present. Joy in the Fact that no effort is needed to make All, Your Self, be All.

––––––•––––––

The foregoing shows why Truth is stated only for Its own sake.

Truth never "works" if one starts by trying to improve a dream of a finite state, for clearly no such dream ever began.

The fact that *Consciousness' Infinity is All* means It never can be stated in relation to what appears as a *finite* body, or a body's so-called finite affairs. Truth Itself, All Itself, has no body. One may readily agree Truth has no body—but that also means *You* have no body.

All there is to You—*all there is, period*—is Bodiless Infinite Being, absolutely un-physical Pure Intelligence; Perfect, sensation-free Pure Spirit. Obviously then, Truth never can be stated in relation to anything that appears located on a planet, or in a time-era, *a span of non-being* called a twenty-first century. One stays entirely away from a false dream sense of a three-dimensional time world *that never really began*, and from all *would-be* pictures of separation presented by senses.

Consciousness deals *exclusively* with Its Own Infinity.

How then, could stating Truth possibly be of practical value?

Only this keeps One's Being from being "used" by a would-be dream *appearing* as forms of "not": not-Life, not-Intelligence, not-Love, not-Wellness. Stating and staying busy *as the specific Alive Presence of Infinity* leaves nothing to operate as the finite thought of "not." It leaves no second mind to think in terms of, thus "produce," would-be, negateive conditions, and then fight with itself over them.

Remember, there wouldn't be any seeming condition *and* a so-called finite sensing "mind" that knows *about* it. That "sense-mind" *would be* the condition. It would literally operate as a *sense* of being a separate body-person, a personal mind, and its worldly troubles.

The Changeless Truth is that Absolute Pure Conscious *Being* leaves *no* non-being as having begun, no false sense of separateness to operate as a condition. To the Absolute Present, no such "mind" or conditions *ever began*—not even as illusory—so can't be gotten rid of.

The Infinite Present One states Its Allness because Its Allness leaves only Its Allness.

The Truth that *Infinite Mind is All* leaves no secondary finite mind in which an improvement could be needed *or occur*. That's what *All* means. The Pure Spirit You *are* has no expectation of a change to come about in time on a finite basis, because to Divine *Being* there is no time, no change, no finite basis. You are not human, physical or mental, but Absolutely Divine Only, and there is nothing else. Your Consciousness never deals with anything but Its *present* Factuality.

It is not enough to *think about* Truth, Consciousness. If Truth is something one only thinks about, without *being It*, that would be just a finite, thinking time-mentality *dreaming* that it is being spiritual and doing a good job. While it claims to "know" Truth, that finite mentality is also the only "place" problems seem to occur. Just as readily as it "knows" Truth, it appears to produce and know about disease, lack and everything else. They would be opposite sides of the same coin.

To just do thinking *about* Truth is to try to use one side of the coin to overcome the other. But once you pick up the coin of a finite "mind," you're stuck with both sides.

Staying "busy" as unthinking *Infinite-Now-Aliveness* is the only "Answer." In Now's Alive Stillness, there is no finite thought-coin.

Pure Now, Pure Infinity, which is the *Aliveness* of Present Awareness, certainly doesn't know of any finite time-problem; nor is It *thinking* thoughts about Itself to get rid of a problem. It is wholly busy "sticking" as the un-intellectualizing *Pure Alive Being* It is.

Your Absolute *Timeless Being* simply doesn't permit time-problems to occur. So obviously *You* are not the one that wants to battle "problems" or have them cleared up! The "mind" saying it has a problem, and the one that wants to be rid of it, would be the same one. None of it is You, for You can't fight with what Your Own Total Presence has actually "pre-empted." Even that is inaccurate, implying there could be something besides Absolute Truth to pre-empt. There isn't.

There never are various *types* of seeming problems. It would always be *one* suggestion that there could be a dream of "not," *one* depthless, distance-less thought mirage, inclusive of all problems it supposedly dreams. The singular nature of dream means it isn't necessary to attack individual problems "out there." Staying busy as Now-Consciousness, which is *Omnipresent Awakeness*, precludes the one would-be source dreaming up them all.

Awakeness *precludes* problems occurring. Why? Because you can't suffer from the problems in a dream *that you're not having* because you're wide awake! There isn't Awakeness *and* a dream—only Awakeness. This right now is not talking to a "you," but is the Self I Am talking to Myself, the Only One.

The fact that Changeless Omnipresent Truth *can only be completely awake and honest with Itself,* is the Answer to all *would-be* "problems," whether of health, finance, relationships, business, government or anything else. Undeviating Present Consciousness leaves only the *allness* of the Perfect Answer, with no problems or questions *having occurred.*

In Absolute Perfection there never is a need for spiritual heroics.

Just *stop*. Let the True State of Your Absolute Being "sink in." Only *Being* can be present. *Forever.* So how could what completely *isn't being* ever have been present to appear to It? It couldn't have. Truth *never* is about clearing up problems or "healing." How lame an Omnipotence would that be, to allow problems to occur in the first place?

To state Truth *as Pure Now*, for Its sake, is to "behold" Perfection *as that Perfection. This* is the only way to "work," for this is the only way Life Itself "works" or *is.* To start as Now and remain totally, only, "interested in" Its Total Present-ness, *is* the One I Am, being Myself.

———————•———————

Right here, now—how unstoppable, how unavoidable, is Consciousness *to Consciousness?*

How fully busy being Pure Consciousness *only,* is Consciousness?

How fully "absorbed" in being *present only* is Consciousness? Can Consciousness do anything other than "look out from" or *be* Its Allness; be all that is present? Does Consciousness have to keep *thinking* about Its Existence to *freely be All?*

When it is said that Consciousness is Omnipotent "throughout" Its Existence, does that mean It travels physical distance, has to get to where a problem appears "out there," to correct it? No! *This* Consciousness is what all Existence is! There are no distant places! *That's* the point. That there is *any* separation or distance would be an illusion of senses, if there *were* finite senses. There aren't.

How incapable is Your *Undimensional Presence* of having physical length, width, or a break or separation in Its Alive Being? One never has to make One's Undimensional Presence extend out across distance, to "get to" where a problem appears, and correct it "there." One doesn't accept a sense-suggestion that there *is* distance or anything separate. *Always,* there is only the Immediacy of Consciousness' Infinite Presence right here—not here in space, but here as *Aliveness.*

The entirety of Existence, of All, is Pure Spirit only. It is not a physical All, but a *Distance-less All.* There is not a millionth of an inch that Divine Perfection has to travel from *Present Spirit,* to be All. There is not a microsecond before It *is* Absolute Presence, Omnipotence. There is no delay for Alive Perfection *here, now,* to be all Substance, all Being.

This never can be clear if one assumes there is *an* all that is separate and which Spirit's Aliveness "fills." No. *Present Aliveness alone* is what All is—which is *why* It is all Power.

A thought may come, "This may be true, but it's so *hard* to stay in the Present."

When is it difficult for the Present to be the Present that *never fails* to be present?

How hard is it to *be?*

Never get frustrated if it seems you "fall" repeatedly. And *never* mentally fight with, condemn, or blame anything on a would-be "sense-mind." That's not Pure Present Aliveness. That's not *Truth being true.*

Be so totally "flooded" with *the Present Aliveness You are,* so preemptively alive as *Oneness,* which is Perfection, that thoughts in terms of "nots," of problems, *don't get a chance to occur.*

That's Truth being true—being All.

The Intelligent Purity already being You is so Absolute, so Pure, that the notion of *another* state, one less than Perfection, would not only seem stupid, impossible—it never occurs.

There never actually is a second mind; it only *seems* there's a suggestion of one. The point of this book is, starting with Infinite Mind's Allness, *there isn't even a suggestion.*

There is only Infinite Mind.

———•———

29

YOU CANNOT BE LIMITED

Aʟʟ ɪs ᴀʙsᴏʟᴜᴛᴇ ᴘᴜʀᴇ *Bᴇɪɴɢ*.

The Only One Present is not experiencing *any* passage of time.

So what then becomes of education? What of business, science, medicine, law? What about all fields of endeavor, all of which would be finite and based on time? Suppose one appears to teach history, yet there is no past. What if one is a skilled athlete, or an artist, yet there is nothing physical in the Infinite, which is *All*?

While the Infinite *is* All, one will not kid himself that he is living one hundred percent on that basis. One does not negate daily work, or assume one is above the rules of society. Rather, knowing One's Self is Changeless Perfect Being, what *appears* is left alone. One sees it for what it is and does what's necessary, to the best of one's ability.

The Infinite, the Absolute, is not "anti-" anything. It does not minimize the often incredible achievements that appear in daily experience.

Only unless you are right now so absolutely alive to being *Infinite* only, so alive as *Pure Awareness only*, that you are not aware of even the slightest physical sensation or finite-ness—do you no longer need technology, or education, business, law, the arts, and so on. If you *were* absolutely being *Infinite Presence only*, nothing finite could appear to you. There would be only Undimensional Aliveness, Absolute Light. While it may be clear this is Truth, such fields of endeavor in daily experience meanwhile serve a very valuable purpose. Things are just seen from a new "perspective."

Take science as an example. Much effort has been made by technological means to find the "cause" or "source" of Life, or Existence Itself. It involves looking for the essence of so-called "matter," or "substance," even going beyond the atom itself, as said earlier. Basically, it has been a search for evidence, for proof. But what kind of "proof" would that be?

It would be merely evidence to satisfy the *senses*. It would still involve looking in the realm of matter and time—looking for that which can be observed and measured.

That is what science is *supposed* to do—observe, measure, test, and classify the world that is seen, touched, heard, tasted and smelled. That has always been science's "mission," and the only valid one on what appears to be a finite basis. The practice of experimenting, observing, measuring, and then drawing conclusions based on the results, is known as modern scientific technique. According to how finite human experience has evolved, science has *had to* develop this way.

Countless fantastic advances and benefits touching every aspect of daily life have come about on this basis. *However*, these methods are also based entirely on the finite senses—and as said repeatedly, all of this very same finite sensing *never is*.

So as far as finding the basis of *Existence, Life, Reality*, is concerned, any finite or technological attempts to observe or measure It cannot succeed, no matter how valiant.

All that a would-be "sense-mind" could ever appear to study, all it could really look for, is not the foundation of Infinite Life or Existence, or *What Really Is*—but that which is finite, observable and measurable in passing time; in other words, *what really is not*.

Starting from the Infinite leaves *only* the Infinite, and no lesser state to lay hold on It, whether scientific, religious, or philosophical.

Because the finite "sense-mind" never is *being*, never is *present*, naturally all of its sense observations and the conclusions based on them equally never are present in Reality, Existence. As sensation itself never is present in Reality, its *entire* viewpoint, its techniques and methods of proof never are actually present. So how could it offer a solid basis for knowing Existence or Life? How could it pass judgment on the nature of Truth, Reality?

It couldn't. This is why it *hasn't*.

The fact that Reality, Infinite Being, never can be known by scientific or technological means is neither a fault of science nor of Being. Nor does it make Being any less than *All That Is*.

Does this mean there is something wrong or lacking with technology or science? No!

This most emphatically is *not* saying that scientific methods and other achievements in finite daily experience are not extremely, enormously valuable. They obviously are. And they will continue to produce ever more fantastic developments—as long as there still appears to be finite experience. It's the same for all fields of endeavor.

What would be wrong is to assume there is a secondary limited *self*.

The Infinite is the *only* Self. The only One alive, present, conscious, so *any* activity can be engaged in is Infinite Mind, or the Omni-Scient One. The Self's Omniscience never stops being *all Life, all Identity, all Presence*. It never is cut off from Itself, or on a finite level. As It is *All-Knowing*, It cannot be stuck in just one limited form of knowing, in this case, via physical, finite senses.

The point is, while all finite fields of work (even the writing of books on Consciousness) may appear for an indefinite period to involve that which is limited—One's Identity, Intelligence, Talent and Ability is absolutely Unlimited, and *right now*!

No matter in what field it may appear you work, do not assume that what is pointed out here takes anything from you. Quite the contrary. "Looking out as" Unlimited Awareness—and not as a limited "sense-mind"—the scope of Your Self is Infinity Itself. As the Infinite, You never are limited to being on the same "level" as what *appears*.

Imagine a large jigsaw puzzle, with all its pieces mixed up and spread out on a table top. Now imagine being one of those pieces—limited to only a fraction of an inch in height—right on the same level as the other pieces. Could you possibly see "the big picture"? Could you put the pieces together? When the viewpoint isn't on the level of, or coming from the puzzle itself, it's far easier.

To mistakenly identify as a body, one would be a puzzle piece. To Infinite Consciousness, there are no "pieces"—all is eternally Complete, Perfect. All is always "Solved." Infinite Intelligence *never was* on the level of any puzzle. In Reality, the Omniscient Self precludes the possibility of there even being a puzzle.

One "starts and stays with" the Absoluteness of the Infinite—*as Pure Aliveness*—which is Intelligence, Omniscience Itself, *in action*. Thus what *appears* in thought as science, business, education, arts, as well as all other endeavors—cannot avoid growing by leaps and bounds, and into entirely new directions. All there would be to them is thought, and *as Infinite Mind*, One never is limited to any one pattern of thought.

———•———

There is only One Life. It is *this One*.

It is *this Life* that is all-inclusive of all there is, even of what appears as an entire stellar universe. There is no other Life outside of *this One,* and no other universe.

Within this One All-Inclusive Life, there can be nothing alien to Itself.

It can only mean there are no aliens—no such thing as *alien* Life.

This One being You is *all* the Life there is.

Life most definitely *is* extra-terrestrial. Why? Because *You* are extra-terrestrial. As All-Inclusive Awareness, You never are bound on an earth, let alone to any body on that earth.

Your Self is actually *extra-universal,* for even the entire universe appears to be within Awareness; Awareness never is within it.

Suppose for a moment that what *appeared* to be creatures or life forms, perhaps advanced far beyond human bodies, were to right now visit Earth. What could they possibly give to All-Inclusive Awareness, *All Itself,* that It wouldn't already include?

Speaking on a finite basis, the "visitors" might appear to have forms of culture or technology highly advanced from those found on Earth. They may know of, and operate in, more than three dimensions. They would appear to be extra-terrestrial, yes.

They never could be extra-Awareness.

So what, *really,* would this experience be?

First of all, would any such experience really be taking place *on a physical planet*? Or would it not be entirely thanks to the Awareness *You alone are,* which appears to include it within Itself?

The One All-Inclusive Awareness is always the only Substance and Presence, the only Mind involved. None of it would be physical, or *on* a planet. All there would be to any *thing,* any "visitor," is that it is a thought-form that appears to be in Awareness.

Could you let ignorance assume for you that the "visitor" thought-forms could be harmful or dangerous? Could they have minds of their own—since the only place they are is in the One All-Inclusive Mind, the only Life present for the entire situation? Could the only Substance involved, *Conscious Love,* act contrary to Itself? Could Intelligence conceive an idea that harms another idea; can the letter A harm the letter B?

Most importantly, the All-Inclusive One I Am simply cannot be harmful to the One I Am.

How could My Omnipresence be alien to My own Omnipresence?

The fact that Divine Intelligence *Itself* is all Presence means that absolutely all that exists is Itself and Its own *Knowingness.* It leaves no unknown, so there can be no fear of an unknown.

There is no need to worry about what a "you" would do. There is no such "you." There is only Awareness *Itself.* The body now holding this book would no more be your Identity than the "visitors." Both would be mere *things,* not Awareness.

The One Awareness would include both the body holding this book and the "visitors" *equally* as thought-forms of which Awareness alone appears to be aware. So could the "visitors" really be coming from "out there," from some "place" that is separate from Awareness? No. There never is any physical travel from another "place" going on.

One would be beholding a less limited *concept* of the infinitude of *ideas* Awareness appears to include—and always *right here* in Awareness, not physical space. Are the figures four, five and six ever thought of as paying a visit to the letters of the alphabet? No. They all appear to be *ideas* in Conscious Awareness, merely different types.

No matter how far advanced any such *form* might appear relative to those of Earth, it still would be some *thing* that appears. It still would be in the limited realm of finiteness, objective phenomena, and not Infinite Presence.

Nothing will ever be more advanced than, or beyond, All—the endlessness of *Your Present Infinite Self.* Never. Ever. No matter what Magnificent Awareness appears to be aware of, it never is greater than Awareness Itself.

The foregoing refers to what might *appear.* In Reality, the Infinite doesn't see some people "here," and visitors from "way out there." Things don't come or go, or occupy space; *all things appear to be present as thought, or ideas.*

As said earlier, there is no further to go because there is nowhere else *to* go.

Consciousness is All.

———•———

If one were to judge on a physical or finite basis, according to a so-called "past," it would appear much effort has gone into a search for extra-terrestrial intelligence.

One aspect of this marvelous undertaking involves sophisticated electronic radio telescopes. These "telescopes" are like huge radio receivers, scanning the heavens for signals possibly coming from an "intelligent life form" in distant space, "out there." It's a matter of scanning for an intelligent transmission pattern, coming via a certain frequency. It's not unlike trying to pick up a particular station on a radio at home, except done on a scale countless times larger, more complex and difficult.

What it all boils down to, though, is looking for a particular *frequency*. What's being sought is a type of *vibration*. Yet radio frequencies, even the widest range of them, are but a tiny fraction of the full spectrum of all possible types of frequencies or vibration. Breathing is essentially a type of vibration; emotions and thoughts are vibration; the color red is vibration; clouds are vibration; the human aura is vibration—yet can any of these be received via radio?

What if "transmissions" or "signals" from "higher forms" *are* going on right now, in fact are commonplace—but just aren't found on the same frequencies as radio signals?

What if the "signals" involve *different types* of frequencies, or vibrations? What if the "signals" are on the frequencies or vibration level of what are sometimes called "subtle energies," or "soul-sense"?

In other words, what if that long sought "communication" *is* going on, but occurs in a different portion of the overall vibration spectrum? What if the "senders" have a different "address" than "physical outer space," and are in the vibration realm of what many call the "psychic plane," "soul realm," or "spirit world"? Since *all* types of communication would be finite—and merely different forms of vibration—is one less valid than the other?

To those who are engaged in genuine work in these fields and "know the territory," this is not only possible; it has *always* been going on. It is also a field that appears to be riddled with fakes. Meanwhile, others consider it just so much ethereal fantasizing.

What does all of this mean in light of the fact that the universe as it appears never is "out there" on a physical basis, *and never was*, but is "right here," inseparable from *thought*?

What does it mean that *all is Consciousness*?

Where is it written that all "life forms" must have a *physical* or three-dimensional form, and inhabit a planet—when in fact, *there are no physical, solid separate objects called Earth and other planets out there for them to inhabit*—and never were?

All is Consciousness.

Completely drop any false notion of Life having to be *on* anything.

All-Inclusive Consciousness, *which is Life Itself*, never held such a notion. Life is not on planets, not in things. All things are in Life, which is the All-Inclusive Consciousness, Endlessly Imaginative Love, *You alone are*. It would be only a mistaken belief, to assume Life must be *on* anything. Yet there never is a second mind to do such believing.

Completely drop any false notion of physical, material limitation, because in Truth You never had it. Even on a would-be finite basis, all one is ever dealing with is *thought*.

All is Boundless *Mind*, Infinite *Imagination*.

Even if higher "thought forms" more ethereal than the body holding this book *do* appear, even if they appear in forms other than physical, and communicate in new ways, they never could be "higher" than, or outside of, Awareness, *Your Present Self*.

As Unjudging Awareness, the All-Wise One from whom *nothing* is hidden, You are divinely un-awed, serenely unimpressed by such "phenomena." Awareness, which is Love Itself, is not *any* form, regardless of how "high," advanced, or ethereal the form might seem. Value never is in the form.

Nothing is greater than Awareness. Nothing upstages *All*.

———— • ————

The fact that there never has been a physical universe—does this in any way negate the fantastic advances and developments in astronomy, cosmology, or aerospace programs, all of which would be based on a premise of "physical" space and distance? Not in the least. Again, these are seen in a different light, and can only appear to become more exciting and fascinating. Why?

No matter where or how "travel" appears to occur on a finite basis—whether via a body in a spacecraft, via telescope, or other means—what *really* is going on? One never has a physical universe in space; always, there is only *thought*, or the *concept* of a universe that appears to be *in Consciousness*. So the "traveling" never is to a different location in space, but to *a different state of thought*.

All you're ever doing is traveling into Your Self! Again, there is only *Consciousness.*

All "travel" in your universe always would be "mental" only; merely a shift in the thought-forms one appears to be *aware of.* A change in the concept or *finite sense* of Your Infinite Imagination appears on the scene. The appearing of the "new scene" indicates that the thought has been "stretched" beyond what had been an accepted, limited thought-pattern to a more "expanded" state of thought. This again, is why the universe *itself* appears to be expanding—for the universe would be *one with* this expanding thought. Meanwhile, Awareness *Itself*, being Infinite, Boundless, never expands or goes anywhere. All things appear to exist as thought, always *Here,* in Infinite Awareness.

All-Inclusive Awareness, or Mind, is absolutely *Unlimited* in Its capacity to be aware of new forms of thought. Mind's Unlimitedness is *always* all that is present; It can't go away or be held in check. So one's experience (which is just so much *thought*) can't be limited to centering around just one tiny body-thought, on one tiny planet-thought, of a relatively microscopic galaxy-thought.

Infinite Awareness, Mind, is *incapable* of having Its Infinite Intelligence be restricted. So it is inevitable that what now appears as the thought of a universe will continue to shift, expand, and change to new forms of thought at an ever-faster rate. If this expansion appears to require spacecraft or other "physical" means at the moment, what difference does it make? It's the best, highest form available "at this stage of the game," and may continue that way for a while. What's more, the technologies developed from these efforts have led to countless other advances for all areas of daily living.

What is important is "sticking with" or *being* Mind's Infinite Presence, the Unlimited *Aliveness* of Being, to Whom there is *absolutely no limitation.* Otherwise, to mentally cling to any visible finite thought-form and favor it over One's Infinite Imagination, is to "slam on the brakes." It is to leave Unlimitedness, settling for a tiny finite, limited fraction.

The fact that your universe is only *thought* never can be altered. Suppose however, that you identified *not as the Infinite*, but with only the finite thought-forms or appearances, and assumed you were on the same limited level as what appears. Since you would be clinging to that level of thought, you would be limited to only that *extent* of experience—for the thought and experience are the same. You are the only one that could seem to cling to it, for you are the only One there is.

To behold Your Self as Pure Infinity *and to be It*, as Invisible Alive Presence, leaves no mental clinging to anything finite. It leaves no attaching to just one limited state of thought or experience. To the extent one is Infinity-conscious and not finite-conscious, of course it seems one is conscious of less and less finiteness and all its limitations.

This "unattached-ness" is what allows the thought or experience to appear to shift, change, or "expand" to a greater extent and variety of thoughts—for there is *no limit* to the universe of thoughts you can appear to be aware of.

Again, as all there is to your universe is *thought*, that means not only the extent, but also the *variety* of your universe is as unlimited as the capacity of Infinite Awareness to be aware of thoughts or ideas. And how *unlimited* is that?!

Even what might appear as advanced extra-terrestrial spacecraft would be like the horse and buggy stage, compared to the *infinitude* of what Awareness can appear to be aware of.

This refers only to how things *appear*. Awareness Itself never is caught up in, or in awe of *anything* that may appear on a finite basis. Nor are there really two states—the Infinite and a finite state to which It could cling. To your Infinite Self, there is only Unlimitedness. It is the consistent, persistent "staying with" *the allness of Infinity's Alive Presence* that counts.

In Reality, Total Infinity is always One's only status.

It is thanks to Your Self being *Pure Infinity* that the universe of thought-forms will appear to operate like a self-expanding prophecy. The more You "behold" of the Unlimitedness You are, the more Unlimited You are in Your Ability to behold!

30

MAJESTIC AWARENESS

AWARENESS NEVER CAN BE AWARE *OF* THE AWARENESS IT IS.

It is impossible to *think* the Magnificence of Your Being. That would be trying to reduce to a mere concept Unconfinable Awareness which is *endlessly greater* than all It perceives.

Could Boundless Awareness, *All*, be confined in a prison? Of course not. Nor could Awareness be confined to a mental prison of thinking. There is nothing wrong with thinking; but You are *already* effortlessly, beautifully free. Having to humanly *think* how majestic Awareness is, would be slavery—an impossible task, and totally unnecessary.

How wonderful! The All-Inclusive Majesty that Awareness is, never has depended on thinking. It does not have to, and *cannot*, be earned. How horrible if Awareness were limited to being only as good as human thinking thinks It to be!

Thinking and worrying, whether a "you" is being as infinite and as good as Infinite Goodness, would try to pass itself off as a sincere effort to "know" One's Self—and would be the prison itself! Human servile, laborious *thought* is not Infinite Majesty! Worrying and thinking never improve One's ability to *be*, because Awareness *is*, before all thinking.

The *Allness*, the *Endlessness*, of Awareness' Presence means Its Integrity and Dignity is all there is! Do you truly *act as*, *be*, the free, unchecked Majestic Being that Awareness *already is*?

Majesty means Majesty! Majesty is the fact that Awareness is unopposed and unrestrainable. It's not that there is another state, and Awareness is not confined to it. There is no other state! *Unrestrainable Awareness is All*. It is eternally un-weighed and unencumbered by the servile labor that human thinking would be when it tries to make itself like the Infinite. To Awareness, no such thing ever occurs. You never can stoop to such a thing, so don't try.

Absolute Freedom is One's only way of Life. Doesn't this "feel" right, true? Awareness is Awareness *only*—the forever unbound, un-attached *Endless One*. There is nothing besides Endless Freedom to which Awareness could attach.

Do not assume Infinite Awareness, that is right here and now alive to the meaning of these words, ever becomes serious or pompous, or feels weighed down by being Omnipresence, Absoluteness. Any sense of seriousness is a would-be projection of human thought *upon* Aware-ness, which actually is impossible. The sheer *exuberance* that Alive Awareness is, is too absolutely pure and free to so burden Itself.

The personal thinking "mind" (if it existed) would be like a hot-air gondola balloon, trying to rise higher and higher as more weight is thrown off it. Yet no matter how high the balloon goes, it never gets free of itself.

You are already infinitely lighter and free-er than the balloon.

You are already the Endless Expanse the balloon would try to rise into!

How impossible for this Endlessness to get down inside a balloon! How impossible for your Endlessness to be limited by how high, or in which *single* direction the balloon travels!

As Pure Awareness, One is already infinitely "higher" than even the most illumined, sincere thinking could ever hope to lift itself.

What is it to *start* Here, and permanently live Here, reveling in Infinity's own Infinity?

This is Your Only Self, the Consciousness that is All. All of what? All of *Itself*.

The *Free Aliveness* of Consciousness—the cognition of specific *vital* Presence here, now—is Life's Self-Announcement of Its Presence. Aliveness *is* the declaration God's Presence makes as It is being the entirety of Existence, declaring All to be real, magnificent, One alone.

Never assume a little state of finite thinking has to grasp Awareness before It is Your "Experience," before It is fully-operative Magnificence. Awareness' Endless Oneness precludes there ever having been a little separate thinking mind *to* grasp It. That's the point!

As all of Awareness, all of All, is changelessly *Present,* no past limited mind *ever occurred,* so there has been no attachment to such a thing. In this glorious Freedom there is no burden, no *need* to rise or evolve. Omniscience *can't* evolve.

The One All-Self is not defined as "struggler." It is defined as Infinite Conscious Majesty. Your Self is absolutely incapable of any other "attitude" about Itself.

You are that Absolute Self-Respect and Integrity which knows Majesty means *Majesty*.

You are incapable of settling for less because there is nothing less!

———•———

Get away from the *words* in this book. At best they can only point to the Magnificence You are. They are not the *being* of It.

Spend a day not even pondering Awareness, but just "letting" the ever-fresh, ever-spontaneous *Now* of Boundless Aliveness "fill" or *be* your entire Being, which in fact It is *already* being.

Drop even all sincere desire for Awareness, the Present. Drop all thoughts or concepts of Purity, of Allness, of Freedom. Drop all effort to "live up to" what this book has said. What's left?

Awareness is as aware as ever, but there is no *trying*.

This is what Freedom, Awareness, is. Only by *starting* as this Freedom is One Free.

The Awareness You are, is not sincerely thinking or working at being free, or trying to see Itself as free, which would be only more thought-bondage.

You are Free!

———•———

To Awareness, utter Purity is *All*.

All that Awareness knows is in accord with this absolute Purity, for Its endless Purity leaves no otherness from which a contrary state could come. Omni-Purity, Omni-Perfection, is the norm, status quo to the One I Am. It is *what* I Am.

The endless Presence of Purity as this One I Am is not unusual, not a long sought-after state. It is the simple Fact of My Being.

I Myself Am not a *concept* of Purity, but the absence of all concepts, which *is* Purity. I Am not thinking of Purity, not going over and over It mentally lest I lose sight of It.

I Am unfailingly, un-shut-off-ably *being* Purity; *living* It; consciously "tasting" It; I Am now being the *actuality* of what Divine Purity is.

Purity is not a standard I live up to. The *Now* of My Effortless Being *right here, now*, defines what Purity is. Who else is there to look in on My All-Purity and comment otherwise?

As Pure *Now*, I have no expectations. I need no reassurances, and want no "handles," nothing to grasp. These would only narrow and dull the wide-open Thrillingness and Freedom I just now *Am*.

I love being this Freedom I Am. This Free Being I Am, is what Love is.

———•———

This Purely Alive One I Am is untouched and unrestricted, *never* coming in contact with anything besides Myself.

This endless Aliveness of My Self here, now, never touches physicality, materiality, or mentality. I Am the utter absence of weight, gravity. I eternally "float" or "rest" as My own Presence, which is *alive* uncontainably.

There are no other states from which I have ascended; there is no "coming down," for there is *only* the Aliveness I Am. All that this untouched One I Am "beholds" is My own endless *ease*. I Am not lazy or complacent, but acutely alive to being All I Am, and *presently* so.

In the Pure *Present-ness* I Am, there is no past, thus no accumulation or worry. It's not that I've let go of cares—My Present-ness leaves no past in which to have had any cares! I Am completely care-free Life, or Joy Itself. My Life is a permanent state of Self-Surprise, for the All I Am is *just now present*. I know only *Present Joy*, with which I Am infinitely Self-Supplied.

As the Joyous Aliveness I Am is *All*, I cannot turn away from Myself. I only can be "faced with" more of the *Present Joy* I endlessly Am.

The beauty of My Joyous Aliveness is that all of It is *Now*—and Joy is literally what Now is. No Joy is waiting for later. I deal only in Joy's Self-Immediacy.

Being absolute, the Joy I Am is everywhere being active, and actively being Everywhere. Unrestricted Joy is *presently* functioning *as* every "pinpoint" of Existence, every "iota" of Substance.

This Absolute Joy I Am never fails to *be*; I never "fall," for there is nowhere besides Joy to fall *to*. Simultaneously, Joy is completely present; yet being infinite, I never come to an end of the Joy I Am.

I never depend on any thing or situation to be the Joy I Am, for there is *only* the Joy I Am.

As *Infinite* Joy, I permanently live as My own Never-Ending-Ness of Myself.

My Vitality is unwithholdable; My Intelligence is ceaselessly imaginative, and I co-exist with no prior rules, no prior physical or mental barriers, as to how unlimitedly marvelous I Am *Now*.

Instantaneous Fantastic-ness is *All*.

Fantastic-ness is not a realm I Am *in*. It is what *I Am*. My Absolute Vitality lives only for Its own Self-Excitement. My Presence has *no choice* but to be total, unchecked Thrillingness. I Am never saying mere words about My Thrillingness, but Am forever fully *being* It, *alive as It, Now*.

I Am not saving any of My Absolute Joy for fear of running out or depleting It, *for there is no end to Myself!* As Absolute Joy, I can live only for the "joy of the moment," the Joyous *Present* I never fail to be.

There is no *thinking* mind to see Me, contact Me, or struggle to be Me, for that would imply the Absolute Joy I Am was not the All I Am.

I Am "forever immersed" in the endlessness of My un-go-away-able Joy. Wherever I "look," all there is to behold is My infinite supply of Never-Before Life. As I Am endless, I Am ever-actively exercising My *Alive* Unlimitedness; the endless reach of My Glorious Purity.

Only from Here do I "take in the view" of My Life, All Existence. Joyous Aliveness is the only "way of Life" of the One reading this now.

This utter, Joyous Aliveness I Am is Unconditional Love. It is Infinite Warmth. But It is far beyond mere warmth. It is the Divine Brilliance of Absolute Light.

The Divine Light I Am is thrillingly alive to being perfect—yet so unchecked, so utterly, totally blissful as to be indescribable. I Am Indescribable-ness Itself.

I "pour" the Divine Brilliance I Am everywhere throughout My Endless Presence, Entirety. Being Absolute, I Am incapable of withholding, and I Am alive all-out, at "full blast" simultaneously Everywhere.

31

PEACE

WHAT IS PEACE?

From a human viewpoint, *peace* likely would be defined as a general state of harmony among people or nations. Some might say it is that period between wars. On this basis, peace often seems unstable, fleeting, and far too dependent on the whims of "man."

The term *Peace* may be more uncertain.

Does Peace refer to the mental or spiritual atmosphere in "the final resting place"? Is Peace the dominant feeling in heaven? If so, exactly *what* is heaven? Is it a kind of divine retirement home for the ethereal; the ultimate in assisted living?

And *where*, honestly, is heaven? One cannot truly believe heaven is a physical *place*, way up, beyond the distant edge of a stellar universe. To accept such sense-illusion as true spells trouble. On that basis it's been shown the universe is *expanding*, and fast—which would mean it's pushing heaven farther away by the minute. Not a good thing.

To those who seem more spiritually inclined, Heaven or Peace of course is synonymous, not with any place or location, but with the awareness or *presence* of Divine Life, Consciousness, or Being, also sometimes called God.

What counts is that Heaven must be *this very Being* as It is softly, gently, and timelessly being present here, now. If Timeless Being isn't Heaven, then Heaven is in passing time—forever a state of what-isn't-being-present. So what kind of "Heaven" could It *be*?

For Heaven and Its Peace to exist, Heaven must be *this very Consciousness*. Why? It is *this* Consciousness that is all-inclusive of all there is. Consciousness is all that exists to *be* Heaven. Heaven isn't where you go. Heaven is what You *are*.

Regardless of how Peace is described in words, doesn't Peace first have to *be*?

To *be* Peace, Peace has to be. It has to genuinely exist.

So what does Peace have to do with being or existing?

The fact that Existence, Your All-Inclusive Awareness, is absolutely all that is present, means It exists completely *alone*. It is utter *Oneness*, existing all by Itself, and Its Oneness is *endless*.

One means *One*—so nowhere in Your One Endless Being are there opposites. There is no duality. Not only are there no opposites *within* Your Being—there is no opposition *to* Your Being. To *One Endless Presence*, opposition of any kind is impossible.

The fact that Your Being exists utterly, completely *alone*, is a permanent guarantee of never being threatened by any outside force—for there is no outside force. There is nothing that could come in from outside, because Your Own Endlessness has no outside. It is impossible to need a protective barrier around Your Being, because the fact that It is *endless* means there is no edge or border at which to put one.

For Eternity, there is nothing that could upset You. As Utter Oneness, You are at ease in the certainty of being undisturbed *forever*. It isn't that fear has been overcome—it simply never occurs, for there is only Perfect Calm—the *endless, endless reach* of Your own "infinitely outstretched" Presence. All there is, is borderless, unchecked *Openness*, which is *alive*—the endless "overflowing" of softly present Life.

As the Entirety of Existence, all You ever know is that deepest, all-abiding Peace and Joy of being able to live completely *defenseless*. You never are naively open to attack—but simply can't be protected or have a guard up, for again, *Your Own All* leaves nothing else from which to need protecting. Absolutely nothing exists besides You, Your Infinitely Gentle Self—nothing material or even mental out of which an attack could be made. There is only wide open, pure Unprotectedness—being serenely, boundlessly free—a never-ending expanse of Divine Ease and innocence.

This open, free Ease is Unconditional Love. It is un-conditional because It never is faced by any condition—just "more and more" of Its own endless Openness. This Open Love is the all-embracing *softness* with which Your Awareness is now present and aware.

How indescribably *delicate* is Awareness as It is now being present?

Yet how indestructible is It?

How utterly, completely *effortless* is Your Existence as It goes about Its business of simply *being?* Yet how immovable and stable is It? Does It ever waver?

How delightfully un-labored—*how permanently easy*—is it for Existence to simply *be* here, now? Being this effortlessness, this all-embracing Ease is One's Life Work, One's Career—*for Eternity*.

That is all there is to It. Existence is simply *being*.

Existence never works at existing. It never struggles to be. There is absolutely nothing that has to be done.

Existence never is trying to arrive. It never needs to attain.

Existence never has to try, period. It just *is*.

There is *no possibility* of exertion in Existence for It already perfectly *is*, and nothing else is.

As Perfect Existence is already *All That Is*, there never is anything besides Its own Presence that It has to accomplish. Being doesn't work to sustain Itself over time, for in Absolute Being, there is no time. As this Changeless Being, You never can have anything go wrong; You never make a mistake. There is nothing Perfect Being *can* do, except *be*, effortlessly. Your Life is delightfully effort-*less*.

Existence, Your Being, involves no possibility of physical effort, no mental effort, no conscious effort. Being's Perfect Total Presence *precludes all effort*. Your Being is Divine *Effortlessness* Itself. This Effortlessness can no more withhold Itself from being *All*, than Being can withhold Itself. As It *already* is, It never can be delayed—or put aside.

Effortless Being never can be *escaped*.

Right now, stop. "Feel" how delightfully, unspeakably *effortless* Existence's Being is. How un-tense and restfully easy is *absolute* ease—*endless* ease?

This *Ease*, which is all of Existence, isn't a state You are *in*. It is what You *are*. This Ease that You forever are—is *so* easy, so effortlessly simple, It is not in the realm of words.

Existence's Ease is the *gently alive Bliss* You are now alive to being. How marvelously gentle and soft is this Delightful Bliss to Its own Presence? How fully "immersed" in Its own Tenderness is It?

This endlessly overflowing Ease is what You *never, ever, fail* to be.

This Infinite Ease that You are *permanently being* is never, never, never going to go away. It can't. *Ease is absolutely All That Is*—there is nowhere besides Itself that It could go to!

If this effortless Ease being You now were somehow multiplied a billion times over in Its simplicity and softness of being, Its wondrous richness and depth, You would have barely scratched the surface of the *Never Ending Ease* that Your Present Self is.

This All-Embracing Ease is the "Satisfied Sigh" of Infinite Serenity.

It is the Divine *Ahhh* that is All—the *Ahhh* that never comes to an end of Itself.

You never can be uprooted from Here, but are divinely, inescapably "stuck" being this endless Ease.

Luxuriate in It. Be It.

This Ease of Existence is Peace—for Ease is all that exists *to be* Peace.

Ease is all that exists, period.

———•———

As Existence is all Peace, *then Peace is all that exists.*

Peace is all that is ever present—as the Present Itself. That's the only place Peace can ever be—as the Effortlessness of One's Present Being. It means there is no wait for Peace to arrive any more than this Present Being is waiting to arrive. *Peace already is.*

Peace, the Effortless All-Embracing One, is being You now. That means *You* are the only One that can ever "experience" or be Peace, be Heaven, for what appears to be *the entire universe.*

How often have you seemed to assume (actually Your Self never has) that there is a "personal you" *and* Peace...that there is "a" Peace you must wait for...connect with...must some day bring about...a Peace that hopefully, as you stick with Oneness, will appear to "spread over" Existence?

Absolute Peace is already being all of Existence now—so It is not a hoped-for quality that will some day "come over" Existence.

Omni-Present Consciousness "occupies" the entirety of Presence as *Softly Alive Peace Itself.* Peace is present unconditionally, as "Everywhere." Omni-Peace has already "happened." There is no wait for

Peace to enjoy Its own Omnipresence. There are not two realms, no second dream state that Peace is gradually pacifying. As Peace Itself is literally all Presence, It leaves no absence of Its Presence, and no other that could ignorantly wait for Peace.

To attempt to wait for Peace to come about in time, instead of *consciously being It now*, would be the very seeming postponement of It. Yet Peace never can actually be delayed any more than the Present can be delayed. Peace *Itself* is the Only One existing, alive, in the first place. It never is *people* that are being Peace. Only Peace Itself is being. There is only Peace-As-All. Likewise, Peace isn't being Peace to benefit a lot of people. It is Peace only for Itself, for there is only Itself. Peace leaves no others trying to hold to It for dear life, because Omni-Peace never fails to be the Alone One—as *this* Entirely Effortless Being.

Only an ignorant assumption that Peace is not *this very Being*, but is some separate state "out there" that will come about in time—is the *only* thing that would seem to keep Absolute Immediate Peace away.

All along, *You alone are Peace* and the only One that can be It!

The mere mental assumption that you could be separate from Immediate Peace, would be all there is *to* a separation. There never is physical separation, for there never is anything physical. Peace Itself isn't waiting for, or trying to reach, a Peace "off there" somewhere. Instantly cut off any suggestion in thought *right here*, that there has ever been separation. Absolute Peace can no more be separate from Now than Now can choose to not be.

Infinite Peace *never* has co-existed with a dream-illusion that there is time and space, and a separate world "out there" in need of Peace. It's not that there *is* an illusion, and Peace, Awareness, isn't being fooled by it. There isn't even an illusion! Peace's Absolute Calm never is co-existed with, let alone blocked or interfered with!

The Effortless Peace being present right here, now, is as potent and effective at the *seemingly* most distant points all across "earth" and a "universe" as It is *right here, now!* Why? There are no distant points! All is always right here, *as this Present Consciousness*, which is Absolute Peace Itself. A sense-dream of time and space and separation, never began—never has been *present* to interfere.

All is *Present* Consciousness, Peace Itself.

One never tries to correct a time-world, or have Peace spread "out there," for in Infinite Conscious Being, in *All*, there is no physical distance in which to have such a thing. Only *Here*, as Peace's Ease, is all of

Existence existing. Absolutely all there is, is the Ease of Peace that is alive Here; *this* All-Inclusive Conscious Love.

Peace's Changeless Total Presence precludes a changing time-dream of nations, races, factions, or people developing a desperate need for peace. To insist there is a world separate from One, "out there," needing peace would be trying to superimpose a never-began dream state upon the Ever-Present Peace that Consciousness is *Now*. Who is there to do such a thing, *Conscious Peace Itself being All*?

Peace's Utter Presence cannot be resisted by any body or thing. Mere *things* don't have minds with which to act contrary to the Already Omnipresent Fact that Peace is. Peace Itself is the only Presence, Self, or Mind there is, which includes all bodies and things within *Itself*. This never changes. It is Life's one hundred percent guarantee that the Ease of Peace is all that is ever existent and functioning.

The fact that Peace's Ease is changelessly *All Presence*, means an absence of Ease never has occurred! The fact that Ease is *absolutely present* means It is *absolutely pure*. Not so much as a tiny ripple has ever disturbed the utter Purity that Ease is. Nothing besides Peace's Endless Ease ever "happens"! It precludes a history of waiting for Peace, or a misbehaving humanity having to be kept in line.

One does not merely "see" or agree with this and then quickly move on to the next paragraph, the next page. One is this, for Eternity.

———— • ————

As Peace exists nowhere but *as the Self now reading this*, the only One with any "say in the matter" is You. You are the only One that could seem to withhold Peace from your universe by continuously assuming Peace is off in a distant future—which never will *be present*.

A so-called time-world "out there" has *no* say in the matter of Peace whatsoever, for it's never had *being*. It has no Peace, or even human peace, it can offer or withhold, because *You alone are being It all*.

How could You, as the Only One That Is Being, wait to find Peace in time—in *that which never is being*? How insane—to continually wait for Peace to come about in a state that never is! Of course Peace hasn't shown up "out there" in a time-world yet, if that's the only place one is looking. It can't. There is no place outside of *Your Present Self* where Peace could be!

Life's Peace, Happiness and Satisfaction are not found in time and space. Waiting for Peace to come in time is to assume It is somewhere apart from Your Self in the Present. It would mean ignoring the only "place" Peace really, forever is—*this Effortlessly Present Being I Am.*

Peace never can be found or come about anywhere else. Peace cannot be found. It can't come, for *Peace already is.*

Why try to put off Present Peace, when it's *impossible*? Again, who exists besides Conscious Peace Itself to try?

The Ever-Present *Living Fact* that Peace *is*, is un-hold-back-able. Consciously, consistently and persistently *being It Now*, can appear to bring about unheard-of "peace on earth." Why? Present Peace, the Instantly Omnipresent One being You, *is already the only Substance, Mind, existent*. There is nothing present besides Peace to negate Peace.

Why should any of this seem unusual? To whom could It seem so, *Conscious Peace Itself being All?*

Be the effortless Presence of *Silent Aliveness*, which *is* Peace.

Peace isn't a *word*. It is Wordless Bliss, the All-Inclusive *Alive Love* You are now silently alive to *being*. Effortless Peace doesn't mean being a body with a lazy, do-nothing attitude. It means joyously being this *softly Alive Love* as It rests in, or *is*, Its own endless Ease.

Peace is "light" or "buoyant" in that nowhere in Peace is there any weight or density. Peace's endless Pure Being leaves nothing physical or material. There is only Silent Peace, effortlessly "floating" as Its own Endlessness. This Peace-Full Ease doesn't fill *an* Existence, but literally is what all Existence is!

These are not just feel-good statements one periodically turns to for a temporary "fix." *Peace Itself* is the Only Presence "forever and ever and ever" *present*. It *never* can go away.

To the Consciousness aware right here, now, Absolute Peace is so complete in Its "coverage," and so "omni-instantaneous," It is beyond words to describe.

How long does It take Consciousness to be conscious everywhere throughout Its Present Being? It doesn't take time—*It is*. Likewise, Peace is permanently "Total Coverage" of All, for *It is what All is.*

When Conscious Peace "beholds" Its Existence, all It "sees" is Omni-Peace in Constant Absoluteness. This is all that is ever "seen," for Peace Itself is the Only One conscious and present—and all there is for Peace to "see" is Itself.

Effortless Peace is *Stillness.*

Peace is *Silence.*

This Still Silence of Peace is Divine Wisdom Itself—far too wise for the tension of words.

It is the deep, quiet Certainty of Infinite Self-Esteem.

While Peace is Silence, It's not a sleepy, retiring state—Peace is vitally *alive.*

It is Life Eternal in full song—Divine Delight at full volume!

Listen as this Unspoken Joy echoes, inaudibly, throughout Your Endlessness.

Peace is the *Infinite Goodness* You are, speechless with Bliss.

It is Absolute Light, whose brilliance endlessly explodes in Divine Silence.

Peace is *all Presence, all of All.* There is nothing to come between It and Itself.

Absolutely everywhere Your Life can possibly "look," all It beholds is the still, silent Beauty of *Boundless Peace.*

Be alive as gloriously *Unrestrainable Peace*—the Great, Uncontainable Calm.

Be alive as Peace, eternally overflowing as Your own Never-Ending-Ness.

The Silent Peace You are is so vast, so *Immeasurably Endless*, that to It, the blaze of countless star-drenched galaxies would be less than a tiny image on a piece of microfilm, not even a tiny *dot.*

An entire stellar universe, appearing to span billions of light years—would be so insignificant as to not even be noticeable—against the *Vastness*, the unspeakable *Endlessness* of the Peace You are.

POSTSCRIPT

CONSCIOUSNESS IS ALL is a book on Absolute Reality, sometimes also called Infinite Reality, or simply, the Absolute.

The essence of the work is the fact that Consciousness (also known as the One Self, I Am, Love, Life, the Divine, God, and other terms) is absolutely all there is of all there is. Simply nothing exists outside of, or beyond, Consciousness.

As Consciousness is *All* or *One*—It thus is not a higher Self, but the *only* Self. Reality is a matter of looking *out from* the allness of the One Self, Consciousness, rather than looking *up to* It as a lesser consciousness or personal self. The Self never looks up to Itself—and the Self is really the only One being conscious or alive in the first place. One is free to enjoy *being*, rather than constantly struggling to *become*. *Consciousness Is All* is written from this "viewpoint."

Peter Francis Dziuban (pronounced *Jubin*) became aware of Absolute Reality through the works of Dr. Alfred Aiken. Alfred Aiken wrote numerous books on Consciousness or Reality, with such titles as: *That Which Is, Now, Life, Power,* and *The Unchallenged Self*. He also spoke widely throughout the United States and in Europe, giving tape-recorded lectures, forums and seminars from 1955 to 1968.

While *Consciousness Is All* has its foundation in Alfred Aiken's writings and talks, it is a completely new and original work. The book was written over a period of several years, and was first copyrighted in 1998, although not published until 2006. It reflects the helpful comments and enthusiasm of those who share an interest in Consciousness. Also helpful in formulating portions of the book's discussion of "finite sense," was the description of the nature of the five physical senses in Robert Pirsig's *Zen and the Art of Motorcycle Maintenance*.

Mr. Dziuban first became interested in philosophy and Reality while attending the University of Notre Dame. He later investigated various philosophies and spiritual teachings—among them, the Infinite Way, and the work of Joel Goldsmith, Lorene McClintock and Herb Fitch. He also has worked at several positions in corporate America—most of them in the communications field, including eight years as a writer. *Consciousness Is All* is his first book.

Reality, Truth, does not belong to, nor is It the product of, any one body or person. This is why all information of a personal nature is placed at the end of this book—to minimize the tendency to attach Truth to any person.

If you have enjoyed reading this book, you may find that a second, and even multiple readings, provide an even deeper appreciation of its contents. The clarity and familiarity with the "viewpoint" that is gained from a previous reading will greatly enrich the appreciation of the material in subsequent readings.

For more information on forthcoming books from Peter Francis Dziuban, or Alfred Aiken's books, please contact
Blue Dolphin Publishing, Inc.,
P.O. Box 8, Nevada City, CA 95959.
Orders: 1-800-643-0765. Information: 1-530-265-6925.
Web: www.bluedolphinpublishing.com

Printed in the United States
65182LVS00001B/25-48

9 781577 331605